James Baldwin and the Queer Imagination

James Baldwin

AND THE

Queer Imagination

Matt Brim

The University of Michigan Press
Ann Arbor

This book may not be reproduced, in whole or in part, including illustrations, in any form (beyond that copying permitted by Sections 107 and 108 of the U.S. Copyright Law and except by reviewers for the public press), without written permission from the publisher.

Published in the United States of America by

The University of Michigan Press

Printed and bound by CPI Group (UK) Ltd, Croydon, CR0 4YY

2017   2016   2015   2014   4   3   2   1

A CIP catalog record for this book is available from the British Library.

Library of Congress Cataloging-in-Publication Data

Brim, Matt, author.

James Baldwin and the Queer Imagination / Matt Brim.

pages   cm

Includes bibliographical references and index.

ISBN 978-0-472-07234-7 (hardcover : acid-free paper) — ISBN 978-0-472-05234-9 (pbk. : acid-free paper) — ISBN 978-0-472-12059-8 (e-book)

1. Baldwin, James, 1924–1987—Criticism and interpretation.   2. Gay men's writings, American—History and criticism.   3. African American gays—Intellectual life.   4. Queer theory.   5. Gay men in literature.   I. Title.

PS3552.A45Z596   2014

818'.5409—dc23

2014014522

For D.V.

We do not know enough about the mind
    or how the conundrum of the imagination
dictates, discovers,
or can dismember what we feel,
    or what we find.

     —JAMES BALDWIN, "CONUNDRUM (ON MY BIRTHDAY) (FOR RICO)"

Acknowledgments

In writing this book, I have benefited enormously from the support of colleagues at the City University of New York's College of Staten Island, including Maria Rice Bellamy, Ava Chin, Ashley Dawson, Tim Gray, Edward Miller, and Terry Rowden. Many others have provided comments, direction, and support at various stages of the writing process. I thank Sarah Chinn, Jonathan Elmer, Christine Farris, Matt Flinders, Tom Foster, Steven G. Fullwood, Amin Ghaziani, Donald Hall, Heather Love, Alyce Miller, Jonathan Ned Katz, Ted Leahey, Velina Manolova, Dwight McBride, Bailey McDaniel, Lisa C. Moore, Chris Pepus, Robert Reid-Pharr, Warren Rosenberg, Susan Stryker, Maurice Wallace, Robyn Wiegman, and Thomas Wirth.

Several wonderful, serious, hilarious writing groups helped to push and pull this project along at Indiana University and Duke University, and I heartily thank Johanna Frank, Sarah Murphy, Rod Taylor, Alison Umminger, and Becky Wood, as well as Jason Mahn and Rebecca Walsh. The graduate students in my 2010 Baldwin summer seminar were invaluable resources, as have been my amazing undergraduates in queer studies at CSI. The Global Queerness Conference, hosted by the College of Wooster, enabled me to share several of my queer ideas about Baldwin and receive helpful feedback.

At the University of Michigan Press, Tom Dwyer, Christopher Dreyer, and Aaron McCollough expertly shepherded this project through the publication process. The generous reports of two anonymous readers helped to sharpen its argument. In addition, this book would not have been possible without the support of a series of PSC/CUNY Research Awards from the Research Foundation of the City University of New York and a Mellon Postdoctoral Fellowship from Duke University.

Finally, a few words of special appreciation are in order. Sarah Schulman and David Gerstner deserve more thanks than can be expressed here, for they are stalwart and caring colleagues. Brian Leung was an early collaborator and a trenchant interlocutor, and I thank him for his novelist's eye. Susan Gubar, who has known this project from its infancy, has been an unending source of inspiration as a reader, mentor, scholar, and dear friend. Eric Hartman, I am most thankful to say, came along at just the right time.

Part of chapter 1 appeared as "James Baldwin's Queer Utility" in *ANQ: A Quarterly Journal of Short Articles, Notes, and Reviews* 24, no. 4 (2011): 209–16, published by Taylor & Francis Ltd., and is reprinted by permission of the publisher (Taylor & Francis Ltd., http://www.tandf.co.uk/journals). An early version of chapter 4 appeared as "Papas' Baby: Impossible Paternity in *Going to Meet the Man*" in the *Journal of Modern Literature* 30, no. 1 (2006): 173–98, published by Indiana University Press.

Contents

Introduction

James Baldwin Theory—Seeing the Invisible

At its best, queer theory has always also been something else—something that will be left out of any purely intellectual history of the movement.

—MICHAEL WARNER,
"QUEER AND THEN? THE END OF QUEER THEORY?"

Thus lesbianism, homosexuality, and the societies we form cannot be thought of or spoken of, even though they have always existed. . . . [W]hen thought by the straight mind, homosexuality is nothing but heterosexuality.

—MONIQUE WITTIG, "THE STRAIGHT MIND" AND OTHER ESSAYS

What one can and cannot see says something about you.

—JAMES BALDWIN,
QUOTED IN DAVID LEEMING, JAMES BALDWIN: A BIOGRAPHY

The central figure in black gay literary history, James Baldwin has been made a standard-bearer for queer culture. Baldwin is a queer touchstone within the university as well, especially in the field of queer theory. As a totem figure for this notoriously rowdy discipline, Baldwin nevertheless often functions as a surprisingly untroubled queer signifier. This study will explore the paradoxes of Baldwin's queer exemplarity, an intervention made possible because Baldwin has been productively re-viewed, renewed, renamed, and reclaimed as a queer object of study over the last two decades. That queering has produced a corresponding shift—a "Baldwinization" of queer theory in the form of black queer studies—that has sharpened, darkened, "quared," and repaired the field. But if queer theory has in some ways risen to the challenges of Baldwin, how has it also failed to do so? In turn, what new problems can queer theory pose for Baldwin and his work? And what are the consequences of reformulating these queer relations? These are the driving concerns of *James Baldwin and the Queer Imagination*.

Without much using the word and without the benefit of the theory that would later be constructed around it, James Baldwin imagined much of what theorists mean these days when we use the word "queer." Baldwin, working with and beyond prescribed identity categories, takes as his most enduring subject precisely those illegitimized desires, often between men and often between races, that have been pushed to the very edge of the thinkable and there, inevitably, gripped the erotic unconscious. Queer theory, in part, names the enterprise devoted to the analytical and scholarly reimagining of just such "impossible" desires as Baldwin's fiction attempts to represent. It is easy, then, to imagine Baldwin's work and queer theory as both sensibly and even necessarily folding into each other, with the conceptual framework elucidating the author's fiction anew while the fiction helps the queer interpretive apparatus live up to its theoretical promise. I argue in this book that we can and must imagine more. If one broad goal of this project is to re-introduce Baldwin through queer theory, the work involved in doing so also produces a reciprocal encounter with the "purely intellectual history" that, as Michael Warner's epigraph attests, can never fully capture the spirit of queer theory. In this dialectic, Baldwin and queer theory become an *uneasy* pairing, a sometimes bad fit that produces new critical traction. As I use it in this book, the phrase "the queer imagination" indicates the meeting ground for this re-energized coupling, the field of play on which is negotiated the dynamic relationship between Baldwin's creative capacities and the theoretical interpretive venture, itself creative.

Modeled upon Baldwin's understanding of identity as a multidirectional switchpoint for sameness and difference, my thesis runs counter to itself. On the one hand, Baldwin imagines non-normative desires, and queer theory succeeds in articulating their complexity. On the other hand, the queer imagination continually undermines itself, marked, I will argue, by its own surprising contradictions and unexpected ruptures. The queer Baldwin is not simply the liberatory or the visionary or the multiple Baldwin but rather the paradoxical Baldwin. To read his paradoxicality, queer theory must, to adapt one of Baldwin's prized metaphors, estimate the price of the queer ticket, the price of the incommensurability that is identity. For better or worse, no firm template or consistent methodology for reading queerness can possibly emerge in the discussion that follows, as paradox is hermeneutic inconsistency itself, a puzzle every time. Therefore, the queer theory eminent in this study is not thematic. Rather, the non-trope of queer paradoxicality insists, unhelpfully to be sure, that you will know it *not* when you see and recognize it but when it surprises and confounds you most. Queer paradox offers little predictive value.

Broadly speaking, the imaginative dynamic that I trace here emerges out of what I argue is the vexed relationship that queerness has to normative practices, both representational and disciplinary. I want to trouble that relationship even more by reimagining the queer/norm dyad beyond a liberation/constraint paradigm, as I sense this coupling has become a static conceptual tool in queer theory. The Foucauldian model of power, in which there is no "outside," has provided a foundation for conceptualizing the queer/identity relation, but it has also had the unintended effect of creating a closed interpretive loop—everything is within the field of power. Working in that tradition, theorists rightly aver that the queer creative practices are not simply free; they are free even as they confine and are confined. We say that queer theory is not only liberatory but always under the pressures of normative reinscription and reabsorption. The outstanding new anthology *The Routledge Queer Studies Reader* demonstrates just this operation of internal critique in its first section of essays, "Genealogies," the contents of which provide a brief history of queer theory as an enterprise ceaselessly trying to slip out from under its surprisingly normative self. Exemplary in this regard, as well as in its clarity, is Cathy Cohen's "Punks, Bulldaggers, and Welfare Queens." Perceiving the construction of the queer/hetero binary to be a reappropriation of queerness in order to sustain racial and class inequalities, Cohen confronts the folly of locating queerness easily beyond or in distinction to norms: "In many instances, instead of destabilizing the assumed categories and binaries of sexual identity, queer politics has served to reinforce simple dichotomies between heterosexual and everything 'queer.'"[1] Queerness operates less in distinct opposition to normality than at an unpredictable remove from it, and that distance seems to be ever collapsing. In our field of vision, the queer sky and the normative sea share a broad and blurred horizon, and much of the most influential queer theoretical work has taken place at this line of convergence.

Perhaps the most pervasive critical response to this disheartening recontainment has been to imagine ever-queerer queernesses. Queer theory makes its way by trucking suspicion for hope. The interrogatory subtitle of Cohen's essay, "The Radical Potential of Queer Politics?," dances along this line, both denuding "radical" queer politics and calling for readers to "construct a new political identity that is *truly liberating, transformative, and inclusive* of all those who stand on the outside of the dominant constructed norm of state-sanctioned white middle- and upper-class heterosexuality."[2] Note the dual motion here: the gesture toward liberation, frequently made with reference to the future, futures, and futurity, is itself exemplary of and foundational to a queer theoretical impulse. The late José Esteban Muñoz opens his study of queer futurity by beautifully capturing the more general queer theoretical sentiment that "[q]ueerness is not yet here." "Queerness," writes Muñoz, "is essentially about the rejection of a here and now and an insistence on potentiality or concrete possibility for another world."[3] Yet even as queer theory embraces and privileges radically emancipatory futural projects, it binds itself to normativity not simply because norms create the boundaries through which queerness breaks but, rather, because that rupture is never a clean break. Even—or especially—in what Jasbir Puar calls "queer times," the "fantastical wonders of futurity"[4] are not easily dislocated from the present. Norms and queerness entangle one another and even, as Cohen's example demonstrates, become indistinguishable.[5]

I want to suggest that queer theory's revelation and intersectional analysis of ever-proliferating normative structures might be said to constitute a gross system of sexual and gender normalization from which no queerness is safe. Of course, the largely deconstructive push-pull of queerness and normativity has produced a deeply textured analytic fabric that, to its credit, has refused to tie off its loose ends. But it also has produced a vicious cycle: we must constantly seek out a more liberatory queerness, but the work of doing so inevitably produces a critique that reads the norm back into the queer (as opposed to the early provocations of Judith Butler to "wor[k] the weakness in the norm"[6]). Because this twin critical impulse to queer norms and renormalize queerness has largely come to define the field of queer theory, it is time to consider whether we have been so intent on queering normativity, on revealing it and divesting it of its quiet power, that we have become yoked to normativity itself. The dilemma of how queers should regard this "general" theory of normativity, as opposed to individual norms, is urgent. Valerie Traub, in her critique of the "new unhistoricism" in queer theory, argues that "queer is intelligible only in relation to social norms," social norms themselves being fairly recent inventions. She thus refuses to "celebrate the instability of queer by means of a false universalization of the normal" that, for instance, frames temporality itself as a normative construction to be undermined. She wonders if queer theory attempts "to produce a binary for the sake of deconstructing it."[7] Floating free of their contexts, norms provide a generic metanarrative for queer theory. But is normality queer theory's enemy, the pervasive obstacle to liberation, or does normality function as queer theory's bête noir because queer theory, by ceaselessly constructing and then confronting the beast, remains forever in its shadow?

While grounded in the legacy of queer theory's insights about subversion and constraint,[8] I am drawn here to an alternate power dynamic by which an active relationship of queerness to normativity emerges in queer thought. Structuring this other tension within the queer imagination, as I have suggested, is the element of paradox, which provides a useful framing concept for this study because it names the kind of logical inconsistency that I trace through Baldwin's fiction and that I want to draw out more generally for queer inquiry. The idea that queer is a site of contest and theoretical "trouble" has, of course, been part of its definition since the inception of the field of queer theory and, prior to that, its personal/political reappropriation. Michael Warner, whose recent essay, "Queer and Then?: The End of Queer Theory?," takes stock of twenty years of queer theoretical work, points to "queer theory's ambivalence about itself"—witnessed through its constant self-critique, its institutional discontents—as perhaps its most long-standing attribute.[9] But I want to suggest that a special paradoxicality, a dynamic sharper than ambivalence, deeply marks queer thought.

Conceptually, paradox offers a pointed tool for thinking about queerness because even as it rejects "[t]he process of ignoring or at least downplaying queers' varying relationships to power,"[10] it also refuses simply to dismiss queer's recurrent normativities as "unqueer" moments within a "properly" progressive trajectory of queer liberation. Instead, paradox offers a framework for incorporating those "outlier" moments into queer thought without simply resorting to the real but hyper-ready charges of homonormativity and unexamined privilege. As I refuse to excise the unqueer from queerness, I also will not argue that Baldwin occupied (nor will I try to use Baldwin to ascend to) a theoretical position of "queerer than thou." That kind of competiveness, which Warner identifies as a pervasive trend in queer academe, is itself excessively available to the paradoxical critique offered here, a critique that insists on and does not try to chastise or suppress the sporadic pulse of an unqueer undercurrent within the queer imagination.

If queer paradox refuses to efface the unqueer, it also does not allow for a tepid, enfeebling compromise by which queer creative energies are kept on the normative tether of "the possible," as in celebrations of (often politically defanged) irony. In fact, I believe that queer's liberatory impulses often create breathtakingly successful theories and practices, a fact that cannot be easily reconciled with queer's constant failures. In the world of queer creativity, Jack Halberstam reminds us, "possibility and disappointment often live side by side."[11] Paradox, capable of compassing extremities without remaking or reducing them, can help to articulate that conundrum. Further, paradox surpasses the blithe construction of non-normativity and normativity as a "mutually constitutive" binary, the deconstruction of which produces difference as a predictable building block of meaning. While I accept the poststructuralist intervention that insists on the collapse of all binaries under the weight of their own faulty reasoning, that formulation is no longer sufficient for conceptualizing the queer/unqueer relationship. My intent has been to leverage the strange obstinance of that binary rather than to explore its slippages, for beyond the oppositional complementarity of queer binarisms lies a radical incommensurability. Queerness and normality are shockingly, incompatibly, compellingly—in short, paradoxically—sustained, and they are therefore in need of a new tensile logic. How, queer paradox forces us to ask, have these things possibly come together here? Baldwin, in his oeuvre, his critical reception, and his theoretical utility, offers a flash point for this kind of radical coupling that eclipses a subversion/constraint or oppositional paradigm. I am fascinated by Baldwin because his work extends the moment when the queer and the unqueer exist in unpredictable, unresolvable, untenable relation.

Paradoxes, then, are interesting and useful because they require and are defined by unscripted and bizarre tensions and differences. They derive their interpretive potential from their resistance to logical explanation or structural consistency. No theoretical exercise in wordplay, paradox, as I use it here, illuminates a deep and productive troubling of queer imaginative acts. Rather than participating in the queer "gotcha" game, the goal of which is to assert or invent a new queerness, a queerer queerness, I suggest that we might look with a curious eye toward "queer normativities"—a paradoxical phrase, to be sure—not in order to expunge normativity from queerness (which is impossible) or to luxuriate in our guilt and abrade ourselves on the sharpened edges of our endless self-critique but in order to de-energize those very cyclonic winds in which the field seems to spin, sometimes out of control. In short, by charting the paradoxical ruptures of normativity within the queer imagination, we might become self-critical in new ways.[12]

My argument is not that queerness is always paradoxical (although I believe it very often is). Instead, I suggest that paradox offers one of the more complex and interesting access points for thinking across the spectrum of queer creative thought. My use of the phrase "the queer imagination" in this book's title announces the kind of logical inconsistency akin to paradox taken up here, for its definite article "the" refers to what, by almost any account, must be considered an indefinite noun, "queer imagination." Against the apparent multiplicity of queer imagination, this use of "the" attempts to maintain an odd sense of discretion, for I work singularly with Baldwin and with a finite number of queer approaches to his work. But as much as anything else, this use of "the" points to my own individual and limited queer imagination, a reality that will be evident throughout the book. Still, out of the small and insistent truth that enables (forces) one to recognize one's own situatedness within acts of queer imagination emerges a larger lesson: queer thought is often strangely conflicted. Queer thought is strangely conflicted even for the brilliant Baldwin, and the same proves true for queer theory of the "highest" order and queer politics of the most progressive kind. I am fascinated by that conflict. I hope that this book builds toward a theory of queer paradox that might prove useful beyond the various limitations of my own queer imagination, on which, paradoxically enough, it relies.

One way I have structured my analysis is through a series of neologisms and chapter titles meant to render the paradoxicality of the queer imagination visible in linguistically concrete terms. The remainder of this introduction uses Baldwin's own trope of seeing the invisible, perceiving "the evidence of things not seen," to argue for the expansiveness of his queer imagination and the increasing intricacy by which queer studies generally and black queer studies specifically have explored the far corners of that imagination. I begin, therefore, by privileging the liberatory vein of the queer paradox. This book's chapters then take up the task of analyzing Baldwin and his work from a variety of more acute angles. Chapter 1 addresses the paradox of "queer utility" by which Baldwin and his work have become useful for a variety of purposes quite opposed to the goals he set out for himself as a writer. Chapter 2 explores the tensions among queer, gay, and transgender interpretive frameworks, arguing that the three are largely incommensurate and unassimilable yet also interanimating and individually insufficient. The result is an analytic that refuses either a ready conflation of the three (as, for instance, "Queer") or their resolute categorical separation according to the politics, identity, and ideology that motivate one's interpretation. Chapter 3 casts as paradoxical the terms "gay sex" and "gay love" as they are made to stand in for the abstraction that is straight male-straight male sex in Baldwin's third novel, *Another Country*. Chapter 4 examines the related paradoxical figure of "Papas' Baby," the fantastically racialized offspring of the white male and black male dyad that is perhaps the author's most privileged figure. Finally, this book's conclusion turns most explicitly to the surprising ways queerness seems to be so very strangely pierced by the normative. It operates as a bookend to the queer liberatory claims of the introduction by tracing the ways Baldwin, caught in the normative undertow of his own queer imagination, invisibilizes the visible through a failure to represent lesbians in his fiction, even while he deeply engages with them in public dialogue.

Queer theory is a fascinatingly imperfect tool, its leverage offering up both good and bad surprises. Through the notion of queer paradox, I have tried to identify the most surprising and "impossible" moments in Baldwin, to elaborate the inconstancy by which the queer imagination succeeds and fails, and to glean meaning about that dynamic. Throughout, I maintain that the wide-ranging field of queer studies must discern and critically sustain, rather than simply override, the paradoxical tensions inherent in the queer imagination.

SEEING THE UNSEEN

James Baldwin and the Queer Imagination argues that twentieth-century American writer James Baldwin had a paradoxical queer imagination. The book suggests that the author's fiction proceeds unevenly, in ways that can be as restrictive as they are revelatory, and that his work therefore exemplifies an "unqueer" undercurrent in queer creative thought. In the remainder of the introduction, however, I emphasize the more immediately striking aspect of Baldwin's queer imagination: the ability, the vision, and the daring to confront desires that exist in the cultural imaginary yet have simultaneously been made culturally unintelligible. I want to expand the discussion of Baldwin's status as witness to twentieth-century America, a much-invoked moniker for his racial positioning, to focus on his ability to marshal the "evidence of things not seen" into a case for queer reality. Indeed, I suggest that Baldwin's most unfailing characteristic as a writer—his investment in drawing "impossible" yet undeniable desires into the realm of literary representation—is this method of figuring unseen reality, which I take to be central to queer imaginative work.

By virtue of the author's status in American letters and the very public nature of what might be called his critical writing persona, the title of my book and the thesis toward which it gestures may seem either obvious or overreaching. On the one hand, for the many readers who have chosen to learn and know it, Baldwin has made black gay literature synonymous with queer creative culture. On the other hand, many scholars and cultural arbiters have "known" Baldwin only by deferring that very racial/sexual knowledge, holding it at bay, making it someone else's business. Navigating between these two knowledges, one intimate and the other estranged, I argue both that Baldwin's queer imagination is anything but obvious and that queer ideation is inextricable from his work. In fact, it is precisely by reclaiming queerness for Baldwin that we can discover the broad regions and readerships to which his queer imagination lays claim. My insistence that Baldwin's queer imagination has broad cultural implications therefore contains within it the call for queer cultures to re-energize their relationships to Baldwin's writing, as well as an indictment of the ways dominant culture invisibilizes its relationship to queer thought.

To queer Baldwin is, first, to release him from a history of particularly tight-fisted reading practices. Traditionally (and often, still) critics have squandered our opportunities to understand Baldwin as a black queer male writer. As a site of multiple subjectivities, Baldwin's complex identity as a black queer male writer might have been explored early in the young author's career with the publication of Go *Tell It on the Mountain* in 1953 and of *Giovanni's Room* in 1956. Yet for many critics and canon makers, these novels have made an odd and incompatible pair. The first book would become a much-taught "black experience novel,"[13] while the second would become, quite distinctly, a staple of the "gay canon.""[B]y privileging *either* race *or* sex," Magdalena Zaborowska notes, "[w]e have . . . inherited and been haunted by the black writer from Harlem of Go *Tell It on the Mountain* or the gay writer from Paris of *Giovanni's Room*."[14] The relationship between these works, each a classic in its own right, points to one of the long-standing problems in Baldwin criticism, a problem summed up by the misleading question: which Baldwin are we reading? The publishers of Go *Tell It on the Mountain* rejected the *Giovanni's Room* manuscript as a threat to the literary future of a promising young author whose calling seemed so clearly linked to his powerful, if still emerging, black voice. While *Giovanni's Room* was largely seen as a "curious little detour" whose reception in the popular press was "cautiously positive," that reception required its own disavowals.

The press's curiosity often rested invisibly on a tolerance made possible by white critical distance. Marlon Ross asks ironically, "What did white men have to lose from mildly praising such a novel?"[15] As Baldwin's works moved into the academy through African American literary studies and gay literary studies—just the fields one might expect to offer the most nuanced theoretical frameworks for reading Baldwin—each discipline instead performed its own disavowals. While "in the context of African American literary and cultural studies, historically [Giovanni's Room] has been alternately dismissed or ignored altogether, stumblingly acknowledged or viciously attacked,"[16] Go Tell It on the Mountain has been a core text. That Giovanni's Room contains no black characters has allowed most gay literary scholars to avoid discussions of how dramatically raced the narrative is, while Go Tell It on the Mountain has been made, impossibly, black not queer.[17] Baldwin's writing has led an "odd double life."[18]

The distorted double life of Baldwin's writing, initially created by reviewers but then sustained by a model of academic disciplinarity that formed around the politics of identity, would be somewhat reconciled by the field of cultural studies. As a result, the question of which Baldwin to address found a critically nuanced response: "All of them." Cultural studies, as the important 1999 collection of essays titled James Baldwin Now makes clear, has provided a more dynamic, responsive model for intellectual inquiry into the multiplicity or intersectionality of identity that characterizes Baldwin and informs his work. Editor Dwight McBride suggests that "[g]iven the advent of cultural studies in the academy—with its focus on interdisciplinarity or transdisciplinarity, critical theory, and an ever-broadening notion of 'culture'—it seems more possible today than ever before to engage Baldwin in all of the complexity he represents to critical inquiry, considering the various roles he has occupied."[19] Baldwin certainly suggests such an approach, for in confronting and articulating the complexities of identity, he is at his most rigorous, most persistent best. Crucial to his repositioning in the academy has been Baldwin's own principle of locating difference, the engine of identity, not without but within. Much has been made of Baldwin's expression of his deeply held belief in all people's shared humanity, by which he meant not that we are all alike but, rather, that the fates of those that seem most different—the oppressed and the oppressor can stand as the most general example—are irrevocably intertwined. One of Baldwin's personal insights, a poststructuralist commonplace today, is that the racial, sexual, and gendered other is created necessarily as an aspect of the self. In one of his last essays, the ostensible topic of which is androgyny and the actual topic of which is the refusal to confront the terrifying otherness in the self, Baldwin writes, "But we are all androgynous, not only because we are all born of a woman impregnated by the seed of a man but because each of us, helplessly and forever, contains the other—male in female, female in male, white in black and black in white. We are part of each other. Many of my countrymen appear to find this fact exceedingly inconvenient and even unfair, and so, very often, do I. But none of us can do anything about it."[20]

In a less well-known example from his extended analysis of Hollywood films, *The Devil Finds Work*, Baldwin frames the complex matter of identity more directly as a confrontation instigated by the outside other but then fully realized through an interiorization of that stranger. Baldwin writes, "An identity is questioned only when it is menaced, as when the mighty begin to fall, or when the wretched begin to rise, or when the stranger enters the gates, never, thereafter, to be a stranger: the stranger's presence making *you* the stranger, less to the stranger than to yourself."[21] As I will argue more thoroughly in chapter 4 of this book, this perspective allows for a reverse intervention by acting as a critical wedge into regimes of the normal and making possible such intellectual enterprises as whiteness studies. The more general point here, one that will be made in different ways throughout this book, is that identity for Baldwin is less a marker of static sameness and difference than of unrecognized, painfully assimilable otherness within the self. While the multiplicity of identities that we can associate with the marker "black gay male writer" would seem to suggest an integration of human experience, this composite of terms was troubling for Baldwin, as was the ceaseless interplay of those terms. Paradoxically, attending to the specificity of one's intersectional identity—race, sexuality, gender, nationality—both orients and disorients, by locating the self in the tumultuous seat of difference. Rather than answering the question of which Baldwin to address, the response that we should include all of them in our analysis raises new and thornier questions.

When Hilton Als refers to "the way in which [Baldwin] alchemized the singularity of his perspective into art,"[22] he hits the mark, for alchemy implies a transformation, more magic than science, of individual parts into something greater than their whole. The ever-slippery, ever-unique alchemy of individual identity that Baldwin describes simply as "a person"—"a person is more important than anything else, anything else"[23]—requires an equally nimble interpretive approach. Representing the disciplinary intervention with which I will most directly be concerned here, Robert Corber helpfully suggests that "[t]he category 'queer' which has recently emerged in literary studies to describe identities, desires, and practices rendered illegible by the available sexual taxonomies seems more appropriate to the study of Baldwin. Such a category acknowledges, as Baldwin himself did, the limitation of identity categories without discarding them altogether."[24] Synthesizing Als's aesthetic perpective and Corber's academic one, I offer "the queer imagination" as a way of registering the alchemic dynamic by which "a person" emerges, fails to emerge, or refuses to emerge amidst socially prescribed identity categories.

The two most deeply intermixed alchemic "ingredients" in Baldwin's queer imagination were race and sex. In his 1961 "love letter" to Norman Mailer published as "The Black Boy Looks at the White Boy," for example, Baldwin distinguishes the "absolutely naked" truth of the black struggle for identity from the unconscious expectation of white men that the world would "help them in the achievement of their identity." "[T]o become a Negro man, let alone a Negro artist," Baldwin writes, "one had to make oneself up as one went along. This had to be done in the not-at-all-metaphorical teeth of the world's determination to destroy you."[25] I want to draw attention to Baldwin's dual motion in this passage, accomplished through the simultaneous refusal of metaphoricity and appropriation of the power of metaphor. The world has teeth—not just guns or racist cops or drugs, but teeth. The starkness of the de-metaphorized metaphor corresponds to the black man's nakedness in the world, and the power of Baldwin's vision lies less in his figurative language than in his assertion of the literal truth of the figuration: the world's teeth bite black flesh. Expanding elsewhere on the ways white men's "private fears and longings"[26] are projected onto black men as part of an erotics of denial and erasure, Baldwin explicitly raises this same problem of paradoxical representation: "The brutality with which Negroes are treated in this country simply cannot be overstated, however unwilling white men may be to hear it. . . . For the horrors of the American Negro's life there has been almost no language."[27] In Baldwin's formulation, what "cannot be overstated" is also, contradictorily, beyond words. Yet the language of Baldwin's love letter, written in the space of charged masculinity that attracted America's premier literary black and white "boys" to each other, becomes that language. Baldwin's act of witnessing does not so much record that relationship as realize it with the written word. In reverse fashion, even as he achieved recognition as "author James Baldwin" by the American public, a perpetual state of namelessness emerged out of Baldwin's most profound perceptions of self and nation, informed, as they were, by race and sex. In search of love and in search of his name, Baldwin therefore becomes emblematic of the complex erotic relations that he names as the unnameable, the literal metaphor.

From this perspective, Baldwin stakes his claim in something of a queer imaginative wilderness. Where dominant culture refuses to imagine, cannot bear to imagine, or "simply" does not think to imagine erotic bonds, Baldwin intervenes with a remarkable complexity of mind. If, for example, homosexuality has been "the love that dare not speak its name," Baldwin simultaneously breaks that code of silence and recodes same-sex love not as shamefully unspeakable but as nearly unspeakably complicated, variously a forced confession and a state of transcendence. When he writes, in the raced context of the Atlanta child murders of the late 1970s and early 1980s, that "the imagination is poorly equipped to accommodate an action in which one, instinctively, recognizes the orgasmic release of self-hatred,"[28] Baldwin captures the paradoxical relationship that creates yet another inarticulate state, temperamentally and politically: Americans seem to be imaginatively exiled from their strongest, most powerful, most self-defining desires, perhaps especially the desire for their own annihilation. Baldwin's insight was not entirely new, although his exploration of it might well be the most important such contribution in all of American letters. D. H. Lawrence opens his important 1923 *Studies in Classic American Literature* by making essentially the same point: "'The world is a great dodger, and the American the greatest. Because they dodge their own very selves."[29] "Duplicity," Lawrence later adds, is the "fatal flaw" in American literature, for Americans give "[t]ight mental allegiance . . . to a morality which the passional self repudiates."[30] In the vacuum created when desire is expunged from thought, Baldwin creates language, figuring that which lies outside the target of the known and pushing the symbolic register into the resisting queer real.

To help me briefly explain Baldwin's transformation of unthinkable erotics into language, I turn to David Gerstner's recent book *Queer Pollen: White Seduction, Black Male Homosexuality, and the Cinematic.* If part of my own argument is that Baldwin literalizes (literally puts into language) ubiquitous but unnameable cultural desires, thereby rendering visible key truths that have been constructed as unimaginable, Gerstner offers a compelling alternative theory of queer representation in Baldwin. Gerstner, a cinema studies professor and queer theorist, reads Baldwin as working in a hybrid genre, at once literary and extra-literary, that enables him to meet the representational demands of his time. Specifically, Baldwin responds to the way that, according to Gerstner, "[f]or queer black men of the twentieth century, a new sensual language was . . . in order . . . , a new language to emphasize the visual and the aural—or what I identify as the cinematic."[31] By reading Baldwin's fiction through the visual/aural lens of the cinematic, Gerstner offers an important model for not only conceptualizing but concretizing the insistent vagueness of what I call the queer imagination. This is no easy task, for it requires the theorist to articulate, as does Gerstner (pointing to Derrida), the artist's own rendering of the "possibility of the impossible."[32] It is in that space of (im)possibility, Gerstner suggests, that "Baldwin's 'cinema of the mind' makes available a queer black 'real.'"[33]

To understand Baldwin's "queer black 'real'" and to understand the larger queer imaginative project of which he is an important part, one must first try to grasp the sheer force of creative will necessary to outrun the gravitational pull or interpretive drag of the raced heteronormative imagination. The apparent paltriness, the inflexibility, the rut of race- and sex-normative thought would not be so remarkable but for its unmeasured and seemingly immeasurable capacity to impoverish the imagination. It has a particularly thinning effect on the possibilities of and for desire. Audre Lorde, Baldwin's younger contemporary and interlocutor, articulates this problem in "Uses of the Erotic: The Erotic as Power," a contribution that must be contextualized within the feminist sex/porn debates of the 1970s and 1980s. "The need for sharing deep human feeling is a human need," recognizes Lorde, "[b]ut within the european-american tradition, this need is satisfied by certain proscribed erotic comings-together. These occasions are almost always characterized by a simultaneous looking away, a pretense of calling them something else, whether a religion, a fit, mob violence, or even playing doctor. And this misnaming of the need and the deed gives rise to . . . the abuse of feeling."[34] The instances of "misnaming" that Lorde identifies are neither random nor limited to or by the terms of the particular conversation in which she was engaged. Baldwin recognized them as well and, indeed, drew the reader's eye back precisely to scenes of misrecognized "erotic comings-together," not only in the church, the lynch mob, and the child's exploration that normative adult sexuality supposedly resolves, but also in national American identity, the hungry stomach, and the raced family tree. For Baldwin, all of these locations represent states of desire, sites where the power of the erotic, so eloquently invoked by Lorde, both threatens and enlivens. Baldwin made it his job to reveal these possibilities, the promise and the peril of misnamed desire.

It would be commendable to recognize and then write intelligently about the nuances of human desire in the absence of the erotic proscriptions created by crushing homophobia, crafty heterosexism, and enduring racism. That Baldwin did so in their presence makes him especially deserving of sustained queer theoretical attention. This does not mean that theorists should simply heap queer praise on Baldwin as a black gay literary pioneer, a designation that is, at any rate, itself a point of contention. Rather, more generally, the variety of pressures under which queer works are created—gender and race were especially in play for Baldwin—requires that literary interpreters generously address the limitations of (even as they are taught to think anew by) those ever-remarkable queer imaginative acts. Even at his finest, Baldwin—"the language animal"[35]—at times grapples to bring the complexities of unnamed desire to light, just as he misses opportunities for self-revelation.

Undoubtedly, some of the most difficult negotiations I make in this study involve the question of how to occupy the space of Baldwin's own absent critique. I have tried to address this tension explicitly when and where it emerges in my analysis, while trying to be mindful of the need for literary interpreters to do justice to the creative writers who make our work possible and necessary. For me, fair treatment involves the consideration that arises in the absence of mutuality in my literary relationship with Baldwin, and it requires a critical rerouting by which I align my interpretive eye with the author's so as to best gauge and represent the stakes when our visions diverge.[36] This book is by no means, then, an homage. It is, most generally, a recognition of the fact that Baldwin gives queer thinkers a lot of work to do. Tracing Baldwin's imagination is about articulating what he enables us to see, not just what he shows us. His vision can be problematic, but the field of vision he clears creates a usable space in which to read and respond. My larger argument about the importance of Baldwin's queer imagination to American letters relies, therefore, on the unpredictable dynamic between Baldwin's fiction and the ever-expanding constellation of queer thought it makes possible.

Part of the wonder of reading Baldwin comes in realizing the audacity required for a writer to undertake the project of representing unrepresentable erotic relationships so unflaggingly and despite myriad silencing forces. Reading Baldwin consequently demands that one enter his queer imagination, learning to think the unthinkable. Put differently, it relies on the ability to recognize the barely perceptible incarnations that restrictive anti-queer logics take. In his book *No Future: Queer Theory and the Death Drive*, Lee Edelman describes the logic of "reproductive futurism" as just such a curb on what can be imagined. Reproductive futurism, bending and bowing to the inviolable figure of "the Child," "impose[s] an ideological limit on political discourse as such, preserving in the process the absolute privilege of heteronormativity by rendering unthinkable, by casting outside the political domain, the possibility of queer resistance to this organizing principle of communal relations."[37] While Edelman specifically discusses the limitations on what counts as the political, his point has a more general utility in that it encourages the reader to see an outside where no inside/outside opposition was originally perceptible: "Impossibly, against all reason, my project stakes its claim to the very space that 'politics' makes unthinkable: the space outside the framework within which politics as we know it appears."[38] Like Monique Wittig, whom I turn to shortly, Edelman dramatically argues for a radical queer repositioning vis-à-vis pervasive systems of unexamined normalcy. I argue neither for a yet-unimagined queer future nor for a queer rejection of futurity. Rather, taking Edelman's cue, I suggest that if the project of heteronormativity can be framed as an imperative to unthink possibilities for nonheteronormative practices, ideas, politics, and lives and if "queer" can be defined not only as marking sexual or erotic practice but as an imaginative act or impulse or investment that pushes back against the impoverishing heteronormative construction of reality, Baldwin had a fiercely queer imagination, the ability to think states of desire that operate "impossibly, against all reason."[39]

Robyn Wiegman has repeatedly addressed the imaginative potential of queer theory through an ongoing analysis of queer disciplinarity and the evolution of related fields.[40] Addressing Jack Halberstam's *Female Masculinity*, which performs the queer work of formulating "alternative political imaginaries," Wiegman suggests that Halberstam's brand of queer scholarship requires us to recognize that "lived practices are far more complicated and unpredictable than the languages that critics often use to describe them."[41] Wiegman dramatizes this aspect of the late Monique Wittig's work as well. In "un-remembering" the contributions of the foundational lesbian thinker, Wiegman cites Wittig's "absolute refusal to concede to the conditions of the known" and her "relentless . . . struggle against compulsory meaning."[42] Wiegman, Halberstam, and Wittig all gesture toward the additional way in which the queer imagination takes on meaning for me in the present book.

It describes not only the creative energies that produce the primary texts under analysis but also the critical approaches that must meet the interpretive challenges laid down by Baldwin's work. A key attribute of queer theoretical inquiry as I deploy it here is its capacity for reading imaginatively, identifying non-normative erotic relations, and even daring to queerly rewrite Baldwin—to reconstruct the stories almost told, those fictions of desire keenly desired yet not fully elaborated. Queer theory, I argue, can and must take up the imaginative work of reading the impossible narratives in Baldwin's fiction into being. As much as this is a book about James Baldwin, it is also a book that tries to address the possibilities for queer theoretical work while also, as I discuss below, challenging some of the ways the queer intellectual enterprise has become institutionalized and even dogmatic. My hope, in any case, is that the dynamic relationship between my subject and my critical framework will prove clearly imagined throughout.

Yet Wiegman raises additional questions for me about just how clear the relationship ought to be between my subject and my critical orientation when she queries, "[W]hat it is we expect our relationship to our objects of study to *do*."⁴³ Interrogating her own assessment of Wittig, Wiegman agitates against simply incorporating thinkers from the past into queer theory of the present in an effort to build coherence or wholeness into a (critically and otherwise) incoherent world: "Is this what outliving begets to us, a present tense that we presume is capable of capturing the complexity of the world?"⁴⁴ Wiegman ultimately concludes,

> [L]et's not "remember" [Wittig]. Let's not incorporate her into queer studies by memorializing her into the current habits of critique, or confer status on her by making her queer theory's theoretical precursor, as if giving her queer theoretical thoughts before the fact makes her work of more value. Let's not use her as a feminist weapon against queer theory, as if the only thing interesting about second-wave feminist thought was the tug of war it offers to every iteration of post-structuralist thought. Let's refuse the lure of saying that Wittig either knew queer theory, instinctively, before we did, or that she knew more than queer theory ever did. Let's take Wittig at her word and imagine having the ability to imagine other possibilities instead.⁴⁵

The challenge of "un-remembering" Wittig is precisely the challenge of keeping open the potential for queer imagination, at times thanks to and at times despite Wittig, and at times thanks to and at times despite queer theory. Quite the same can be said of remembering Baldwin, who has become black queer literature's poster boy, forefather, prophet, and palimpsest. In further queering Baldwin, I do not wish to attempt the shortsighted and, in fact, impossible critical task of foreclosing other treatments and readings. As a reader and theorist, I find it thrilling to realize that my subject, like Wiegman's, often exceeds the cast of my critical net. It is equally thrilling to realize that I have thrown the net in just the right spot. If I overreach in appropriating Baldwin for queer theory, I do so with the recognition of the inevitable partiality of that appropriation.

In any case, Baldwin will not be so easily appropriated by queer theory and the purely deconstructive methodologies it often employs. Indeed, Baldwin is quite useful in helping me to navigate the theoretical cul-de-sac created when the work of deconstructing identity seems too formulaic, critically unreflective, or unresponsive to the text at hand. In this work, I follow Kathryn Bond Stockton, who also writes at the intersection "where 'black' meets 'queer,'" in her book *Beautiful Bottom, Beautiful Shame*. Stockton "emphasize[s] the obvious switching of signifying tracks that occurs when a sign that is generally attached to black, let's say, flashes in the signifying field of 'queer'.... Each switchpoint is a kind of off-rhyme ...: a point at which we intellectually sense how one sign ... lends its force to another."[46] Having noted the often idiosyncratic nature of meaning making, however, she astutely critiques "a focus once so generative but now too familiar and too imprecise: that much more watery and indistinct form of meaning-redirection, going under the name of 'instability.'" Intersectionality, Stockton reminds us, can be anything but unstable, anything but slippery. She therefore argues that "it is time now to shift from this focus [on instability]—shift from its status as destination—so that we may explore more specific collisions, collusions, and borrowings between the signs that identities, however unstable, may be fond of, or even despise."[47] Rather than automatically eschewing identity in favor of a theory of instability, Stockton advocates that we "theorize from deep within"[48] the fictions we interpret, be those fictions disciplinary, identitarian, or literary.

In my work and in the queer theoretical field generally, this tension between fictional and critical (in)stability often erupts as some version of the gay-versus-queer debate.[49] I both engage that debate here and try to think beyond it. To engage it means recognizing the value of each position. Running through queer theory is a liberatory, anti-identitarian thread that deconstructs sexual and gender binaries by, for example, historicizing them.

Absent the "truth" of these naturalized categories, queer theorists have attended both to the possibility and the reality of shifting, multiple, and sometimes contradictory identifications and desires. The project of destabilizing prescriptive norms, especially those that attempt to solder together sex, gender, and sexual identity, has been one of queer theory's most long-standing investments. Yet despite the success of that deconstructive effort and the allure of unscripted queer non-identity, gay and lesbian identities retain extra-normative (that is, "beyond normative") meaning, even for and among queers. For instance, to be gay often feels to me like a deeply radical state of being, as far from normative as it could be. Undoubtedly, what feels radical to me will look normal (and normative) to others, just as coming out will seem alternately possible or not, desirable or not, liberating or not, depending on one's situation. On the one hand, gays and lesbians, through uncritical participation in normalizing regimes of identity, risk foreclosing possibilities for change, or what Butler calls the "future uses of the sign."[50] On the other hand, queers, through their disruption and disavowal of stable markers of identity, risk the personal and political efficacy that can accrue quite literally under the banner of gay and lesbian identity. Drilling down one more level, the reclamation of "queer" as a marker of affiliation and as a critical framework has sometimes reproduced the dominant-culture, masculinist dynamic by which lesbians, feminists, and transgender people are again invisibilized. I use queer theory as a tool for mediating these tensions, for critiquing the exclusions required by normative gay identity, for valuing the differences invisibilized by those exclusions, for imagining the possibilities beyond identity, and for reflecting on the ramifications, both positive and negative, of that queer liberation.

BLACK QUEER STUDIES; OR, QUEER STUDIES . . .

I have already mentioned the important collection *James Baldwin Now*, which productively situates Baldwin at the disciplinary intersections of cultural studies. An equally important anthology narrows that focus and suggests a possible reason for the absence of more queer Baldwin books. *Black Queer Studies: A Critical Anthology* breaks new ground as a "critical intervention in the discourses of black studies and queer studies."[51] It seeks to draw out the "interanimat[ing]"[52] potential in these two disciplines, the former of which, by successfully translating activism into academic standing in the 1970s and 1980s, became a model of disciplinarity for the latter in the 1990s and beyond.[53] With the advent of black queer studies, "quare" studies, and queer of color critique, Baldwin's work has achieved a new presence, not because the composite term "black queer" somehow succeeds in stabilizing an intersection—though as Stockton notes, it may—but precisely because such terms often operate in unpredicatably elaborate and productive relationship to each other. Black queer studies recognizes that multidimensional relationship, just as it anticipates the terms (of class, gender, nation) that it inevitably, if only momentarily, holds in abeyance. Far from a totalizing impulse, black queer studies energizes Baldwin studies by marking a racial and sexual connection, the specifics of which inevitably enrich (and often explode) the very terms used to frame the debate. It is no surprise that of the seventeen essays that comprise *Black Queer Studies*, three focus primarily (and others secondarily) on the work and influence of James Baldwin.

This is all to say that I have been keenly aware of my own omissions and deferrals in framing my approach to Baldwin. The question I have often returned to is, does queering Baldwin as a primary mode of analysis risk underplaying the importance of race, even if only until the queer analysis is recognized as necessarily multidimensional? More specifically, should the title of this volume be *James Baldwin and the Queer Black Imagination*, or can the term "queer" alone concretely suggest the study of racialized sexuality? If my choice of title seems inattentive to race, I must ask the reader's patience. It is because considerations of race run so thoroughly through this study that I feel (somewhat) justified in foregrounding queerness alone in the title. Perhaps my title even raises interesting questions about the extent to which the term "queer" can seem to foreclose "black," when, in fact, such a foreclosure is impossible. If one of the criticisms of queer theory has been that it can invisibly recenter whiteness, I should be clear that I take race studies to be implicit within queer studies done well, and vice versa. To the extent that this volume will make the term "black queer" evoke difference but also operate as a kind of redundancy, I will have succeeded in conveying this complexity. As McBride argues, "Baldwin reminds us that whenever we are speaking of race, we are always already speaking about gender, sexuality, and class."[54] I argue, further, that whenever we speak of queerness, we are always already speaking in all of these registers.

But I want to keep an eye on the assumptive risks of "the implicit," for just the opposite meaning can be made of the term "queer." E. Patrick Johnson reminds us that if the queer umbrella holds out the promise of recognizing and validating all sorts of differences under its inclusive dome, it can also undermine its own goal (and politics) by dislocating specific queer identities from the cultural contexts that give them meaning. Finding this "culture-specific positionality . . . absent from the dominant and more conventional usage of 'queer,' particularly in its most recent theoretical reappropriation in the academy," Johnson instead draws on "the vernacular roots implicit in [his] grandmother's use of the word ["quare"] to devise a strategy for theorizing racialized sexuality."[55] The same dangerous hypocrisy of inclusivity emerges in queer studies as, for instance, in women's studies and disability studies: in advocating for the inclusion into the academy of subjects excluded from primary canonical fields of study, scholars have sometimes mimicked exclusionary practices. Barbara Christian's important essay "The Race for Theory" argues that this paradox is replayed with particular poignancy when theory is the coin of the realm. Queer theory in particular not only demands to be included in the homophobic academy but also purports to be defined by a sweeping inclusivity of marginalized subjects and ideas. Johnson and Christian remind us that we must apply continuous, multidirectional critical pressure if we are to fulfill that mission.

In framing my study of Baldwin, I have borne in mind this sense of the potential for growth as well as the potential pitfalls of queer theory. Without diminishing race and without subsuming race under queerness, I have chosen to privilege queerness in my title not only because it has seemed to me a strangely used and strangely useful signifier in Baldwin criticism but because Baldwin's work presents glaring opportunities for queer theory. With the important exception of black queer studies, sustained queer critiques of Baldwin have been absent. What exists is a variety of queer readings of Baldwin by scholars across the disciplines, including literary critics, sociologists, African Americanists, memoirists, cultural critics, historians, and feminist scholars. Baldwin's work has attracted thinkers in a remarkably multidisciplinary fashion. This has been especially true when scholars familiar with Baldwin want to venture into the amorphous field of queer theory, where Baldwin has become, for various audiences with various agendas, a queer gatekeeper. Baldwin, it seems, makes for good queer interpretation, allowing many of us to "cut our queer teeth," so to speak, on his fiction, gaining interpretive experience, sharpening our analytic skills, and practicing some of the methodologies and learning the nomenclature of queer theoretical inquiry. Likewise, for more full-throated queer theorists in the academy, Baldwin's work has offered a kind of depth capable of supporting even the most sophisticated and expert, but nevertheless pointed and discrete, analyses. The odd result is that while there have been important queer contributions to Baldwin scholarship by queers—indeed, one almost inevitably passes through Baldwin in the queer academy—Baldwin's larger oeuvre has yet to be fully theorized *as* queer.

My students have often wondered about the practicality of queer theory, as have I. Queer theory is sometimes (but, I want to emphasize, not always) abstract and unwieldy. It problematizes its own disciplinary construction in an endless act of remaking itself. Queer theorists are accused of being inaccessible in some settings and overly personal in others. Michael Warner's inaugural question "What do queers want?" continues to give us fits twenty years in.[56] But Baldwin has helped me to come to terms with the question of queer practicality. His queer imagination has helped me to realize an important relationship between the scope of a problem and the scope of the imagination needed to address that problem. If queer theory is abstract and unwieldy, are not sexism, heterosexism, homophobia, and transphobia supremely abstract and unwieldy, their visible manifestations but a fraction of their broad spectrum? If queer theory ranges from the critically inaccessible to the vulnerably personal, does this breadth not speak to its own dire necessity, the need for every possible kind of response to a status quo that allows for so few voices to be heard and so few visions to be shared? Ultimately, I find queer theory daring in much the same way that I find Baldwin daring. They each recognize the scope of the crisis, they each dare to share that dangerous information, and they each imagine that things could be otherwise.

CHAPTER I

James Baldwin's Queer Utility

Black Gay Male Literary Tradition
and Go Tell It on the Mountain

> Identity would seem to be the garment with which one covers the nakedness
> of the self: in which case, it is best that the garment be loose, a little like the
> robes of the desert, through which robes one's nakedness can always be felt,
> and, sometimes, discerned. This trust in one's nakedness is all that gives one the
> power to change one's robes.
>
> —JAMES BALDWIN, THE DEVIL FINDS WORK

> [W]e don't have many names for our radical dependence on the past, how it
> facilitates even our sharpest breaks with it.
>
> —CHRISTOPHER NEALON, "QUEER TRADITION"

> Once our traditions have been sullied, once they carry the taint of an all-too-
> modern homosexual funkiness, it becomes that much more apparent that we
> are continually in a process of choosing whether and how to continue those
> traditions.
>
> —ROBERT REID-PHARR, ONCE YOU GO BLACK: DESIRE, CHOICE,
> AND BLACK MASCULINITY IN POST-WAR AMERICA

In the introduction, I prefaced the ways that James Baldwin has been alternately and distinctly situated within an African American literary canon and
a gay literary canon. That "apparent" incommensurability has been created
by strange bedfellows. In his 1991 discussion of the homophobic reception of
Baldwin's fiction, Emmanuel Nelson argues, "Critically engaging Baldwin's
fiction proves to be too much of a challenge for many white heterosexual
critics, although there are notable exceptions. . . . But to many the task of
examining the perspective of a novelist who is both Black and gay is too tax-
ing on their imaginative resources. . . . Their reactions range from mild dis-

comfort to shock, angry dismissal and hysteria, and studied silence."[1] Nelson thoroughly documents the racialized homophobia present in white reviewers' assessments of Baldwin's fiction. White straight reviewers "seem generally comfortable with Baldwin's non-fiction prose [which rarely mentions the subject of homosexuality] but are often uncomfortable with his fiction [in which homosexuality is often present]."[2] In other words, critics' negative *homophobic* reviews (including no review at all) effectively popularize and privilege Baldwin as an exclusively *black* mouthpiece. This occurs precisely to the extent that anti-racist, anti-homophobic "imaginative resources" fail them. Robert Reid-Pharr suggests another reason why homosexuality in Baldwin's fiction (and life) has gone un-reviewed by literary critics when compared to race, though he approaches the matter from the other direction. Gently parroting the critics, Reid-Pharr writes, "One must remember always that Baldwin is *the* black author, the paragon of the Black American intellect, the nation's prophet of racial tolerance, one whose queer sexuality presumably stands in such anomalous relation to his racial presence, intellectual and otherwise, that it works only as the exception proving the rule."[3] The complex rationale at play here, according to Reid-Pharr, is that Baldwin's positioning as "the" black writer not only results from the critics' failure to pursue homosexual themes but also rests on their unwillingness to interrogate, as Baldwin would have them do, whiteness in relation to blackness. In this scenario, both whiteness and homosexuality become intangible through the insistence on Baldwin's black authorial presence.

While these twin, white critical disavowals, the first of Baldwin's homosexuality and the second of Baldwin's insights into the construction of whiteness, have perhaps resulted in the author's racialization as black, disavowals have also come from quarters of black literary and cultural criticism. I want to acknowledge that, like the white straight critics whom Nelson takes to task, black critics have sometimes exhibited the same homophobic reactions to Baldwin, "from mild discomfort to shock, angry dismissal and hysteria, and studied silence." But I want to turn to Sharon Patricia Holland's important analysis of African American literary tradition and its relationship to black gay writing to deepen the conversation about black critics' appropriation of black gay writers as (primarily or exclusively) black writers. In the fourth chapter of her book *Raising the Dead: Readings of Death and (Black) Subjectivity*, Holland explicitly seeks to "foste[r] a procreative black imaginative terrain"[4] that does not excise black gay subjectivity, including that found in her primary textual example, Randall Kenan's novel *A Visitation of Spirits*.

Holland argues that one primary obstacle standing in the way of the rec-lamation of the novel's black gay presence is the African American social and literary critic's strong desire to solidify a black literary tradition. Just as such a tradition has been subverted by racist constructions of an "Ameri-can" (read "white") national literature, African American critics' need for a tradition of "their own" quite often returns us to "territories where power is utilized in its most 'traditional' form."[5] In both cases, homophobic exclusion becomes a tradition-defining strategy. But further, part of the difficulty in trying to situate black gay literature within a black literary tradition extends from the fact that "the word *tradition*, in the African American sense, en-compasses all that is surely black and procreative."[6] Black critics, privileging family narratives within the text and deploying genealogical tropes to set texts in relation to each other, thus reassert a traditional power structure by relying on a heterosexualized hermeneutics. Linking the need for an African American literary tradition to the larger field of play in which "tradition" reinscribes normative relations, Holland concludes that "the gay, lesbian, or bisexual (sub)text of critical and literary endeavors, and therefore the Afri-can American *canon*, is somehow treated as secondary to developing a lit-erary project emphasizing its procreative aspects. The relegation of queer subjects to the unproductive end of black literary production places them in a liminal space. Such disinheriting from the procreative process contradicts a communal desire to bring back (all) black subjects from the dead, from the place of silence."[7] While my extended treatment of the vexed relationship between race and procreation appears in chapter 4 of this book, I want to mark here the important links Holland makes between retrieving an Afri-can American literary genealogy and reclaiming procreative rights denied to African Americans under the many-layered system of American racism. Yet finding "no precedent" either in black literature or the lesbian and gay canon for Kenan's story of a black gay Southern youth's suicide and ghostly return, Holland looks to Baldwin's *Giovanni's Room*, where "the tradition unfolded itself in a queer configuration of black and white."[8]

Despite the problems she identifies with "tradition," Holland resists jetti-soning that critical framework, a decision that has several implications. Her reading attempts to signify off of the unwelcoming metaphors of hetero-sexual procreation in order to "embrace Kenan's novel as hopeful progeny in a long line of sons and daughters."[9] Not only can we question the success of the resignification of familial metaphors in this context, but we can also consider the genealogical irony involved. The queer "progeny" exemplified by

A Visitation of Spirits joins the "long line of sons and daughters" not through birth but through death, a highly suspect insinuation of queer blackness into familial history that seems more a rupture of that line than an integration into it. Standing against the hopefulness of Holland's formulation is her final realization that inclusion within the broader African American literary tradition requires of Kenan "the ultimate *erasing* of black subjectivity in order to actualize a queer project,"[10] for his black gay protagonist must resort to suicide in hopes that speaking from the dead will "force a community to see what it has left behind."[11] Perhaps despite her critical motivations, then, Holland raises the possibility that black gay literature cannot be incorporated into the field of African American literature as long as the latter is framed as a "tradition." Assimilation into that "tradition" may require that black gay presence be made visible only through a concomitant rendering as invisible—in Kenan's case, a ghosting that results in the absent presence of his black gay protagonist. Against this absence, Holland reads Baldwin as making Kenan's narrative more present.

Holland's work offers a compelling example of a scholar's deep investment in reimagining her field of study—"the African American literary tradition, to which," she writes, "I had directed my life's work for the last ten years"[12]—to include queer perspectives. My initial point, which may at first seem innocuous, is that Holland, like so many other readers, turns to Baldwin to facilitate that reconciliation. He functions as foundational to the architecture of two now mutually buttressing edifices, being both the conduit for reading black gay male writers into the larger African American literary tradition and, simultaneously, the cornerstone of the black gay literary tradition itself. The excellence of his writing and its unparalleled critical and popular success provide the internal logic that justifies and enables that positioning. A black tradition cannot ignore him, and a black gay tradition cannot exist without him.

In fact, neither of the preceding statements is indisputable. But Baldwin makes it seem as though they are. More precisely, Baldwin's critical positioning is now such that these statements have become, effectively, obvious. For this reason, Baldwin's work has achieved a broad and even pervasive critical utility for scholars, like Holland and myself, who work at the theoretical intersection of black queer studies. In this chapter, I will analyze the status Baldwin has achieved in black queer studies, not by questioning the sometimes problematic ways his work has been used to integrate black gay writing into the African American tradition but by interrogating the other, perhaps more obvious, use that has been made of him as the father figure of the black gay male literary tradition. As I have already suggested, even an essay such as Holland's that explicitly attends to the dangers of constructing literary traditions risks naturalizing Baldwin as the core of black gay writing. Rather than an isolated instance, this case can be made more generally: as black queer studies has variously identified the intersections, overlaps, and dependencies of black literary canons and gay literary canons, it has, as a consequence, also (re)constructed a black gay male literary tradition. Within that tradition, one pattern is unmistakable: critics and creative writers alike have conceptualized the work of black gay male writers by thinking, as though inevitably, through Baldwin. Yet, as Holland implicitly argues, we must question the power plays by which all traditions are constructed. If Baldwin has been made to anchor or organize a black gay male literary tradition, in what ways, perhaps unavoidably, has "power [been] utilized in its most 'traditional' form" in the creation of that tradition?[13] Might we need to rethink how certain queer constructions paradoxically follow traditional ideologies? What might a black queer literary tradition look like, and what is Baldwin's place in it? In this chapter, I complicate Baldwin's pivotal positioning within black gay male writing by arguing that he operates, on the one hand, as the necessary central figure in the field and, on the other hand, as an unstable signifier of an always-rupturing tradition.

A NECESSARY REFERENCE

If it is nearly impossible to think of a black gay male literary tradition without thinking of and through James Baldwin, it is nevertheless quite possible to know the work of James Baldwin well—including his fiction, plays, essays, and his many interviews—without having almost any sense of the broader tradition that he has been made to anchor. In light of this asymmetry, I want first to reflect in some detail various moments in which Baldwin has been situated at the center of black gay male literature by other writers in that tradition, paying special attention to the metaphors used to conceptualize his centrality. An important volume of black gay male writing published in the spring of 1988, *Other Countries: Black Gay Voices*, contains the following dedication:

In celebration of their lives:
JAMES BALDWIN (1924–1987)
RICHARD BRUCE NUGENT (1906–1987)
BAYARD RUSTIN (1912–1987)

The collection begins with an introduction by Colin Robinson, who edited this first volume of *Other Countries* along with Cary Alan Johnson and Terence Taylor. The introduction begins,

Welcome to a birth. In your hands is the latest addition to the small but growing canon of Black Gay Male literature, the new manchild in a family whose dead and living forefathers, brothers and cousins include B, BGM, Black and Queer (by Adrian Sanford), Blackbird and Eight Days a Week (by Larry Duplechan), Blackheart, Blacklight, Black/Out, Brothers, Change of Territory (by Melvin Dixon), Conditions and Earth Life (by Essex Hemphill), Diplomat, Habari-Daftari, In the Life, Moja: Black and Gay, Rafiki, "Smoke, Lilies and Jade" (by Richard Bruce Nugent), Tongues Untied, Yemonja, and the many works of James Baldwin and Samuel Delany."

Performing the task of "birthing" a "new manchild" into the "family" of "forefathers," "brothers," and "cousins," the introduction ends by further metaphorizing *Other Countries*, describing it as "a vision" and "a difficult journey into new territory," as well as an "excavation of a past that has been lost, hidden, stolen." Building on this new/old framework, Robinson returns, in the end, to more familial metaphors to characterize the publication: "It is a [*sic*] homage to our forebears—like Richard Bruce Nugent and James Baldwin," "a pride in our immediate parentage in *Blackheart*," and a "legacy to go beyond [this] country."[14]

In the lineage described by Robinson, Baldwin stands shoulder to shoulder with several other "forefathers," Richard Bruce Nugent and Bayard Rustin most notably, as the dedication in *Other Countries* makes clear. Nevertheless, Baldwin is more often represented as occupying a unique position, even in such intimate and elevated company. Nelson, writing in a legitimized, encyclopedic context, can thus repeat what has become a critical commonplace, that "[a]lthough [Baldwin] occupies an important place in African-American as well as gay American literatures, the significance of his life and work in the specific context of the black gay male literary tradition is immeasurable. He continues to be its defining figure."[15] But even in the much more personal and idiosyncratic context of a blog, accomplished black gay experimental writer John Keene commits to the same basic argument, that although Baldwin is "the source of an ongoing 'agon'" for certain writers, "every Black gay male writer writes under the star (in all senses of that word) of Baldwin (and Hughes, and Nugent, and Cullen, etc.)." This interesting parenthetical both broadens the "stars" in the black gay literary firmament beyond Baldwin and suggests that perhaps Baldwin's star shines with a special light, illuminating the past, present, and future like no other black gay writer. Though he is "aware of [Baldwin's] literary failings and his personal imperfections," Keene maintains, "[F]or me, as for so many writers, [Baldwin remains] a towering and essential figure. He was, I should add, the spark that lit the fire that became the Dark Room Writers Collective, among other things, though his influence was also central to Other Countries and related [black queer] writing groups of the 1980s."[16]

A synthesis of the two preceding paragraphs reveals a powerful composite picture of Baldwin: the "defining," "towering," "essential" "forefather" standing at the center, chronologically as well as figuratively, of the black gay male literary tradition in the United States. He has been made the fulcrum on which the plank of the black gay male literary tradition has tipped, located as he is in the middle of the last century, halfway between the ambiguously queer writers of the Harlem Renaissance and the productivity, much of it cut short by AIDS, of the gay eighties and nineties. No one casts a longer shadow; no one ignites a brighter spark. Again, I will question (even as I employ and test) the familial/genealogical renderings on which *Other Countries* relies and the notion of the author's primacy that Keene posits. It is clear, though, that such constructions have been not only extremely prevalent but, more important, terribly useful. Indeed Baldwin, I will argue, has a protean and multifaceted "queer utility," a usefulness for a complex variety of reading audiences. I want to inquire into that queer utility by, first, analyzing an extended example of Baldwin's usefulness to two writers in particular, Essex Hemphill and Joseph Beam. I choose these men for several reasons. Both have been inestimably important to black gay literature as writers themselves and as readers and editors of writing by other gay men of color. Hemphill particularly stands out, in much the same way as Baldwin, for the often devastating power of his social vision and the beauty of his writing. Thomas Glave's invocation of Hemphill's ever-presence, captured in the term "(re)recalling" that weds memory to "always, now," suggests that

Hemphill's death from AIDS marked a rupture into a "giantless time."[17] I argue, however, that both Hemphill and Beam looked to Baldwin in ways that ultimately make his "giant" presence in the black gay writing tradition at once unquestionable and problematic. I therefore frame Hemphill and Beam as exemplary figures of the watershed moment of black gay male writing in the 1980s and early 1990s that secured yet another heritage for Baldwin to disavow.

In his introduction to the 1991 collection *Brother to Brother: New Writings by Black Gay Men*,[18] Essex Hemphill recalls his search for "the evidence of being" as a lonely and sometimes disabling attempt to uncover writing by and about black gay men.

> My search for evidence of things not seen, evidence of black gay experiences on record, evidence of "being" to contradict the pervasive invisibility of black gay men, at times proved futile. I was often frustrated by codes of secrecy, obstructed by pretenses of discretion, or led astray by constructions of silence, constructions fabricated of illusions and perhaps cowardice. But I persevered. I continued to seek affirmation, reflection, and identity. I continued seeking the *necessary* historical reference for my desires.[19]

"As I approached the mid-1980s," recounts Hemphill, "I began to wonder if gay men of African descent existed in literature at all, beyond the works of Baldwin and Bruce Nugent, or the closeted works of writers of the Harlem Renaissance." He then continues by singling Baldwin out for special mention, noting that Baldwin

> created some of the most significant works to be presented by an "acknowledged" black gay man in this century. . . . [I]n the specific context of black gay literature, Baldwin's special legacy serves as role model, as source of inspiration pointing toward the possibility of being *and* excellence. The legacy he leaves us to draw from is a precious gift for us to hold tight as we persevere.[20]

For Hemphill (and undoubtedly for countless others), Baldwin symbolizes the very possibility of being a black gay male writer, in that his visibility enables Hemphill's own self-awareness; Hemphill sees *himself* thanks to the evidence Baldwin has left behind. In characterizing as "necessary" the visible reference that might reflect his raced homoerotic desire, Hemphill suggests that his own artistic identity somehow depends on a literary fore-runner such as Baldwin, whose "precious gift," in Hemphill's astute estima-tion, is his legacy as a black gay male "role model" for the younger writer. Even Hemphill's narrative style in his appropriation and redeployment of Baldwin's phrase "the evidence of things not seen" evinces Baldwin as the referent for the act of making black gay male experience legible. The idea at work here is that we are enabled or even created by our desiring forebears (or contemporaries) and the traces they leave behind.

Joseph Beam, whose groundbreaking 1986 anthology, *In the Life: A Black Gay Anthology*, was the first collection to make the visibility of black gay men its primary focus, raises the same issue of self-representation in the introduction to that volume, demonstrating the centrality of the theme of living in and as a shadow.[21] Myriam Chancy notes that for Beam the artist, "the painful absence of representation in popular culture of Black gay life" proved especially disabling. "As a writer himself, Beam [sought] ... Black gay authors whom to emulate," while refusing "to read those white gay writers who have rendered him invisible within the pages of their texts."[22] Yet Beam laments, "How many times could I read Baldwin's *Just Above My Head*?"[23] What Hemphill and Beam sought was a lineage, literary and historical, raced and queer.

The black queer gaze that retrospectively seeks out and finds a forebear in Baldwin simultaneously projects itself into the future to form an ongoing lineage of black gay male writers. That forward-looking dynamic is often framed in the language of familial obligation. "If there is to be evidence of our experiences," concludes Hemphill, "we learned by the close of the 1980s that our own self-sufficiency must ensure it, so that future generations of black gay men will have references for their desires."[24] Beam also addresses the generational discontinuity black gay men have faced, namely, "making ourselves from scratch." Beam narrates his experience of looking at "a world not created in my image" yet having to do that world's bidding, only to be faced at day's end with the task of "rush[ing] home to do my own: creating myself from scratch as a black gay man."[25] Like Hemphill, Beam writes with an eye toward the future so that others will be able to look to the past with a sense of familiarity.

What is it that we are passing along to our cousin from North Carolina, the boy down the block, our nephew who is a year old, or our sons who may follow us in this life? What is it that we leave them beyond this shadow-play: the search for a candlelit romance in a poorly lit bar, the rhythm and the beat, the furtive sex in the back street? What is it that we pass along to them or do they, too, need to start from scratch?[26]

Both writers link themselves to Baldwin by constructing a larger, still-materializing tradition; they vow to "carry the word."[27]

I want to take seriously the need so eloquently recorded by Hemphill, Beam, and other black gay writers of the late twentieth century. To do so, I believe we must follow those writers in their understanding of the feminist truth that "the personal is the political."[28] In their difficult searches that eventually led them to reconstruct a black gay literary inheritance around the work and person of Baldwin, many black gay men responded in deeply personal yet strikingly similar ways to the dramatic political punishments of social homophobia and, often, familial dispossession, both of which were also shaped by dominant cultural racism. Likewise, in their "reclaiming" of a tradition, they responded to an increasingly cohesive cultural context that, combined with their resolutely avowed needs, allowed for the articulation of a black gay male subjectivity and, therefore, literary genealogy. "Reclaiming" tradition, in other words, belies complicated acts of invention, acts of queer (because complicated) utility. Steven G. Fullwood, writer, archivist for the Schomburg Center for Research in Black Culture, and founder of the Black Gay and Lesbian Archive, suggests that writers of Hemphill's era had to "claim gay" explicitly as part of a politics of presence initiated by black lesbians such as Audre Lorde, Barbara Smith, and Cheryl Clarke. That politics, encapsulated in Clarke's call to "[w]rite for our lives," allowed for certain trajectories and traditions to be articulated. Those traditions, however, would be very different from any legacy available to Baldwin, who "had to say 'gay' to get past it" and who, as I will discuss in this book's conclusion, often stands at odds with black and lesbian feminist thought. Many black gay male writers of the 1980s, however, returned to black lesbian feminism, especially as it helped to articulate the possibilities for black queer collectivity. Thus "the definition of, and necessity of, 'tradition' changes," according to Fullwood, "as does the necessity of black queer presence."[29] Writing for one's black gay life in the 1980s and after inevitably meant something new. It meant writing in a cultural context infused with feminist thought but also radicalized by sociopolitical conservatism, its renewed racism, and its primary weapon of homophobia, AIDS. For black gay men to remain invisible under these "liberated" conditions, conditions that had failed to liberate, would have required new and unacceptable forms of self-deception. It would have required hiding from the fact that one was being killed *as* a black queer—homophobia, racism, and sexism having sharpened themselves anew on each other in that decade. The response of many black queers to the overtly threatening culture that explicitly sought their erasure was to claim identity in their work. For many black gay men in particular, "tradition"—far from a quaint notion—became a lifeline.

Discussing Baldwin's "black" first novel and his "homosexual" second novel, Marlon Ross joins Fullwood in attributing Baldwin's stature as black gay male role model to the broader cultural conditions in which Hemphill and Beam sought him out as much as to the personal needs of individual black artists bereft of a queer heritage. Ross writes, "Only with the emergence of a more autonomous gay black sociopolitical consciousness in the early 1980s did a public discourse arise that began to integrate Baldwin's 'gay' novel into an African American context. It is as if only an openly gay black readership could give a valid racial identity to a novel otherwise cut off from black experience, and it is no surprise that Baldwin's work as a whole has been a major cultural resource for people who identify as black and gay."[30] In Ross's formulation, Baldwin becomes a "valid" black gay writer retroactively, once the kind of readership exists that can make that demand of him. If Baldwin was a forefather to the many writers of the 1980s (and after) who looked to him as such, it is also true, and not contradictory, to say that their "looking to" Baldwin echoes with a procreative, forefather-making energy.

That potentially queer construction of black gay male literary genealogy goes largely unexplored, however, overdetermined as Baldwin's queer utility has been by the conceptual limitations of "tradition." Recognizing the normalizing power that attends the uses to which Baldwin is so often put, Ross immediately argues, "Nonetheless, the easy categorization of [*Go Tell It on the Mountain* and *Giovanni's Room*] projects onto them the very denials that Baldwin was attempting to bring to the surface, and the potential ghettoization of Baldwin as an author 'for' black gay people also contains assumptions against which his work struggles."[31] In another context, Dwight McBride specifically notes Hemphill's reliance on claims to identity when he writes, "[Hemphill] demonstrates his access to the various categories of [black gay male] identity he claims, [but he] does not critique ... the idea of the categories themselves ... [as he] plays the 'race/sexuality' card."[32] In this, Hemphill appears at least partially to employ the "guard and keep" strategy of identity that Baldwin saw as widespread and relatively unquestioned: "Most people guard and keep; they suppose that it is they themselves and what they identify with themselves that they are guarding and keeping, whereas what they are actually guarding and keeping is their system of reality and what they assume themselves to be."[33] Hemphill sees Baldwin standing at the nexus of "black gay man" precisely because he adopts "the idea" of a black gay male role model that Baldwin, to the contrary, refused to be. Implicit in the argument for generational continuity among black gay men is a reliance on the notion of a recognizable, if sometimes undiscovered, identity.

In their difficult search for self, Hemphill and Beam take hope thanks to the evidence left behind by Baldwin, and in doing so they run oddly parallel to another "traditional" use to which Baldwin has been put. For Hemphill, Baldwin exemplifies black gay male "being *and* excellence"; in much the same way, for reviewers and scholars, he has exemplified *black* "being and excellence" or, more frequently, "the voice of black experience," supposedly demonstrated par excellence by the author's first novel, *Go Tell It on the Mountain*. D. Quentin Miller notes that three of Baldwin's works consistently appear in anthologies and on college syllabi: the 1953 novel *Go Tell It on the Mountain*, the 1955 essay collection *Notes of a Native Son*, and the 1957 short story "Sonny's Blues."[34] Chosen, surely, not only for their quality but, as their common themes and overarching concerns suggest, for their excellence as expressions of African American experience and "black consciousness," these works have established Baldwin as an essential American writer by virtue of their "verisimilitude," their "sense of reality and vitality" in representing blackness (and pointedly not black gayness). *Go Tell It on the Mountain* has been held up as Baldwin's most powerful expression of the "black experience" and advertised as proof that he truly "knows Harlem, his people, and the language they use."[35] The claims to authenticity forwarded by Hemphill as well as most reviewers thus reveal another similarity: they each know what they are looking for in their subjects. In fact, they each see what they hope to find—a black gay role model and a "Negro" spokesman, respectively. Paradoxically, Baldwin, so galvanizing a figure for various audiences, undermined the possibility that he or his work should become representative. Nevertheless, the authority that accrues with semi-autobiographical writing such as Baldwin's can threaten to overshadow its exploratory nature, as when, for example, *Go Tell It on the Mountain* is (still) made to signify as a "black experience" novel or even a black proto-gay novel rather than the mode of inquiry that it truly was for Baldwin. Though he knew that in "clarify[ing] something" for himself in *Go Tell It on the Mountain* he would inevitably connect his experiences to that of others, it was nevertheless true that "[t]hroughout his career . . . [Baldwin] took pains to remind friends and interviewers that he was Jimmy Baldwin rather than the representative of some group."[36]

I have been arguing that the genealogy imagined by Hemphill—a connection among black gay male writers made amid the strains of cultural presence and absence—becomes problematic not only because it remakes Baldwin in Hemphill's own much-needed image without interrogating the "truth" of the identity categories that undergird that image but, more important, because that re-creation is so clearly useful to the younger writer and cannot be dismissed even in the wake of the large-scale critique of identity offered by poststructuralist scholars. Steven Seidman reflects this difficult negotiation in *Difference Troubles*, his study of how difference might be more productively conceptualized in social theory and sexual politics than it is at present. The key standoff Seidman explores is between identity politics, which serves a self-enabling but also normalizing function in society, and a poststructuralist "non-identity," which disrupts the illusory unity of identity at the risk of remaining an empty political or critical gesture. Yet even while he joins poststructuralist queer thinkers such as Judith Butler in their critique of identity, Seidman refuses to dismiss outright appeals to those stabilizing structures, arguing that "[i]dentity constructions are not disciplining and regulatory only in a self-limiting and oppressive way; they are also personally, socially, and politically enabling; it is this moment that is captured by identity political standpoints that seems untheorized in the poststructural critique." Ultimately Seidman asks, "Queer theory . . . to what end?"—thereby gesturing toward a heretofore unarticulated queer intellectual ethic that might respond to lived experience as part of crafting a usable theory.[37] That impulse guides my thinking about the ways Hemphill and others remake Baldwin in their own image, for that image was necessary and essential for a generation who saw the futility of making itself from scratch and who, in response, bravely found the individual and collective voices to do otherwise. Yet that necessity cannot be the final word. Is there a way, I want to ask, that Baldwin can be a historical reference for Hemphill's desire without having to be identified as a black gay role model? How might we otherwise reformulate the relationship between a self-identified black gay man and his forerunner who disavowed that identity?

BALDWIN'S QUEER GENEALOGY

That Baldwin has become uniquely necessary as a reference who makes other artists' own raced homoerotic desires imaginable speaks to what I call his powerful "queer utility," his not only enduring and enabling but also problematic presence in the work of queer imagination. To explore Baldwin's paradoxical status, I will integrate a discussion of his queer literary genealogy with a pointed analysis of his debut novel, Go Tell It on the Mountain, the author's most famous novelistic treatment of the themes of tradition and inheritance. I read Go Tell It on the Mountain as a text that helps to negotiate the impasse of Baldwin's place in the black gay literary tradition, an impasse that has been largely overlooked even though Baldwin eschewed his "tradition-al" voices—the black representative heralded by largely white liberal audiences and the black gay role model so necessary to writers of the 1980s—in favor of the voice of a "witness" who refuses to assume either of those identities. In fact, Baldwin's most celebrated "black book" lends itself to queer interpretive strategies such that the authority that issues from the "black experience" is called into question. More to the point of this chapter, Go Tell It on the Mountain can become an instrument for similarly rethinking Baldwin's place in black gay male literature.

Elsewhere in Brother to Brother, in an essay that is equally tribute, literary genealogy, and reverent critique, Beam acknowledges Baldwin's indispensable yet sometimes vexing queer presence. While honoring the writer, Beam also registers his desire that Baldwin would have been more attuned to the lesbian feminist analyses by contemporaries such as Audre Lorde and thereby would have become more feminist himself. Beam's title, "James Baldwin: Not a Bad Legacy, Brother," thus signifies with the multiple meanings that define Baldwin's queer utility. The title's primary effect is that of understatement, a choice that throws into queer relief Baldwin's unquestioned "excellence." Yet the title can function as understatement only because of the very security of Baldwin's legacy, and the brotherly form of address resonates with the intimate recognition of just how important Baldwin's legacy has been. Gently, then, Beam begins the work of re-evaluating the lineage that connects him to Baldwin.

Quincy Troupe's collection of remembrances, James Baldwin: The Legacy, would at first seem straightforwardly to verify that Baldwin has indeed left a legacy. The book contains many detailed personal reflections on Baldwin and his capacity to touch others, revealing anew, through the idiosyncratic voices of its contributors, his ability to alter the very field of the imaginable, especially in terms of race relations. Several selections are by gay men, both black and white. A beautiful and, I think, telling memory by Caryl Phillips raises questions about how Baldwin's sexuality contributed to his solitude. More explicit is a 1984 interview by Richard Goldstein (reprinted from the *Village Voice*) in which Baldwin at least partially addresses those questions of queer isolation. In doing so, however, he deeply problematizes his status as black gay male forebear and complicates the uses to which he has so necessarily been put by those seeking a literary, cultural, and personal inheritance.

For example, asked by Goldstein about being gay, Baldwin characteristically disavows the identity: "The word 'gay' has always rubbed me the wrong way. I never understood exactly what is meant by it. I don't want to sound distant or patronizing because I don't really feel that. I simply feel it's a word that has very little to do with me, with where I did my growing up. I was never at home in it."[38] Baldwin here replays his long-managed distancing (and even dissociation) from gay terminology, or what he called "labels." In an interview twenty years earlier, for instance, he claimed that "those terms, homosexual, bisexual, heterosexual are 20th-century terms which, for me, really have very little meaning. I've never, myself, in watching myself and watching other people, watching life, been able to discern exactly where the barriers were. Life being what life is, passion being what passion is."[39] What strikes one in both of these interviews is that Baldwin seems to exist out of time, somehow beyond the reach of the terms that in fact lent powerful meaning to twentieth-century American life. He undermines the meaningfulness of sexual terminology and thereby exempts himself from meaningful association with such terms by focusing on the ambiguity of the "barriers" or boundaries that fail, in his estimation, to hold up to scrutiny. Tellingly, Baldwin avoids confronting the potentially more stable meanings that exist nearer the "center" of sexual identities. Instead, he makes borderlessness representative of or central to identity rather than an idiosyncratic complication of the ways identities, at their edges, can extend into each other and blur. Baldwin explains his inability to identify with sexual labels by framing the matter of sexuality as "very personal, absolutely personal."[40] Asked by Goldstein about "gay life, which is so group-oriented, so tribal," he replies, "And I am not that kind of person at all. . . . I feel remote from it. . . . You see, I am not a member of anything." At the same time, he attests to feeling "very strongly for my brothers and sisters" and having a special responsibility "[t]oward the phenomenon we call gay . . . because I [knew that I] would have to be a kind of witness to it." Baldwin's compromise, which allowed him to uphold this responsibility without being beholden to the terms of the debate and which also allowed him once more to strategically position himself and his reputation beyond the politicization of homosexuality, was to make a "public announcement that we're private."[41]

The genealogical act of imagination performed by Hemphill might profitably account for Baldwin's own reticence to identify as gay and thereby marry the kinds of personal and public acts of meaning making that would allow him to figure prominently and unproblematically within a broader tradition of black gay male writing. Where Hemphill finds Baldwin—in relation to black gay creative community—Baldwin will not be found or fixed, as he writes neither from nor explicitly for that community. Yet crucially, we cannot simply dismiss the power of the uses to which Hemphill puts Baldwin. Any critique of identity must acknowledge the impetus for the genealogical excavation that seeks it. Indeed, in this case, the elaborately produced cultural absence of public black gay male identity creates the very conditions in which the signifier seems to offer a solution to what is experienced as a crisis of being. The queer utility of Baldwin here rests on the paradox that he disavows and thus engenders a critique of gay identity while simultaneously recognizing a responsibility to those who re-create him in the image of the black gay man they so need him to be.

Perhaps more disruptive to Baldwin's place in the lineage imagined by black gay men of the 1980s is a comment mentioned in passing in Goldstein's introduction to his interview. Goldstein found—not surprisingly, given Baldwin's self-described "maverick" status—that the author "knew very little about the state of American gay life today: What's a 'clone,' he wanted to know." Baldwin then asked, "how is AIDS transmitted?"[42] When we read that Baldwin claimed later in the interview that he was unaware of homophobia in the black church—"I don't know of anyone who has ever denied his brother or his sister because they were gay"[43]—doubts about Baldwin's relevance begin to emerge. Again, the year of the interview is 1984. If the defiant and affirming homosexuality of Hemphill and Beam strikes a discordant but not false note of identification with Baldwin, the prevalence of HIV/AIDS among black gay men (first Beam and then Hemphill would die in the epidemic, along with more than half of the contributors to *Other Countries*) and the record of religion-based homophobic shaming and abandonment to which *Brother to Brother* itself testifies stand starkly against Baldwin's knowledge and experience. When Baldwin's remarks are framed against this evidence, one is compelled to ask, what was Baldwin's legacy indeed? What are the implications, moreover, when the centrality of a touchstone such as Baldwin is not a purely academic matter of canonicity— specifically, when Baldwin's importance as a "brother-forebear"[44] takes on lifesaving, life-giving utility? Furthermore, what does it mean that the lives Baldwin helped to save were then threatened by certain forces from which the brother-forebear was so admittedly disconnected? Finally, how did Baldwin actually look to the black gay past, and how did he imagine his role in creating a black gay literary future? A backward glance is instructive.

The genealogy "should" begin with the "gay voices of the Harlem Renaissance,"[45] including Langston Hughes, Countee Cullen (Baldwin's grade school teacher), Claude McKay, and Richard Bruce Nugent. Born in Harlem in 1924, Baldwin inhabited the space and time of these early queer writers. Yet neither they nor any other queer black writers were recognized by Baldwin as his major influences. Herb Boyd, in *Baldwin's Harlem*, offers a detailed account of Baldwin's relationships to Cullen and to Hughes, the latter of which was important, but equivocally so.[46] Certainly Baldwin saw neither of these men as an indispensable professional or personal mentor. At one point, he explains that lack of connection with reference to class distinctions, recalling, "I knew of Langston and Countee Cullen, they were the only other black writers whose work I knew [as a youth], but for some reason they did not attract me. I'm not putting them down, but the world they were describing had nothing to do with me, at that time in my life. . . . The black middle class was essentially an abstraction to me."[47] It is perhaps curious that Baldwin would not have seen reflected in much of Hughes's poetry the Harlem street life with which he was surrounded. Even more intriguing is that while the work of black, closeted, Harlem-based Cullen, whose poetry certainly models more classical forms and themes, did not resonate with Baldwin, the highly mannered novels of white, closeted, expatriated Henry James would lead Baldwin, upon his own expatriation, to claim James as his great literary influence.[48] Richard Wright, of course, was the "father figure" that many critics saw Baldwin as having to "kill" in order to take his place, but Baldwin always thought that claim was overblown.[49] Both Baldwin's well-documented "agon" with Wright and his choice of James are indicative, however, of the more general case of Baldwin's primary literary and intellectual engagements. Though Baldwin was one of twentieth-century America's

great interlocutors, none of his most famous public dialogues were with other black gay men. Wright, Eldridge Cleaver, Malcolm X, Norman Mailer,
and William F. Buckley Jr. offered Baldwin straight and/or white male figures against whom he could define himself and his work (precisely through
the deployment, interestingly, of what one may call an oppositional erotics),
while Lorraine Hansberry, Margaret Mead, Nikki Giovanni, and Audre
Lorde provided sometimes sympathetic and often antagonistic points of intervention into Baldwin's thinking about race and gender. Absent throughout his career is an extended black gay male dialogue.

One keenly wants the record to include, for example, a "rap on queer race"
among Baldwin and his black gay contemporaries. Samuel Delany springs to
mind. In the years before Baldwin died, Delany had already published some
twenty-five books, including fourteen novels, several novellas, collections of
short stories, critical works, and a memoir. For Delany, Baldwin had been
an example of a gay writer working within yet painfully at odds with the
language he had been given in order to articulate a "personal honesty." As
he searched for his own voice in the 1960s, Delany "thought about Baldwin
and Vidal and Gide and Cocteau and Tellier again. They, at least, had talked
about [homosexuality]. And however full of death and darkness their accounts had been, they'd at least essayed a certain personal honesty. And the
thing about honesty is that all of ours is different. Maybe I just had to try my
own."[50] Delany seems to indicate here that it was partly despite and partly
because of Baldwin's example that he chose not to write queer literature for
many years. He reminds Beam in an interview contained in the latter's anthology In the Life, "[R]emember, my first five science fiction novels were
written as 'heterosexually' as any homophobe could wish."[51] Delany has since
become one of the most trenchant and certainly the most decorated of queer
black male writers and cultural critics working today. That the very different
black gay voices of Baldwin and Delany do not exist in direct and extended
conversation, even though the two men were contemporaries, only further
complicates and very well may undermine the construction of a queer black
male literary tradition.

One wants, too, the voice of Bayard Rustin joined with Baldwin's in
shared thought. Asked in a March 1987 interview by Redvers Jeanmarie
whether he knew Baldwin, Rustin replied," Oh yes, I know Jimmy very well
and I do read him. We were very close in the 1960s when he was in New
York."[52] But where is the collaboration that might plumb the depths of that
relationship, sharpening and broadening our understanding of the American

black gay male experience? Both Baldwin and Rustin would be dead by the year's end, as would be Richard Bruce Nugent, who becomes especially interesting in this regard. Nugent's short story "Smoke, Lilies, and Jade," which appeared in the first and only issue of *Fire!!* magazine in November of 1926, was the first explicitly homoerotic story published by an African American writer. Nugent's friend and editor Thomas H. Wirth notes that Baldwin's 1956 novel *Giovanni's Room* was the second.[53] Though published thirty years apart, these works would seem to connect two important pioneers. The further historical coincidence that Baldwin and Nugent each died in 1987 provides a final point of literary and biographical connection. One seeks to put these men, somehow, in relationship. Yet they were never to communicate.[54] Where one thinks to find a direct line of influence connecting Baldwin to a black queer literary predecessor or contemporary, none exists.

When Baldwin did attempt to situate himself within an artistic tradition, he most often looked not to literature but to music. Douglas Field notes that as early as 1959, "Baldwin acknowledged his debt, not to his literary antecedents of the Harlem Renaissance but to the blues singer Bessie Smith."[55] Indeed, Baldwin often described himself as an artist in terms more musical than writerly, most typically comparing himself precisely to singers such as Smith. That break with a specifically literary heritage becomes less figurative when integrated into the larger discussion of the "slippery"[56] legacy of black gay writing that I am examining. When Pinckney suggests that upon moving to France in 1948, Baldwin "was thrown back onto his own speech, which was closer to that of Bessie Smith than it was to that of Henry James"[57] (in whose tradition Baldwin sometimes claimed to write), a trajectory of black gay male writing from the Harlem Renaissance to Baldwin disappears altogether.

The introduction to Baldwin's essay collection *The Price of the Ticket* offers the most explicit evidence that Baldwin, too, benefited from the influence of a black gay male mentor. Written in 1985, two years before the author's death, the piece details the lifesaving presence of the man who, writes Baldwin, "in a less blasphemous place . . . would have been recognized as my Master and I as his Pupil."[58] That man was black gay painter Beauford Delaney, whom Baldwin credits with saving his life by showing him—or rather, by assuming—that he had inherent value. Delaney's life and the lives of great black musicians from Louis Armstrong to Marian Anderson were opened to Baldwin, he tells us, "as part of my inheritance."[59] What Baldwin inherited, to be more specific, was a sense of responsibility to defy the terms used by others to define his existence: "black," "gay," "male," "writer"—terms of contestation, not connection.

Baldwin, like his would-be inheritors, keenly felt the necessity of self-creation as he confronted the faulty mirror held up before him by society. Similarly preoccupied, as the title of one of his early essays attests, with "a question of identity," he pursued this question in much more oblique relation to a black gay male artistic lineage than did Hemphill and Beam. Most typically, Baldwin frames his search for identity in terms of the racial distortions with which he has been presented.

> Obviously I wasn't white—it wasn't so much a question of wanting to be white—but I didn't quite know anymore what being *black* meant. I couldn't accept what I had been told. All you are ever told in this country about being black is that it is a terrible, terrible thing to be. Now, in order to survive this, you have to really dig down into yourself and re-create yourself, really, according to no image which yet exists in America. You have to impose, in fact—this may sound very strange—you have to *decide* who you are, and force the world to deal with you, not with its *idea* of you.[60]

To today's "empowered" audience, the action Baldwin calls for in this passage may seem difficult but nonetheless straightforward. Do not buy into "labels," particularly racial ones. Indeed, to offer but two examples, this sage advice has been followed in the most dangerous and crippling of ways by "post-race" ideologues who mouth words purposefully distant from reality and by a generation of young people unsure of how to identify and discuss the pervasive, subtle, and often liberal forms of what Ann Ducille calls "periracism" (aka racism). Baldwin, by contrast, insists that the act of self-recreation, indicatively raced, requires a sustained and even forced confrontation both with "oneself" ("you have to really dig down into yourself") and with the world ("with its idea of you"). Baldwin's writerly obsession with tropes of naming reflects the endless, multidirectional confrontation that is the search for self. Spelling his proper name would become Baldwin's lifelong project, an almost infinitely complex rectification of terms. His essays include "Nobody Knows My Name" and "No Name in the Street"; his favorite maxim was "Know whence you came"; and he characterized his namelessness best, perhaps, in calling himself a "Bastard of the West," the progeny of a country that dared not face the terrifying terms of its union. Certainly Baldwin spent a lifetime telling and retelling his own story. In his fiction, essays, speeches, and interviews, Baldwin endlessly reconstructed the terms of his existence in a remarkable effort not to be dominated by them.

More than finding or discovering his name (or his identity), then, Baldwin understood his charge to be the even greater necessity—and responsibility—of *inventing* his name. That act of creation takes place throughout his oeuvre, but a special relationship exists between Baldwin's fiction and acts of self-creation. This is not because Baldwin's fiction allowed him freedom from reality but, rather, because he understood it as allowing for a kind of radical re-viewing of the self. *Go Tell It on the Mountain* represents Baldwin's first sustained effort at "deciding" who he was. Because the novel also appears to be his most autobiographical, it offers a special opportunity to foreground the idea that Baldwin's fiction operates not as a reflection of the self or reality but as a mode of inquiry by which he addressed the incessant question of identity *for* himself and *in the presence of* the public. Reid-Pharr, in his analysis of "desire, choice, and black masculinity in post-war America," thus sees Baldwin's aesthetic (especially in his late work *Just Above My Head*) primarily as a black intellectual's reclamation of the freedom of "choosing and re-choosing" one's identity amid the social boundaries, including literary ones, of what constitutes a legitimate subject. For Reid-Pharr, Baldwin's lesson is that "[t]he privacy and sacredness of the individual and the individual's body must be maintained even and especially at the moment at which that individual offers up his own life story as a potent metaphor for the reality and the promise of the human condition."[61]

GO TELL IT ON THE MOUNTAIN
AS A MODE OF INQUIRY

If "tradition" offers an unsatisfactory model, how might we differently conceptualize Baldwin's queer utility? What guidance does the author himself offer in his fiction to help us understand the tradition he centers but does not reference? Sylvander rightly argues that "[t]he point [of *Go Tell It on the Mountain*] is the impact of history—personal and collective—on an individual, whether or not that individual is aware of the history."[62] In a gesture that would become part of what he considered a social imperative, Baldwin looks to the past in *Go Tell It on the Mountain*. Specifically, he turns to a story of familial inheritance, in an effort not merely to locate but to re-create himself and, in turn, his relations to others.

The epigraph to Go Tell It on the Mountain—"I looked down the line, And I wondered"—helps to introduce and underscore the novel's concern about historical location as understood through John Grimes's positioning within his family. The "I" in this epigraph surely refers to the novel's young protagonist, and these lines indicate that John is on the threshold of a journey. On the brink of his adolescence, he has come to a doubly anticipatory moment, expected by his church congregation to follow his father in the pulpit, yet urged by puberty and disdain for his father toward more worldly, including sexual, explorations. John looks down the line and wonders what his future path will be, but the ambiguous first paragraph of the novel tells us that by the time John had really begun to think about it, "it was already too late."[63] Family history had long since arrived to set John on his course. Troubling his place within that history, John's homoerotic inclinations shortly become undeniable. His masturbatory fantasies of slightly older boys represent one clear site of confrontation between his burgeoning sexuality and the Pentecostal religious tradition that defines those new longings as "sinful."

If John is looking ahead, Baldwin—the other "I"—is looking down the line, too. But the writer's gaze is cast backward, in an effort to understand whence he came. The novel thus represents a particular kind of personal history, an exploration, through fiction, of Baldwin's own place amid his predecessors. Although Go Tell It on the Mountain may seem autobiographical, Baldwin saw a more nuanced relationship to the novel.

> Go Tell It on the Mountain was about my relationship to my father and to the church, which is the same thing really. It was an attempt to exorcise something, to find out what happened to my father, what happened to all of us, what had happened to me—to John—and how we were to move from one place to another. Of course it seems rather personal, but the book is not *about* John, the book is not *about* me.[64]

In effect, just where a black man—or, as I will argue, a black gay man—might think he has found a novel explicitly *about* him, Baldwin hedges, unwilling to make a straightforward identification. Rather, the metaphor he chooses connotes a separation from within the self: an exorcism.

Go Tell It on the Mountain is not a recollection and portrayal of authentic experience or identity, be that identity "black" or "black gay male"; rather, it represents a mode of historical inquiry. That inquiry is not personal, not "about" John/Baldwin, because Baldwin cannot say who he is—precisely because he does not know—in order to write about himself. He knows only that the names he has been given, like those given to his ancestors, are powerful historical fictions. Stuart Hall's definition of identity—"[i]dentities are the names we give to the different ways we are positioned by, and position ourselves within, narratives of the past"[65]—summarizes Baldwin's own, for Baldwin consistently discusses identity with reference to history, as in a 1965 essay entitled "White Man's Guilt." I quote it at length to demonstrate Baldwin's sustained attention to the issue, as well as to provide a sense of the eloquence with which he conducted his critique of historical identity.

> White man, hear me! History, as nearly no one seems to know, is not merely something to be read. And it does not refer merely, or even principally, to the past. On the contrary, the great force of history comes from the fact that we carry it within us, are unconsciously controlled by it in many ways, and history is literally *present* in all that we do. It could scarcely be otherwise, since it is to history that we owe our frames of reference, our identities, and our aspirations. And it is with great pain and terror that one begins to realize this. In great pain and terror one begins to assess the history which has placed one where one is and formed one's point of view. In great pain and terror because, therefore, one enters into battle with that historical creation, Oneself, and attempts to recreate oneself according to a principle more humane and more liberating; one begins the attempt to achieve a level of personal maturity and freedom which robs history of its tyrannical power, and also changes history.[66]

The lesson learned by those creatures "despised by history" is that the past must be excavated, rather than merely retold, if one's humanity is to be liberated. Baldwin would distill this message into one of his most famous warnings: "Know whence you came." In the first of two epistles joined to form the book *The Fire Next Time*, Baldwin repeats this advice. The letter, entitled "My Dungeon Shook," is written to Baldwin's nephew "on the One-Hundredth Anniversary of the Emancipation," revealing Baldwin's own sense that we can somehow help future generations to "go behind the white man's definitions . . . [and] to spell your proper name,"[67] thus changing history and one's place/name in it.

By extension, the connection Baldwin seeks and encourages in readers does not rely on an ethnic identity model of the "self." But what does it mean when the act of positioning or imagining oneself historically within the particular narrative of the past made manifest by one's family history, as Baldwin does in Go Tell It on the Mountain, reneges on its ties to the expressly personal—"the book is not about me"—and endeavors instead toward less "personal" connections to others? Put another way, just how are people connected by experiences, especially their experiences of love and desire, that do not rely on the logic of identity? Baldwin well understood the identity trouble exposed by this question, casting that trouble once again in racial terms in his 1977 essay "Every Good-Bye Ain't Gone." How, he wonders, when "[s]ome things had happened to me because I was black, and some things had happened to me because I was me," was he "to discover the demarcation line, if there was one"? He continues,

> How to perceive, define, a line nearly too thin for the naked eye, so mercurial, and so mighty. . . . Being black affected one's life span, insurance rates, blood pressure, lovers, children, every dangerous hour of every dangerous day. There was absolutely no way not to be black without ceasing to exist. But it frequently seemed that there was no way to be black, either, without ceasing to exist.[68]

As a story that navigates the space between "me" and "blackness"—and "gayness" as well—Go Tell It on the Mountain functions as a radical and fundamentally queer genealogy whereby reconstructing a family's history of desire becomes a means of crafting historical connections and affiliations beyond one's own "family," where family stands both as a marker of black identity and, in its now-familiar reappropriation, as a trope for gay communal identity. The novel therefore offers the opportunity for a localized investigation that takes the specific institution of the African American family as the site at which sexual identity formations can be fictionally and historically contested as new relations are articulated. In that it promotes a vision of connections that both are and are not identity based, Baldwin's inquiry into family history becomes the context through which extra-textual tensions between black/gay identity and queer non-identity can be exploited and explored.

HOMOSEXUALITY, THE AFRICAN AMERICAN FAMILY, AND NON-TRADITION

I turn now to Roderick Ferguson, who offers an important model for situating black gay men within what might be called a "non-tradition." Strikingly,

Ferguson reads black gay men as fully immersed within and even represen-tative of the seemingly traditional context of the black family. To do so, he relies on the crucial reformulation of the African American family as a non-heteronormative construct, arguing that "[l]ocating African-American racial formation outside the boundaries of the heteropatriarchal household com-pels an alignment between blackness and other nonheteronormative forma-tions such as homosexuality." Refusing to "discus[s] the intersections of race and sexuality without addressing homosexual difference," Ferguson main-tains instead "that homosexuality is at the center of such an intervention."[69] With Ferguson's aid, I thus draw together the terms "non-traditional" and "nonheteronormative," as each connotes alternative relationships to domi-nant, "traditional" power structures. In other words, the concept of non-heteronormativity allows me to follow Ferguson's queer of color critique in connecting black gay men to each other and to the black family in non-traditional ways.

Working at the intersection of American sociology and African Ameri-can literature in his essay "The Nightmares of the Heteronormative," Fer-guson treats African American difference not as natural but as that which is to be explained. Ferguson argues that black difference is the product of a rationalizing Enlightenment discourse that locates the defining mark of race via the construction of the nonheteronormative black family.

> African-American familial forms and gender relations have been re-garded as perversions of the American family ideal. To resituate the authority of those ideals, questions concerning material exclusion—as they pertain to African-Americans—have historically been displaced onto African-American sexual and familial practices, conceptualizing African-American racial difference as a violation of the heteronormative demands that underlie liberal values. As figures of nonheteronormative perversions, straight African-Americans were reproductive rather than *productive*, heterosexual but never *heteronormative*. This construction of African-American sexuality as wild, unstable, and undomesticated lo-cates African-American sexuality within the irrational and therefore out-side the bounds of the citizenship machinery. Though African-American homosexuality, unlike its heterosexual counterpart, symbolized a rejec-tion of heterosexuality, neither could claim heteronormativity.[70]

Ferguson's argument helpfully changes the terms of the debate about John's sexuality in Go *Tell It on the Mountain* and, by extension, the sexuality of "black gay male" readers who perhaps identify with him or with Baldwin. While he recognizes heterosexual/homosexual difference within African American families, Ferguson changes the perspective from which that difference is viewed. He moves beyond the explanatory power of the heterosexual/homosexual paradigm by arguing that the sexuality of all African Americans has been reoriented through the construction of the nonheteronormative black family. One primary goal and effect of that construction has been the material exclusion of African American families, although that disenfranchisement has usually then been interpreted only as the result and not as the cause of the African American familial "disorganization." Ferguson argues that nonheteronormative black households took a variety of forms, but what these "perverse" family units had in common was their distance from ideals of the capitalist state: "Common law marriage, out-of-wedlock births, lodgers, single-headed families, and unattached individuals are all indicators of African-American disorganization defined in terms of its distance from heterosexual and nuclear intimate arrangements that are rationalized through American law and cultural norms that valorize heterosexual monogamy and patriarchal domesticity."[71] He concludes that "[i]n the United States of the early twentieth century, the heteronormative household was rendered as almost a 'material impossibility' for people of color."[72]

Ferguson interprets the finale of Go Tell It on the Mountain as Baldwin's most straightforward confrontation with the myths of the Enlightenment, "those fictions of progress, universal access, and universal identity that disavow particularities even as they articulate them."[73] Baldwin's response, according to Ferguson, was to redeploy the very terms by which black families have been disenfranchised, privileging and making productive their status as nonheteronormative subjects: "The re-articulation of queer identity posits a new valuation of black inner-city communities as sites of a regenerative nonheteronormativity, establishing a link between reconfigurations of African-American queer identity and African-American culture."[74] I find Ferguson's argument that black meets queer on a common ground to be a powerfully reorienting and productive critique, especially in that it implicitly responds to Holland's call to reformulate "tradition" to include black gay representation.

Tracing the Grimes family's genealogy of desire reveals at least as many materially and figuratively "queer" connections as heteronormative ones, as many loves that dare not speak their name as ones that are publicly respectable. To understand John's desire, one must view it in the context of these other unspeakable unions, each of which bequeaths to John a history of desire as struggle—a struggle far beyond the realm of sexual identity catego-ries. John's mother, Elizabeth, struggles with the illicit desire of a young girl lodging with an unconcerned aunt who is more interested in holding séances than chaperoning her niece. Unparented and unrestrained, the young Eliza-beth falls in love with Richard, a poor, defiantly self-educated man who has been made paranoid by racial bias and a lifetime of being "sent down the line" by black relatives. Although their child is conceived out of wedlock after Richard's suicide, Elizabeth is unrepentant; Richard's voice thus continues to haunt Elizabeth, pleasurably, and betrays her lack of faith not only in the strength of God's love but also in the ideals of a stable nuclear family. John's stepfather, Gabriel, harbors, in his youth, an illicit desire for the servant girl whom he impregnates but casts away. His subsequent attachment to his first wife, Deborah, stems not from normative love but from the need for self-aggrandizement. He marries her in the spirit of holy one-upsmanship: "It came to him that, as the Lord had given him Deborah, to help him to stand, so the Lord had sent him to her, to raise her up, to release her from that dishonor which was hers in the eyes of men" (105). With their marriage already marked as unconventional because Deborah is barren, Gabriel's pro-posal is exposed as a form of masturbatory self-pleasure, the pleasure he takes in condescending to marry the social outcast. Florence, John's aunt and Gabriel's sister, embraces a self-defeating and destructive love, for in her inability to hold strong against the "common" charms of her husband, Frank, she turns against her own principle of hating poor black men. With neither love nor hate capable of sustaining her, Florence waits to die alone in a rented room, on the fringes of both her family and society.

Following Ferguson, we see that the desires of John's relatives, created and complicated by race, class, and gender as much as any sexual identity, cannot be viewed as simply heterosexual. This is true not only when com-pared to heteronormative social relations but when compared to each oth-er, for desire is not normative in *Go Tell It on the Mountain*. Amid, rather than strictly against, these non-normative loves emerges John's desire. He stands, in other words, within a genealogy in which one incessantly strug-gles with, rather than merely naming, one's erotic impulses. Because Baldwin recognizes that black communities in Harlem are already queer, his sexual queerness neither places him automatically outside that cultural system nor causes him necessarily to reach beyond it in his search for queer identity. Rather, Harlem's queer layering provides a richness capable of sustaining that act of discovery.

Implicit in Ferguson's writing is the unpredictability of the space of queer re-articulation. That very unpredictability, however, compels a critical departure from Ferguson's queer impulse to revalue or "reaffirm" the nonheteronormative at the moment of John's "salvation." As is typical of my larger study of queer paradox, I here want to resist the slippage between positing a nonheteronormative location and assuming queer liberation. As I will argue in chapter 3, seemingly queer contact zones can dangerously reinforce normative power relations. John's trial and ultimate redemption in part 3 of the novel, "The Threshing Floor," need not—and, I think, do not—result in his "rebirth into nonheteronormative affirmation."[75] Rather, the novel ends with a vision of contested awakenings and cyclical struggle. After his long night lying before the altar with the saints standing over him and with the slightly older and much-adored Elisha in particular "praying him through," John is saved. As the church members walk home in twos and threes—John with Elisha; his father, Gabriel, with his Aunt Florence; and his mother, Elizabeth, with several sisters of the small congregation—Harlem briefly becomes a world of revelation, a world revealed within a world. John looks around himself with new eyes and perceives that "[n]ow the storm was over. And the avenue, like any landscape that has endured a storm, lay changed under Heaven, exhausted and clean, and new. Not again, forever, could it return to the avenue it once had been" (219–20). The young man with a "new name [written] down in glory" (225) believes in this moment that his outward vision reflects his own transformation. John feels physically changed, "for his hands were new, and his feet were new, and he moved in a new and Heaven-bright air" (209). Helping John to stand fast is Elisha, who, walking him to his door, "kissed John on the forehead, a holy kiss. . . . The sun had come full awake. . . . It fell over Elisha like a golden robe, and struck John's forehead, where Elisha had kissed him, like a seal ineffaceable forever" (225).

If "John's newfound wholeness is consecrated by Elisha giving John a 'holy kiss,'"[76] however, that wholeness surely will not last. Readers must here recall Gabriel's own conversion experience, during which the rural landscape seemed similarly changed—"here was a new beginning, a blood-washed day!"—just as Gabriel's hands seemed to become "new hands" and his feet to become "new feet." Yet Gabriel fell from that spiritual height, just as John, too, will fall. Almost immediately John's vision of the "exhausted and clean, and new" avenue partially dissolves, becoming a double vision.

Yet the houses were there, as they had been; the windows, like a thousand, blinded eyes, stared outward at the morning—at the morning that was the same for them as the mornings of John's innocence, and the mornings before his birth. The water ran in the gutters with a small, disconnected sound; on the water traveled paper, burnt matches, sodden cigarette-ends; gobs of spittle, green-yellow, brown, and pearly, the leavings of a dog, the vomit of a drunken man, the dead sperm, trapped in a rubber, of one abandoned to his lust. (220)

The avenue so quickly has returned to what it once had been; in fact, it has never changed, though John's relationship to it has. The great "eyes" of the urban landscape look upon John, unmoved, and the voices of the neighborhood boys will continue to ring out cruelly, "Hey, Frog-eyes!" John senses in this moment not that he is one with the neighborhood, his family, and its history but rather that has must struggle anew within them: "[h]e would weep again, . . . for now his weeping had begun; he would rage again, said the shifting air, for the lions of rage had been unloosened; he would be in darkness again, in fire again, now that he had seen the fire and the darkness" (220–21). If nonheteronormativity is regenerative here, it is nevertheless a brutally isolating rebirth. Baldwin's imagery projects even starker reminders of the deprivations of racial disenfranchisement and religious homophobia because they are set against John's new vision of Harlem redeemed and his new badge of honor, Elisha's kiss. Even this queer, holy kiss, witnessed by the threatening stepfather, takes its place in a cycle of struggle: "Out of joy strength came, strength that was fashioned to bear sorrow: sorrow brought forth joy. Forever? This was Ezekiel's wheel, in the middle of the burning air forever" (221).

Ferguson also argues that John's rebirth in "The Threshing Floor" partially results from the subject of the preceding chapter, "Elizabeth's Prayer." That rebirth, he writes, "refers to Elizabeth's understanding that freely chosen love [as opposed to heteronormative, institutionalized love] is an index of personal freedom. In this context, Baldwin begins to re-articulate the meaning of African-American nonheteronormativity via a reinterpretation of Christian salvation."[77] But Elizabeth's attitude on the walk home is so darkly ambivalent that it is difficult to attribute to her a vision of John's "self-affirmation." As the church sisters counsel Elizabeth that "the Lord done raised you up a holy son. He going to comfort your gray hairs" (212), Elizabeth cries slow, bitter tears. For even as the sisters praise God, she hears speaking to her heart her first lover, John's biological father, Richard, dead by suicide after unjust imprisonment: "*You remember that day when you come into the store? . . . Well—you was mighty pretty*" (213). This voice reminds

Elizabeth that she had loved and attempted to save Richard once and could not; neither can she now save John: "[S]he knew that her weeping and her prayers were in vain. What was coming would surely come; nothing could stop it" (177). In Elizabeth's eyes at least, there has been no reconfiguration of African American identity; she sees no "emergent identifications and social relations." Even to John, his mother's "smile remained unreadable; he could not tell what it hid" (225). Rather than an inheritance of queer freedom, Elizebeth's smile hides the queer history of love's ongoing struggle to be free.

How else, then, other than through tropes of liberation that characterize the queer theoretical imagination, can John's salvation be read with reference to the nonheteronormative genealogy of desire of which he is a part? Does nonheteronormativity need to be made regenerative in response to its racist, capitalist construction? Baldwin criticized Enlightenment thinking in places too numerous to mention. But I am questioning whether an affirmational nonheteronormativity must replace the terms ("disorganization," "perversion," "reproduction") in which the Enlightenment has cloaked African American queerness. Rather than reading Baldwin's first novel as an attempt at an inverted revaluation of queer family ties, I read it as a search for new terms that he does not yet find. The much-interpreted "holy kiss" offers a prime example of the unclear, multiple, mediated messages that swarm around John at the novel's end. In writing that "Baldwin's own position as a subject who is racialized as black triggered an estrangement from the Enlightenment that became the site within which new epistemologies, new historiographies, and new aesthetics were yearned for and elaborated,"[78] Ferguson perfectly lays out the background of Baldwin's fictional inquiry. We might stop short, though, of claims that in Go Tell It on the Mountain Baldwin imagined into being the new knowledges he knew must be invented.

The line I am trying to draw Ferguson's queer of color critique back toward is one of complex emergence, the dynamic area where "emergent identifications and social relations" need not lead one to posit "a new valuation of black inner-city communities as sites of a regenerative nonheteronormativity." It is the same line I will draw between "gay" and "queer" in a variety of ways in this book, where the former seems the sign of normative oppression (i.e., identity) and the latter seems the revalued reformulation that escapes the trap of identity. I think that neither characterization is always accurate and that the supposed trajectory from the first to the second employs a potentially dangerous teleology of progress and liberation. The line or marginal space I have identified is what Christopher Nealon, in a wonderful essay titled "Queer Tradition," calls "the residual gap between *gay* and *queer*."[79] This residual gap represents "a zone between articulate tradition and inarticulate yearning, and stages the becoming-articulate of something that had seemed too simple or obvious or painful to survive passage into language."[80] I represent that gap as the space between history and the individual; between the tradition that Hemphill searched for and the "always, now" that bursts through that tradition in (re)recalling him and his work; between queer utility and queer imagination.

Ferguson is strikingly important in that he offers a way not only to reread John's desire but to rethink black gay male desire by placing each within its larger context of—or better, one of its larger contexts of—desirous and intimate relations. By contextualizing the differences made by black gay male identity within a broader understanding of nonheteronormative relations—and I have tried explicitly to contrast that with how black gay male identity has been situated in the larger tradition of African American literature—Ferguson unsettles the stability of that identity. Crucially, he disrupts black gay male identity not by casting it—and identity generally—aside but by reconnecting it to other identity formations constructed in the same racialized socio-economic space, the space of the African American family. To be a black gay man is to be different, but the meaning of that difference is at least partially created by a *relation of similarity* to other nonheteronormative, including heterosexual, positions. In other words, in the context of the nonheteronormative African American family, the black gay man signifies not only as racially same and sexually different but also as sexually same (nonheteronormative).[81] This complication of identity through the contextualization of desire, or what I have also called the construction of a genealogy of desire, can be said to produce a queer subject, one not completely removed from the benefits and perils of sexual identity but also not beholden to that sexual identity as the only or most useful way of understanding desire and connections with others.

By producing John as a desiring subject in Go *Tell It on the Mountain*, Baldwin teaches that even though one may not exist within a sexual category (even though one may be queer), queerness nevertheless has a context. John is probably gay, but by virtue of his family's history of desire, he is also, perhaps more importantly, queer. Non-identity, so privileged by queer poststructuralists, does not spring from nothing; it is not an absence. Rather, a queer subjectivity emerges out of the web of desires that have touched us in particular ways, as within African American family life. To the extent that we are ignorant of our genealogies of desire and our queer traditions, we will more readily feel alone and, inevitably, will more readily seek out the kinds of identity-based connections that Hemphill saw as necessary. But to the extent that we can construct our histories of desire (whether we look to our family histories, our sexual histories, or other contexts) and to the extent that we can contextualize our desires broadly rather than thinking of them strictly in line with or in opposition to other desires, we can potentially achieve a rewarding queer subject position outside of—but not out of sight of—sexual identities.

I have suggested here that interactions in and with literature can help to construct subcultural domains in which the paradox of queer tradition can be negotiated. The African American family, as Ferguson points out, is another of those subcultural locations. The artist's imagined relationship to his or her forerunners can be yet another node through which queer connections that draw on but do not entirely depend on racial and sexual identity can be made and exploited. Ultimately, queer genealogies stand necessarily alongside of the ethnic identity model of sexuality, helping to orient and connect individuals as they seek to explain their experiences of desire.

CHAPTER 2

Paradoxical Reading Practices

Giovanni's Room as Queer/Gay/Trans Novel

American males are the only people I've ever encountered in the world who are
willing to go on the needle before they'll go to bed with each other. . . . I've
known people who literally died out of this panic.

—JAMES BALDWIN, INTERVIEW

Still, there's a long way to go from reveling in queer theory's possibilities to
exacting its theoretic purchase, especially given the untimely interruption
of everything we cannot control, including our unruly selves and the world's
haunting ability to resurrect, against our best intentions, *its version* of itself. So
let's not assume—to make the *first* of several points—that as a form of internal
critique, queer theory bears a truth that identity's inaugural form does not.

—ROBYN WIEGMAN, *OBJECT LESSONS*

EX-GI BECOMES BLONDE BEAUTY: OPERATIONS TRANSFORM
BRONX YOUTH

—*NEW YORK DAILY NEWS* HEADLINE, DECEMBER 1, 1952

If chapter 1 offered a sense of the paradoxical positions from which Baldwin's larger oeuvre has been and must be read, chapter 2 homes in on a
single Baldwin novel, *Giovanni's Room* (1956). I bring that work into focus
by approaching it from three of the critical orientations that have been gath-
ered together under the "big tent" or LGBT formulation of "queer." These
critical orientations are queer theory, gay studies, and transgender analysis.
On a basic level, my methodology implicitly acknowledges the richness of
a novel that invites sustained attention by a number of LGBT interpretive
paradigms. Yet as one reviewer of this chapter noted, the fact that multiple
reading strategies recommend themselves as appropriate to *Giovanni's Room*
may simply suggest that "Baldwin's fine novel is indeed available to us all."

In effect, the idea that the novel has found various LGBT audiences risks seeming benign. I want to pause, then, to interrogate this underwhelming hypothesis, for I think it is striking to say that Baldwin's traditionally "gay novel" is available to us all. What a porous text it must be to invite us all in. How paradoxical, given our queer differences, that we should feel at home in such mixed company.

My argument will be that *Giovanni's Room* offers a particularly productive text for cultivating the queer imagination, not because it repays close readings by individual queers of different stripes, but because it so urgently compels the individual reader to engage incompatible or incommensurable LGBT reading practices. The novel is not simply textually available to queer theory, gay studies, and transgender analysis; rather, it invokes the tensions and contradictions that problematically bind those approaches together. In other words, *Giovanni's Room* indexes the non-identity of queerness and the differences of the queers who are not so much invited as coerced by the text to read from multiple, potentially uncomfortable positions.

The stakes of my thesis are especially high on a personal level as well as a critical one, for *Giovanni's Room* forces readers to situate and resituate themselves, to read both as and also beyond themselves. Enacting its chief thematic, the book engages queer readers in risky self-reflection. We must each ask, how does *my* queer imagination work? What are its characteristic moves and boundaries? How is my reading self a function of my sexual and/ or gender identity, my critical training, my politics, and so on; and therefore, which queernesses do I embrace and which do I reject as a reader? Ironically, these questions come to light because the novel's protagonist, David, represents so dramatic an example of the *inability* to think queerly. Readers must do something with *Giovanni's Room* that Baldwin, through David, does not and cannot do for them: ever unseat themselves.[1] The near-total failure of David's queer imagination therefore creates a blank map on which readers must chart their own coordinates. I argue that in the interpretive void created by David's ignorance, the reader is thrown into a queer reading crisis. The real drama in this chapter's narrative therefore emerges as I articulate my queer, gay, and trans readings of the novel to one another in order to foreground moments of interpretive exchange, overlap, backtracking, and stressful innovation. One of my underlying assumptions is that such moments (and series of moments) in which a reader shifts intellectual stance are themselves worthy of interpretation, perhaps especially for the field of queer studies, which must be so invested in how it is constructed because it has always been and is currently in peril.[2]

A CRITICAL KALEIDOSCOPE: *GIOVANNI'S ROOM*
AS "EXEMPLARY QUEER TEXT"

With *Giovanni's Room*, Baldwin seems to intentionally provoke what theorists now call a queer critique. The novel offers an overt indictment of sexual and gender categories as constructed, confining, and impoverishing, a problem that Baldwin believed undermined the human capacity to give and receive love. Astonishingly, for the novel was published in 1956, Baldwin chooses to stake his (now-queer) claim about the stultifying effects of sexual identity categories on a story of failed love between two men. Yet even as this singular feature drew his publisher's criticism and prevented the novel's initial publication in the United States, Baldwin insisted that "*Giovanni's Room* is not really about homosexuality. . . . It's about what happens to you if you're afraid to love anybody."[3] Far from the "gay novel" it was first derided as and is often celebrated as today, *Giovanni's Room* represents a sustained effort to consider men's sexual and erotic relations queerly, that is, beyond prescribed sexual identity categories and, perhaps most surprisingly, against homosexuality.

Though set in France, *Giovanni's Room* is, in many ways, a typically American novel. With a central male character in flight from suffocating adult sexual relations, the novel retells what Leslie Fiedler has identified as the prototypical story of American manhood: the man on the run. Baldwin's young protagonist, David, like Fiedler's man on the run, attempts to escape from the heteronormative entrapment of marriage, but with a more explicit relationship to the homoerotic attachments to men that typify canonical male characters. David flees from a relentless "bulldog," the terror and humiliating emasculation he associates with his sexual desire for men. But having fled Brooklyn for Paris (and therefore mirroring Baldwin's own journey), David discovers that he cannot escape his same-sex desires and finds himself "brought up short once more before the bulldog in [his] own backyard—the yard, in the meantime, having grown smaller and the bulldog bigger."[4] Elsewhere David reflects, "perhaps home is not a place but simply an irrevocable condition" (92). It is in Paris (but very much with his homeland in mind) that David must finally face his demons, for there he meets and enters into a sexual relationship with Giovanni, an Italian bartender. David's subsequent marriage proposal to his girlfriend, Hella, reflects the unrelenting heteronormative pull of his native American shores, a pull made all the stronger by the "unbearable" freedom that Giovanni represents. "I suppose this was why," muses David, "I asked [Hella] to marry me: to give myself something to be moored to. But people can't, unhappily, invent their mooring posts, their lovers and their friends, anymore than they can invent their parents" (5). Baldwin thus positions his protagonist between diverging forces: on the one hand, a sexual impulse toward men and, in particular, toward the anti-American Giovanni; on the other, the heteronormative social prescription toward marriage, represented by the "very elegant, tense, and glittering," all-American mooring post, Hella.[5]

The association of repressed desire with geography and, more important, with a national American consciousness becomes central to the novel's queer argument. Giovanni's Room is not simply a study in sexual identity crisis but a story of located male struggle, contested first in David's backyard of America and then in Europe, but rooted more distantly. Staring at the reflection of his own white face as the novel opens, David sees his ancestors who "conquered a continent, pushing across the death-laden plains, until they came to an ocean which faced away from Europe into a darker past" (3). Structured as a necessarily backward glance, the novel thus explores a particular and particularly raced American crisis of male sexual identity as a historically produced condition predicated on a refusal of that history. The result of his white countrymen's rejection of their "darker past," for Baldwin, was a gross simplification that manifests in Giovanni's Room as the overpowering American impulse to categorize, define, and thereby limit and pervert complex human emotions, desires, and relationships.

The tension between identity categories and "the human being," first and most famously expressed in his groundbreaking early essay "Everybody's Protest Novel," would become a major theme in much of Baldwin's work. "[T]he failure of the protest novel," Baldwin writes, "lies in its rejection of life, the human being, the denial of his beauty, dread, power, in its insistence that it is his categorization alone which is real and which cannot be transcended."[6] Baldwin would, controversially, distinguish his writing philosophy from the work of Richard Wright and, more kindly, from that of his friend Lorraine Hansberry, whose A Raisin in the Sun (1959) he thought to contain a "flaw . . . not really very different" from that of Wright's Native Son. The novel fails in its "attempt to illuminate ruthlessly as unprecedented a creation as Bigger by means of the stock characters of Jan, the murdered girl's lover, and Max, the white lawyer," because "[t]he force of Bigger's reality makes it impossible to believe in these two." In Baldwin's estimation, A Raisin in the Sun, like Native Son, also "involves the juxtaposition of the essentially stock—certainly familiar—figure of the mother with the intense (and unprecedented) figure of Walter Lee."[7] Marlon Ross summarizes Baldwin's critique of protest fiction, writing that rather than "fictionally *representing* the categories on which . . . injustice is based . . . , Baldwin wants to *explode* those categories, offering not a protest but rather a critique that disables the categories from retaining their oppressive power."[8]

If, as Baldwin intended, David is a more human protagonist than Bigger Thomas, this is because the human drama that surrounds the former more believably resonates with the force of his own reality. Though David often feels isolated by his desires, he sometimes dimly perceives a more general circumstance shared by his fellow men and women. "I began to see," David reflects, that "while what was happening to me was not so strange as it would have comforted me to believe, yet it was strange beyond belief. It was not really so strange, so unprecedented, though voices deep within me boomed, For shame! For shame! that I should be so abruptly, so hideously entangled with a boy; what was strange was that this was but one tiny aspect of the dreadful human tangle, occurring everywhere, without end, forever" (62). The "dreadful human tangle" that David feels a part of offers a particularly helpful image for Baldwin's conception of the relations, interwoven and knotty rather than one-dimensional and stock, that are produced by forces of desire. It reflects Baldwin's unwavering and lifelong belief that people's sexual (and racial, national, and gender) identities are interrelated, interdependent, and shared. To return to an important passage, Baldwin's belief that "we are all androgynous, . . . a part of each other," was "exceedingly inconvenient" but undeniable. The inconvenience for Americans of human interconnectedness was, in fact, so exceeding that Baldwin described it as a panic, one seen "[n]owhere . . . more vividly than in my country and in my generation."[9] These sentiments, written three years before Baldwin's death, represent one of the final and most explicit formulations of the author's universalizing queer perspective on identity categories.

David, the symbol of Baldwin's twenty-something post-war generation, can sustain neither his entanglement with Giovanni nor the larger vision of complex human relationality that he has glimpsed. Although a series of doomed messengers attempts to relay Baldwin's queer message, the young American invariably fails to heed their warnings. One of David's acquaintances and pursuers, the wealthy and lecherous Frenchman Jacques, warns that while "not many people have ever died of love," its absence has certainly proven to be deadly: "[M]ultitudes have perished, and are perishing every hour—and in the oddest places!—for the lack of [love]" (58). Jacques implies that even—or precisely—in queer places, love is a lifeline. "Love [Giovanni]," he exclaims, "love him and let him love you. Do you think anything else under heaven really matters?" (57). Baldwin thus pushes the reader to comprehend the potential for humanity inherent in male-male erotic relations. Further, those relations provide a site for understanding the importance of love in *all* lives "under heaven."

While the dirty old man Jacques acts as a somewhat surprising wisdom figure, Giovanni offers a more pointedly queer critique of David. In their final lovers' quarrel before David leaves him, Giovanni distinguishes his notably anti-American perspective from David's highly taxonomic worldview: "You are the one who keeps talking about *what* I want. But I have only been talking about *who* I want" (142). "Who" versus "what" neatly encapsulates the queer critique of *Giovanni's Room*: we can love not categories but individuals. Eventually, Giovanni's execution and David's crushing alienation literalize the stakes of failing to love queerly. David may not "go on the needle" in order to forestall going to bed with men, a deadly but common substitution according to Baldwin (see the first epigraph to this chapter), but having sacrificed Giovanni, David comes ever closer to his own disastrous end.

Donald Hall, in his introduction to the patchwork field of queer theory, identifies *Giovanni's Room* as an "exemplary 'queer text.'"[10] Hall cements his argument in a wonderfully rich paragraph that familiarizes the reader with a lexicon that has encoded much of queer thought. I quote it at length in order to highlight that queer language (the emphases are mine).

> But certainly the lingering *possibility* that individuals can *resist* by living and loving in *excess* of preexisting *social categories* does make [*Giovanni's Room*] a thoroughly queer [novel]. It suggests that *desire* can manifest itself in the most *surprising* ways and in *nonexclusive* terms. It suggests *mutability* in sexual relationships over time and also in ways that *exceed* a simple *hetero/homo binary*. It suggests strongly that individuals have the ability and responsibility to allow for *human complexity* outside the starkness of *received social definitions and valuations*, even as it does not deny the power of those *contextual forces*. It evokes the *possibility* of a different set of sexual relationships and definitions *without prescribing* exactly what *the future* might hold.[11]

The novice queer theorist, for whom Hall's pedagogical text is generously written, could not ask for a more succinct characterization of the poststructuralist strain of queer theory. The above paragraph, like Baldwin's novel, fairly bristles at the notion of inherently stable, intrinsically meaningful sexual identity categories. William Turner likewise suggests that "[o]ne vastly oversimplified but still useful way to understand queer theory begins with the proposition that many persons do not fit the available categories and that such failure of fit reflects a problem not with the persons but with the categories."[12]

Indeed, David's problems do seem to be category problems. To David's normative mid-twentieth-century mind, only two options, heterosexuality and homosexuality, present themselves as possible futures. Yet each of these futures, Baldwin insists, is really a trap for David. This point is important for queer theoretical readings of the novel: neither straight identity nor gay identity can do justice to the complex realities of erotic life. The former embodies Western culture's heteronormative mandate and, as is typical of norms, veils its own mechanisms of coercion. Baldwin embodies David's straight future in the figure of the pure, clean, soap-stained American man. Waiting with his countrymen for mail at the American Express office in Paris, David observes of American men that "they smelled of soap, which seemed indeed to be their preservative against the dangers and exigencies of any more intimate odor; the boy he had been shone somehow, unsoiled, untouched, unchanged, through the eye of the man of sixty" (89–90). But the antiseptic veneer meant to preserve the boyish innocence of the man is pure shell, a formal front built on an abdication of self that Giovanni, employing the identical metaphor, characterizes as immoral.

> You want to be *clean*. You think you came here covered with soap—and you do not want to *stink*, not even for five minutes, in the meantime. . . . You want to leave Giovanni because he makes you stink. You want to despise Giovanni because he is not afraid of the stink of love. You want to *kill* him in the name of all your lying little moralities. And you—you are *immoral*. (141)

The preoccupation with cleanliness at the heart of this passage suggests a form of American self-alienation, the veil of soap providing a thin but symbolic barrier against bodies and, in turn, bodily desires, both heterosexual and homosexual ones. Baldwin thus traces David's need to be clean back to its American context; the deceptively clean smile signifies one of David's "lying little moralities" that, like soap, spreads out in a sweet-smelling, superficial layer over human flesh. Desires of the flesh, Giovanni implies, are betrayed by a superficial—and thus immoral—American moral code.

Although Giovanni's reading of David takes place within the context of a male-male relationship, cleanliness and American (im)morality must be understood not solely as reactions against homosexual desire but also as equally unfulfilling, idealized states of heterosexual American manhood.[13] Put differently, David fails to be straight not only because his most pressing and authentic sexual yearning is for men but also because heterosexuality itself is a failure. Heterosexuality fails at a structural level—that is, as a category—because it rests on a performative and therefore unstable fiction of American manhood. Chasing an elusive masculinity, Baldwin's protagonist is in the company of other literary "made men." David Leverenz argues that the passage into manhood as reflected by key texts of the American canon is primarily motivated and marked by fear and shame rather than accomplishment. "Any intensified ideology of manhood," writes Leverenz, "is a compensatory response to fears of humiliation."[14] For David, heterosexuality's enticement rests in its promise of emboldening his masculinity, a promise that surely has special significance given David's supposedly emasculating desires for men. On one level, the "straight trap," while it would thwart David's freedom to openly pursue his desire for men, vows to *produce* him as a man. In the vacuum of desire that characterizes the heterosexual option for David, normative gender identity expands to sustain—indeed, define—heterosexual identity. Of course, this product is itself chimerical. David's "manhood," inflated by (i.e., in order to fill the void of) the fiction of heterosexuality, itself becomes a powerfully alienating force. David, still looking at his compatriots, sadly realizes that "beneath these faces, these clothes, accents, rudenesses, was power and sorrow, both unadmitted, unrealized, the power of inventors, the sorrow of the disconnected" (90).

The implications of David making the heterosexual false choice are thus far reaching. Not only does he realize that he is not straight, but he also therefore experiences a traumatic separation from the masculine gender identity that his straight lie attempts to purchase for him. In knowing that he is not straight, David literally cannot know whether he is an American man. But even if David were straight, the heterosexual "option" would cut him off from masculine gender identity at the same time that it attempted to secure it. Whether taking the form of the macho father or of the impeccable, impenetrable sailor, the recurring figure of the American Adam dominates David's imagination as, paradoxically, both the essence of natural masculinity and an unreachable cultural ideal, an impossible, unassailable heterosexuality. The queer question of the novel thus hinges not on the recognition that sexual identity can be fluid or multiple but on a deeper issue: does David realize that, even if he could be straight, straightness would not help him become a "real" man?

If the trap of American heteronormativity simultaneously foists on and denies David and his countrymen masculine identity, Baldwin also creates for David a counterpart to the American Adam. Just as an impossible het-eromasculinist ideal—Mr. Clean—guarantees perpetual identity failure at the top of the hetero/homo binary, another figure even more dramatically represents category failure from below. Baldwin sets the "gay trap" by invert-ing the metaphor of cleanliness, substituting filth in its place. The soap-washed masculine veneer of the straight man becomes the perfume-stained but putrified flesh of the effeminized homosexual, variously associated with a vomitous old queen, a rotting female corpse, a shit-eating monkey, and, as I will explore in depth below, a lascivious zombie—the flaming, living dead. The rank horror of gay effeminacy gives teeth to the threat of homosexuality as a false choice for David, as these portrayals situate the gay man not merely inside a limiting category but as the embodiment of a cultural end point. David cannot *live* as a gay man.

The awakening of David's "insistent possibilities" as a gay man occurs when, in full view of an expectant queer community at a "dubious" bar, he meets the barman Giovanni. The attraction is instant, undeniable, and, most important, public. By the end of the night, David feels, for the first time, that he can no longer escape homosexual categorization. Riding to breakfast through the streets of Paris with Giovanni, Jacques, and the bar owner Guil-laume, the American panics, thinking, "I was in a box for I could see that, no matter how I turned, the hour of confession was upon me and could scarcely be averted; unless of course, I leaped out of the cab, which would be the most terrible confession of all" (47). The "truth" of sexuality, as Foucault suggests, must be told. Ironically, homosexuality represents not a range of "possibilities" but the only possible way for David to understand the trajec-tory of his queer desire. Here, Baldwin seems to argue against homosexual-ity in the same way that one might argue against a forced confession: what else can David possibly say?

But why not just say "it," since "it" is, after all, true: David likes Giovanni. The answer lies back at the bar "of dubious—or perhaps not dubious at all, of rather too emphatic—reputation" (26). Emphatic indeed, the reputation is resounding, forceful, and categorical. To David's impoverished and typi-cal American mind, liking Giovanni would mean, emphatically, identifying with the habitués of the bar, from whom David has until now been able to hold himself apart. It would mean falling into the filth of homosexuality, metaphorized as a "cavern . . . black, full of rumor, suggestion, . . . full of dirty words" (9). The cavern references gay male anality and equates it with a grave in which David, in his nightmares, is pressed against his dead mother's decaying body, "so putrescent, so sickening soft, that it opened, as I clawed and cried, into a breach so enormous as to swallow me alive" (10–11). Homosexual identification would initiate a descent into literal and figurative dirtiness marked by a return to the feminine and a decomposing masculine gender identity.[15]

Two resonant examples demonstrate the categorical failure or impurity—the dirty femininity—of the gay man as depicted in *Giovanni's Room*. Approached in the bar by a shadowy figure, a male with "very large and strong" hands yet wearing mascara, lipstick, foundation cream, and a shirt covered with paper-thin, brightly colored wafers that make it seem as though the stranger "might, at any moment, disappear in flame," David interprets the effeminized male body as a walking corpse: "Now someone whom I had never seen before came out of the shadows toward me. It looked like a mummy or a zombie—this was the first, overwhelming impression—of something walking after it had been put to death" (38). The epitome of what Lee Edelman has characterized as homographic display—the making legible of homosexuality on the body—the zombie embodies feminine gender marks as a way of making himself gay.[16] That cultural inscription simultaneously functions as a form of mummification, of stylized death. The homosexual—coded as a man turned woman—is a dead man. Alternately, he is made to take on those fatal marks and meanings as a symbolic form of violence committed by those, including himself, who insist on the visibility of his difference, in which case the mummification becomes not only suicide but murder by gender.

Smiling at David in the bar, the "flaming" mummy sees to the heart of and articulates David's peril upon meeting Giovanni: "*Il est dangereux, tu sais.* And for a boy like you—he is *very* dangerous." The danger for a boy like David is threefold. First, it is imagined by Baldwin specifically as a *boy's* danger, a case of threatened masculinity. Second, because David has been able to pass as straight, a boy like him risks an especially great fall if he becomes a "marked" man. Third, as the specter/spectacle becomes spectator, he reveals what was, in Baldwin's eyes, the real danger, David's denial of his desire: "'But you, my dear friend—I fear that you shall burn in a very hot fire.' He laughed again. 'Oh, such fire!' He touched his head. 'Here.' And he writhed, as though in torment. 'Every*where*.' And he touched his heart. 'And here.' And he looked at me with malice and mockery and something else; he looked at me as though I was very far away."

The zombie implies that David will burn with the flames of desire but that his denial of that desire will be the American's true torment. His insight—he sees David as though he was "very far away"—reflects distance, and yet his final warning, "You will be very unhappy. Remember that I told you so," suggests an intimate connection between the two. Looking at David, does the phantom fortune-teller not seem to look back on his former self? Does David, looking into the "dark eyes narrowed in spite and fury" (40) not envision his own terrifying future? The danger, then, stems from this moment being an identificatory one. If David's eyes mirror the phantom's own, perhaps the latter's prediction is true. Perhaps David will suffer the same unhappy "death" as the man in front of him. This is, of course, David's greatest fear.

Juxtaposing this scene with another will show the death grip of the association between homosexuality and effeminacy in the novel. In this next scene, David has a brief and largely fantastic interaction with the epitome of masculinity, an American sailor. Gazing at the sailor as he crosses the street, David forgets himself momentarily, only to be all the more forcefully reminded of who he is not and thus must try to be: "I was staring at him, though I did not know it, and wishing I were he. He seemed—somehow—younger than I had ever been, and blonder and more beautiful, and he wore his masculinity as unequivocally as he wore his skin. . . . I wondered . . . if I had ever been like that." David's initial vision is one of difference. The sailor's manhood seems natural compared to David's own. Yet we know that David is a young, blond American, hardly so different from the sailor—even in the way he wears his masculinity, if his own self-assessment is reliable. Of his emasculation, David reflects, "I was too old to suppose that it had anything to do with my walk, or the way I held my hands, or my voice—which, anyway, he had not heard. It was something else and I would never see it. I would never dare to see it. It would be like looking at the sun." David thus naturalizes his difference from the sailor, even though they appear (and perhaps sound and move) the same and though he characterizes the sailor as *wearing* his masculinity. Why, in the face of ostensible sameness, does David not identify with the sailor as I have argued he did with the mummy?

David continues by elaborating his emasculation.

We came abreast and, as though he had seen some all-revealing panic in my eyes, he gave me a look contemptuously lewd and knowing; just such a look as he might have given, but a few hours ago, to the desperately well-dressed nymphomaniac or trollop who was trying to make him believe she was a lady. And in another second, had our contact lasted, I was certain that there would erupt into speech . . . some brutal variation of *Look, baby. I know you*. I felt my face flame. . . . I wondered what he had seen in me to elicit such instantaneous contempt. . . . But, hurrying, and not daring now to look at anyone, male or female, who passed me on the wide sidewalks, I knew that what the sailor had seen in my unguarded eyes was envy and desire: I had seen it often in Jacques' eyes and my reaction and the sailor's had been the same. (92)

The richness and sadness of this passage lie in the startling illogic of David's brand of homosexual panic. He says that he envies the sailor. He wants to be him, yet in the most striking ways, the sailor is already David's double. Not only do they look, or appear, alike, but they look, or see, alike. If the sailor's gaze is "contemptuously lewd" toward David, so has David's been toward other gay men. Further, in the sailor's eyes, David reads, "*Look, baby. I know you,*" words that might be interpreted as connoting not (only) disdain but also desire, perhaps even an invitation offered in the parlance of a shared urban masculinity ("baby"). Nevertheless, David invests the sailor's eyes only with the knowledge, contempt, and power of unimpeachable straightness, which is to say unimpeachable masculinity. When the gay boy looks at the straight boy, his very act of looking proves to be his downfall. The look in his eyes alone turns him into a "well-dressed nymphomaniac or trollop," and thus the look of gay male desire becomes the most telling and most indelible of homographic marks in *Giovanni's Room*. Corresponding with the phenomenon of internalized homophobia, homographesis, Baldwin suggests, can mark the gay man from the inside out. What David fails to realize but what Baldwin puts within our critical grasp is the queer idea offered by Kaja Silverman that "all subjects are necessarily within specularity, even when occupying a viewing position, and that all antithesis of spectator and spectacle are consequently false."[17] Precisely through David's failed queer imagination, Baldwin is able to represent what Silverman calls "male subjectivity at the margins." He casts a new relationship between the "straight" male subject/object who stands at the center of definitions of the masculine and the "gay" male subject/object who stands on the periphery of those definitions.

Key here is the transgressive union of "envy and desire," a transgression that rests on the gender difference—gender being *the* irreconcilable difference—that lays the very foundation for the hetero/homo binary. As Michael Warner argues in "Homo-Narcissism; or, Heterosexuality," "The difference between hetero- and homosexualities is . . . an allegory about gender. . . . [T]he core of the psychoanalytic tradition . . . is the assumption that gender is the phenomenology of difference itself."[18] That David *is like* the sailor cannot sustain the weight of his *desire for* the sailor, for the logic of gender as difference requires that desire structures objects outside of or other than the self and that identification structures subjects as a feature of the self. "Freud's deepest commitment," according to Warner, "is that these two operations will be exclusive, and one will be reserved for each gender. An admission that it would be possible to identify with *and* to desire a gendered image would be the most troubling of all."[19] Following Warner, one queer theory that might be brought to bear on *Giovanni's Room* would posit the possibility of the masculine gay male couple. But unable to manage his simultaneous identification and desire, David rejects his own masculinity. This disidentification with the masculine self affects a regendering or an inversion as David remakes himself in the image of a (female) "trollop." Drawn taught with paradox is the seemingly straightforward question that Mae Henderson identifies as at the heart of *Giovanni's Room*, "What is it to be a homosexual and a man?"[20]

That David can sooner believe that he is a woman because he desires men than believe that he is a man who desires men—the utter impossibility of the latter option—seems sufficiently suspect to make us question the logic of gender sameness and difference on which normative sexuality depends. In fact, the scene encourages the reader to reject the "truth" of gender: that all men are somehow fundamentally the same and that those men who are different are, under the strict rules of the binary, women. In other words, the scene encourages the reader to cast a critical eye on the power of gender to override, by defining the terms by which sexual sameness and difference are understood, erotic differences that would trouble the deployment of gender sameness as a meaningful identity marker. But for David, our first-person narrator, masculine gay men are not merely unrecognizable as gay but, indeed, unthinkable as gay. That ontological void relies not simply on David's stereotypical assumptions that the masculine men he encounters are straight but, rather, on a gender-determinative logic that recodes all gay men as effeminate. In fact, for David, being gay is largely a process of becoming a woman or, as he tells Giovanni, a "little girl" (142). Just as the trap of straight identity attempts to construct an ideal masculine Mr. Clean, the trap of gay identity does not so much reveal as produce the dirty little girl. Sexual identity categories in *Giovanni's Room* become emphatically gender-defining acts. They do not express or naturally correspond to gender identities but instead insist on and determine them.

An extension of the queer theory that would unite, rather than oppose, identification and desire might posit a more flexible and comprehensive relationship between the two. In "The Male Prison," an essay about Andre Gide's homosexual "dilemma" (published in 1954, just prior to *Giovanni's Room*), Baldwin writes that "[t]he great problem is how to be—in the best sense of that kaleidoscopic word—a man."[21] By "kaleidoscopic" man, Baldwin indicates neither a natural state nor a mere category but a subjectivity capable of grappling with both masculinity and femininity to achieve "genuine human involvement,"[22] the highest expression of which is love, with both women and men. The figure of the "kaleidoscopic" man seems to me to best represent the queer vision that hovers over but is never realized in *Giovanni's Room*. With its changing colors and shifting shapes representing the mutable relationship between gender and sexuality, the kaleidoscope metaphorically explodes categories into fragments and reconstitutes them into patterns as complex as life itself.

CRITICAL BACKTRACKING: *GIOVANNI'S ROOM* AS POST-QUEER GAY NOVEL

Reading *Giovanni's Room* as a model queer text makes a great deal of sense. The novel's queer exemplarity stems from Baldwin's insistence time and again that prescribed identity categories invariably betray the complexity of the individual and, by isolating him in their "cells," belie his inescapable state of dependence on the other. As Hall demonstrates, the tools of queer theory are well-honed for explaining this position. It was to my surprise, then, that over time, I found myself resisting the kind of queer theoretical analyses of *Giovanni's Room* that I so value. Rather than the queer text I had been reading and teaching, the novel began to seem downright gay.

In calling *Giovanni's Room* a gay novel, I might seem to be making an obvious claim, central as the work has been to the gay canon. The Publishing Triangle, the association of lesbians and gay men in publishing, offers a fairly representative list of the one hundred best lesbian and gay novels, on which Baldwin appears multiple times. The "Books" section of the *Los Angeles Times* recently released its list "20 Classic Works of Gay Literature," including "books that have provided a richer understanding of the joys and challenges particular to gay life." *Giovanni's Room* tops the list (it was second in the longer, Publishing Triangle ranking), and the embedded picture of Baldwin offers a visual symbol of his ubiquitous presence in the gay canon.[23] More interesting than the assertion that *Giovanni's Room* has become a classic work of gay literature is where this claim falls in my history of reading and teaching the novel. Oddly, my gay reading, which relies on the kinds of identity-based claims that enabled gay studies to flourish, *followed* my queer reading, which uses an anti-identitarian, poststructuralist queer theoretical approach. This was a surprising trajectory, from queer to gay, yet it also seems wonderfully suggestive to me, dynamically pointing both backward and forward. It points to a fruitful evolution in queer reading practices, one surely bolstered by queer theoretical disciplinary innovation and deepened by historical sensitivity, the result of which is a theory of gay difference. As my thinking about the novel evolved, I found myself reordering the usual trajectory from gay to queer that Thomas Piontek associates with the shift from the modern to the postmodern.[24] *Giovanni's Room* became a post-queer gay novel.

Yet the process of rereading and of overwriting deconstructive queer renderings of *Giovanni's Room* with a post-queer gay interpretation was more uneasy for me than I have implied. In fact, I found my scholarly investment in queer theory to be deeply antithetical to my instincts as a gay reader of Baldwin. As an academic, I privileged my intellectual training; as a gay man, I trusted my experience. These threads of "me" were unweaving themselves in a fray of readerly self-difference. To put this another way, as a queer theorist, I was experiencing, to point back to Robyn Wiegman's epigraph, an "untimely interruption" of my "unruly" gay self. The truths of queer theory and of gay identity that informed my two interpretive approaches could not be reconciled. Wary of revisiting chronological arguments about the births of gay studies and its counterpart (offspring? evil twin?) queer theory in the academy, I nevertheless faced the question, In a post-queer context, just how was I making *Giovanni's Room* gay, again? Strange temporalities are presently so associated with liberatory queer theories[25] that thinkers have found themselves needing to work especially hard to re-recover gay pasts that remain impervious to liberation. Heather Love, in *Feeling Backward: Loss and the Politics of Queer History*, argues that readers are incentivized to turn away from early representations of same-sex desire because they archive painful affective readerly experiences of loss, shame, despair, and regret. By holding her gaze on the "stubborn negativity of the past"[26] without the goal of transforming it, Love returns an important legacy of literary response to homophobia to her present-day readers. A similar painful attachment to the homophobic construction of homosexuality in *Giovanni's Room* powerfully held my gay attention and set in motion a process of critical backtracking.

A personal, readerly dilemma arose before me: despite Baldwin's category-busting, kaleidoscopic queer vision and despite my deep investment in queer theory, I started reading David as gay again. This was not an expected or comfortable reading trajectory for me. That I continued over months and indeed years to be nagged by my untimely return to gay from queer seemed increasingly important and worth further exploration. Why did I, despite the treasure trove of queer thought available to me, including my own critique of identitarian need in chapter 1 of this volume, continue to revisit a not-so-queer critical place? The question already answered by queer theory lingered nevertheless: why and how is David *not* gay? Baldwin tries preemptively to answer that question in novelistic terms, writing as early as 1949 that "[i]t is quite impossible to write a worth-while novel about a Jew or a Gentile or a Homosexual, for people refuse, unhappily, to function in so neat and one-dimensional a fashion."[27] *Giovanni's Room*, if it is a worthwhile novel, must not be "about" a homosexual. Readers must not, if we are to appreciate the novel fully, let David's sexual identity obscure or detract from a larger human message, for "[a] novel insistently demands the presence and passion of human beings, who cannot ever be labeled. Once the novelist has created a human being, he has shattered the label and, in transcending the subject matter, is able, for the first time, to tell us something about it and to reveal how profoundly things involving human beings interlock."[28] In essence, Baldwin denies that representation of the oppressed and representation of the dominant are significantly different endeavors.[29] To answer my nagging question, the reason David cannot be gay is because Baldwin will not permit David to *read* as gay—even if he is. At the level of narrative, David cannot inhabit the inert category "gay," because that rendering would—must, it seems—suffocate him in an "airless, labeled cel[l]"[30] and consequently thwart human revelation. Further, at the interpretive level, we must not read David as gay—that is, insist on his gayness—for that would, in turn, produce a suffocating critical gay reading practice, ironically just the kind of reading practice that has elevated a cadre of texts to visibility but that also has created a false distinction between major and minor literatures. If we are to know David as gay, it is only by first following the transcendent representation of David the human being.

We can now begin to understand the meaning and significance of Baldwin's assertion that "*Giovanni's Room* is not really about homosexuality. . . . It's about what happens to you if you're afraid to love anybody." In this claim, which also constitutes an act of disclaiming, Baldwin leverages the considerable powers that construct and enforce a heterosexual/homosexual distinction, while he simultaneously and all the more forcefully attempts to render that distinction unimportant by insisting on the universality of his message. *Giovanni's Room* asks us to understand the universal (love) through the particular and "perverse" (love between men), transposing the terms of the usual integrationist analogy "we (homosexuals) are like them (heterosexuals)" so that it reads "they (heterosexuals) are like us (homosexuals)." The ultimate meaning is that we are all, fundamentally, in the same boat. Among queer theorists, Sedgwick most famously advocates for a related universalizing perspective that regards issues of homosexuality as important to and having impact on people of all sexualities.[31] Baldwin's shift to universality from gay specificity, which is, in effect, a deconstruction, certainly attempts to make erotic and sexual relations between men less differently meaningful than those between men and women and, thus, meaningful to everyone, though as Trudier Harris points out and as I will address more fully in the conclusion to this book, lesbian relationships are nowhere explicitly addressed by Baldwin. From this reverse assimilationist point of view, which takes as its chief tenet the underlying interconnectedness of all people, male sexual relations in *Giovanni's Room* provide the template for understanding larger, typically normative social relations.

In "Letter to My Nephew on the One-Hundredth Anniversary of the Emancipation," which opens the book *The Fire Next Time*, Baldwin explains, in racial terms, another version of reverse integration. About white people, Baldwin writes to his young nephew that "[t]he really terrible thing, old buddy, is that *you* must accept *them*."[32] Near the end of the letter, Baldwin emphasizes the importance of this redefinition, for "if the word *integration* means anything, this is what it means: that we, with love, shall force our brothers to see themselves as they are, to cease fleeing from reality and begin to change it."[33] I want to distinguish Baldwin's perspective on racial integration in *The Fire Next Time*, published just after *Another Country*, from that in *Giovanni's Room*, published seven years earlier. As I will argue in the next chapter, *Another Country's* treatment of (homo)sexuality aligns more closely with the racial advice to his nephew than does that of *Giovanni's Room*, reflecting Baldwin's evolving relationship to gay experience and its place in the larger heteronormative culture. But in *Giovanni's Room*, gay subjectivity offers less of a cultural location from which to "love" and thereby effect social change and more, rather, of a cultural abyss.

While honoring Baldwin's powerfully unifying vision, I hesitate to turn quite so quickly from his critical treatment of the "one-dimensional" gay character, for that character seems to exist off the page for Baldwin as well. Here we enter into the complicated and, as I argued in chapter 1, undertheorized issue of Baldwin's relationship to gay identity. Represented in *Giovanni's Room* as prescriptive and confining and, as the next chapter will demonstrate, elsewhere associated with liberatory potential, gay identity exposes a tension within Baldwin's work and life. Perhaps most kindly but also accurately, we could say that so few positive models of homosexuality existed in the mid-1950s as to make advocating for gay identity painfully distasteful, if not unthinkable. While writing *Giovanni's Room*, Baldwin seems to have held a grim view of the "plight" of the homosexual.

> The really horrible thing about the phenomenon of present-day homosexuality . . . is that today's unlucky deviate can only save himself by the most tremendous exertion of all his forces from falling in to an underworld in which he never meets either men or women, where it is impossible to have either a lover or a friend, where the possibility of genuine human involvement has altogether ceased.[34]

My critique is not that Baldwin mischaracterizes the social circumstances that disable and traumatize gay people. Rather, I question the way he thereby negatively juxtaposes gay identity ("present-day homosexuality") with the possibility of human life ("genuine human involvement" and "growth"). Problematically, that distinction would prove to be a lasting one for Baldwin. When asked in a 1969 interview whether homosexuality is a disease, he first argued that "[t]he fact that Americans consider it a disease says more about them than it says about homosexuality."[35] But he then, oddly, reversed course when prompted to comment further about "societies where homosexuality becomes very open": "When it becomes open as it has here, it becomes a disease. These people are not involved in anything resembling love-making: they're involved in some kind of exhibition of their disaster. It has nothing to do with contact or involvement between two people—which means that the person may change you. That's what people are afraid of. It's impossible to go through life assuming that you know who you're going to fall in love with. You don't."[36] Open homosexuality can only be a disastrous exhibition in this formulation, a manifestation of the "disease" of looking for the love you naively think you want, whereas homosexual "love-making" can apparently only occur in some privatized space that allows for true "contact or involvement." Fifteen years later, Baldwin appears perhaps even more willing to position gay people as culturally dislocated members of a pitiable "underworld." Writing in the midst of the murderously homophobic culture war that fueled and sustained the AIDS crisis, he troublingly disregards the ways sex became, for many gay men, an important and even central expression of gay identity, politics, and pride: "There is nothing more boring, anyway, than sexual activity as an end in itself, and a great many people who came out of the closet should reconsider."[37] Of course, by 1985, when these words were published, going back in the closet was no longer an option for the earliest AIDS dead and the visibly infected. But beyond this, by advocating for the re-closeting of a "great many" gay men, Baldwin suggests that the appropriation of gay identity (here linked explicitly to gay sex for its own sake) produces a more "brutal and dangerous anonymity" than does remaining in the closet. The ease with which he imagines identity-based gay sexual culture to be culturally expendable points to an enduring attitude about the insufficiency of gay identity. What Baldwin cannot imagine, except as oxymoronic, is the concept of gay life.

It might be appropriate at this point to reiterate Baldwin's early and long-standing goal as writer and social witness: "to reveal how profoundly all things involving human beings interlock."[38] The struggle to embrace one's full humanity is a shared struggle for Baldwin, and the extent to which one struggles alone, without recognition of the humanity of others and without one's own humanity recognized, is precisely the measure of our shared failure. I foreground this point in order to stress that, remarkably, Baldwin seems always to have presupposed that queer people are deserving heirs to the interlocking human drama—in short, that queer people are fully human. On the one hand, I find this assumption so radical as to be one of Baldwin's most enduring queer ideas. On the other hand, I wonder about the precise logic of Baldwin's "taking for granted" the humanity of gay people, a logic that replays itself in the "post-gay" liberal sentiment of today.[39] I wonder about the motivations and goals when, in the name of "genuine human involvement" (with whom?), gay identity is assumed away as unnecessary and even destructive.

It is an odd thing to perceive one's sexual identity being set at odds with one's humanity, as Baldwin unambiguously positions it. It is strange to hear that one's resolute (if catalog-like), deeply felt, keenly experienced, and, yes, *singular* gayness could possibly exclude one from a state of transcendent universality, that is, from recognition as nothing less than a human being. Again, on the one hand, Baldwin's assumptions are radical: what, he asks, could the homosexual possibly *mean* short of what he means as a human being? Quite on the other hand, however, in both his fiction and his essays, he imagines that the homosexual can *achieve* full humanity only by transcending homosexual specificity. Fully human beings cannot only or primarily be gay, as though one's humanity must be staked somewhere other than and evidently beyond homosexuality, lest the stakes pull up and one's humanity floats away, free of the mere homosexual.

In my earlier queer formulation, the category "gay" appeared as a limiting element because it obscured the interconnectedness of our "dreadful human tangle." My post-queer gay reading of *Giovanni's Room* argues just the opposite. I think Baldwin's universalizing impulse, which degrades the importance of sexual identity in order to privilege our shared humanity, moves in a dangerous direction. The fundamental problem is that humanity, as anyone who has ever needed to argue for theirs knows, is itself the most banal and meaningless of categories. To be forced to insist on one's humanity, as queers are constantly forced to do—to need to fall back on this most obvious and inarguable of claims and to treat that claim as profound—is the incomparably degrading position. To argue that we are all complex human beings is to argue, literally, nothing. To search for some meaningful and enduring understanding of our commonality at the base level of humanity precisely by denying the baseness of that comparison and elevating "humanity" to an achievement seems to me a poignant but illusory endeavor. Gay as we insistently are, our humanity can never be questioned, can never be partial, can never be "achieved." Being gay is as good as humanity gets.

I propose that one's sexuality is coextensive with one's humanity and that we cannot deconstruct one without deconstructing the other. Putting aside the reasons we might want to do just that, if we want to privilege our humanity, it therefore must be a complex humanity informed by deep knowledge and experience, including the many forms of sexual difference and identity. There is, I argue, no intrinsic shared humanity separate from the engagement with others at their privileged levels of specificity (sexual and otherwise) and at one's own. Losing our sexual identities would mean losing an important opportunity either to connect at a detailed level of human experience or to face the fact of our sustained disconnection.

It would also mean, as Sarah Schulman's unpublished play *The Lady Hamlet* dramatizes, leaving in place the unstated connection between a "universalizable" point of view and heterosexual male privilege. Schulman argues that theater audiences have only been taught to regard the man's drama— Hamlet's being the case in point—as the human drama: "[A man] steps onto the stage and all the world is his to prowl until he exhibits his human flaw. Then, audience gasps. There are no higher stakes than a man's fate."[40] But Hamlet's perspective is specific, not general. When we are trained to interpret his drama as our own, we mistake the act of making meaning out of unique difference for the act of accessing general human truth and experience. The Lady Hamlet, if such a role existed, would require audiences "to universalize to her, as we now universalize to [Hamlet]."[41] If Baldwin's queerer impulse was to generalize away David's gay specificity, the power of the novel compels just the opposite reading: we cannot help but see through David's eyes, to universalize to him, to read and to experience him as gay.

What if it were impossible to imagine "gay" as a limiting category? What if gay identity represented a fully complex, fully human subjectivity? What if we assumed, finally, that gay people exist by virtue of, rather than despite, the specificity of their gayness? Then we could universalize through the particularities of gay experience, which is to argue not that the category "gay" is not a troubled and troubling one but, rather, that gay *life* can be neither reduced *to* a category nor inherently reduced *by* the category. This means that we could craft a reading practice for *Giovanni's Room* that need not reject gay identity. We do not need to queer David to liberate him. Rather, we must face the fact that gay, closeted David is not liberated. He is gay, and in the homophobic world that envelopes him, he is doomed. Further, he is not doomed "like" all unloved and unloving people are doomed. His tragedy is specific, it extends from ungeneralizable motives and social dynamics, and it cannot have universal meaning apart from those details. If we do not allow David to be gay, the novel can teach us nothing, precisely, about gay people. The question is, do we want to learn?

FEELING THE GAY BODY: ON THE NECESSITY OF TRANS-GAY ANALYSIS IN *GIOVANNI'S ROOM*

In the first two sections of this chapter, I have argued for a necessary and productive incompatibility of queer and gay reading strategies. "Post-gay" queer cultural critique both supplants traditional gay readings of *Giovanni's Room* and cedes to a rejuvenated "post-queer" gay interpretive strategy, in a cycle that will assuredly—indeed, must—continue. In this final section, I enrich my previous readings with transgender analysis,[42] a move that I want to characterize as fundamental to this chapter in its potential to disrupt, necessarily, my earlier reading practices and positions. Paradoxically, my trans analysis is incommensurable to, yet inextricable from, my queer and gay readings of the novel. It has no common measure; it tilts on its own axis. Yet it gravitationally draws in and draws toward its companion readings. While I join a chorus of transgender thinkers in questioning the ways transgender has been co-opted by queer academics in hopes of "prolong[ing] the queerness of the moment,"[43] I maintain that trans reading strategies can, in fact, gain saliency when set alongside queer/gay interpretations, and vice versa. This is true not so much because queer/gay analysis and trans analysis are always intimately interrelated forms of meaning making but for the more general reason that opportunities for transgender analysis (like opportunities for racial and class analyses) are woven into the entire fabric of cultural production. Rather than insisting that *Giovanni's Room* is a discrete "transgender text," I am arguing that transgender critique must be considered broadly applicable, appropriate for understanding texts produced and/or consumed under the cultural conditions of gendered existence. In what follows, I employ what might be best termed a "trans-gay" critical framework that moves my discussion away from both queer fluidity and gay identity and toward a focus on the multiple stakes of trans misrepresentation and, ultimately, the issue of embodiment. Specifically, I link David's transphobic worldview as failed reading strategy to his final encounter with his sexed gay body, for at the heart of *Giovanni's Room* is a fundamental corporeal questioning.

To characterize the matter differently, my further reading of *Giovanni's Room* hinges on recognizing and unraveling the logic of another false choice: not the choice between the first two options above that argue alternately for a queer interpretive lens and for a gay interpretive lens, but the choice between those options and anything else. A queer *or* gay framing of the novel is itself a false choice, because it forecloses other possible readings, specifically ones that attend to matters of gendered embodiment as related to but not subsumed within matters of sexual desire. One of the chief insights of transgender studies is that gender has no necessary relation to sexuality. "Why," Susan Stryker asks in her introduction to *The Transgender Studies Reader*, "[has] the entire discussion of 'gender diversity' [been] subsumed within a discussion of sexual desire—as if the only reason to express gender was to signal the mode of one's attractions and availabilities to potential sex partners?"[44] To the extent that we make trans reading strategies available where critics have previously failed to employ them, texts take on extra cultural meaning. Not only are trans narratives culturally important because they exist; they are especially important because they have been hidden and so must first be excavated in order for their importance to be recognized. *Giovanni's Room* reflects widespread fears about homosexuality, to be sure. But in its narrative logic that argues that gender cannot shift on its own terms, the novel's homophobia is founded on transphobia. However, the novel's meta-narrative argument, not fully attributable to Baldwin, potentially posits transgenderism and transsexuality as lively cultural possibilities that must broadly inform queer reading practices.

In casting transgender as an always already available interpretative potentiality, I take my cue from Jay Prosser, who identifies an error that routinely plagues readings of Radclyffe Hall's 1928 classic, *The Well of Loneliness*: namely, the transgender subject and, more specifically, the transsexual one have been read as homosexual. "[T]ransgendering," argues Prosser, "merely symptomatiz[es] homosexuality" for most critics of the novel.[45] Transgender critique speaks pointedly to the need to weaken and often break the link between homosexuality and gender "inversion." Specifically, it reveals the misperception, which I argue is both recirculated and exposed as misperception by *Giovanni's Room*, that inversion can serve as a metaphor for or an indicator of homosexuality. Prosser locates that conflation not at the beginning of the study of inversion but only recently, with the psychopathologizing of homosexual identity around 1900.[46] Prior to Freud, transgender subjects could be treated apart from homosexuality (as well as interconnected with it). Such sexologists as Krafft-Ebing and Ellis were "ambivalent ... about the relation between sexual inversion and homosexuality."[47] Transgender signals not *sexual* confusion (e.g., a desiring subject in the "wrong" body) but, rather, an experience of oneself as a different gender than might be expected or mandated given the perception of one's sexed body.

As gender "inversion" has come to signify homosexual display rather than a subjectivity in its own right, the trans subject has been threatened with erasure. Recall that in *Giovanni's Room*, homosexuality definitionally produces and enforces gender switch. The potentially transgender subject is thus easily mistaken for the homosexual subject, and this is because David imagines gender switch as exclusively a function of the coming-out process. With homosexual identity firmly centered as the referent for transgender, the narrative of the homosexual coming-out process has consequently become the hegemonic transition story in our culture, foreclosing narratives of gender transition. Two competing versions of transgender thus emerge: on the one hand is transgender subjectivity as elucidated through first-person accounts and contemporary theory; on the other is the more prevalent "transgender" misrepresented as an explanation for homosexuality. Further, the impossibility of the gay man being figured as the effeminate, happy queen makes the figure of the transwoman doubly impossible, for transgender analyses is undermined by the figuration of the "tragic" death of the gay man turned monstrous woman. The mummy, the zombie, the walking dead—taken as gay queens, these figures make identification as homosexual unpalatable, even horrifying. But they render transgender subjectivity nearly unthinkable in the absence of a ready, internalized trans reading practice. The "flaming princess," potentially a transwoman, can be nothing other than a gay failure. Transgender analysis reveals that the agent of non-subjectivity that overshadows the novel is not the abject gay or queer man but the cumulative specter of transgenderism. In all of these ways, necessarily linking the gay man who comes out with a burgeoning effeminacy creates a screen behind which the possibility of a male-to-female (MTF) transgender subject is screened out, mistaken as nothing other than the threat undergirding homosexuality. A trans imaginative reading must start by recognizing the erasure of the trans possibility rather than (queerly) championing the demise of categories or (gay-ly) championing their resiliency.

Yet, unlinked as they are, can be, or may be theoretically, gay male effeminacy and MTF transgender possibilities exist in relation to each other in *Giovanni's Room*, just as they often do outside the novel. At issue is a larger question for gay, queer, and trans studies: how are they related? The work of disentangling trans narratives from gay ones and of understanding their potentially stubborn inter-narrativity is complicated. Jack Halberstam asks, "Is it believable in this day and age that [a lesbian butch character] would not have thought of being trans?"[48] He thus reminds us that gay and lesbian identities can organize around gender, whether fundamentally or peripherally, and can sometimes become meaningful in relation to increasingly familiar models of transgender experience,[49] even while processes of gay male emasculation and transgender non-compliance that may appear very similar and may inform each other are by no means identical or set in fixed relation to each other. Still, we can say that potentially transgender characters in *Giovanni's Room* are forced to pass as gay because male effeminacy is yoked to a brand of homosexuality dislocated from trans identity, even though the "gay" "male" patrons of Guillaume's dubious bar might not be having sex with men at all or might not be having sex with men *as men*, a point David seems to confront without at all grasping. Surveying *les folles*, a term meaning "queens" but translated literally as "madwomen," David notes how "they always called each other 'she.'" He then ventures a theory of sexuality about these patrons who "looked like a peacock garden and sounded like a barnyard." "I always found it difficult to believe," reports David, "that they ever went to bed with anybody, for a man who wanted a woman would certainly have rather had a real one and a man who wanted a man would certainly not want one of *them*. Perhaps, indeed, that was why they screamed so loud" (27). David treats gender noncompliance as a sexual problem: the gender-ambiguous "peacock" is a sexual abject. He therefore makes the mistake, to repeat Stryker, of thinking that gender exists for sex and, consequently, that gender "failure" amounts to sexual failure.[50] A different reading of this scene might argue that the stories of sexual escapades told and retold by *les folles* are props used to elaborate a primarily transgender identity and assemble a trans or possibly a trans-gay community. Sex, both real and fictitious, might just exist for gender.

The strong version of the claim I am building here is that beyond asking whether David is gay, straight, or bisexual, we can also ask whether he is a man, a woman, or outside the gender binary. The reason we do not ask the second question is precisely because we are so taken with the first. Gender switch, in the form of inversion, is peremptorily explained with reference to effeminate gay male identity. Gender dysphoria is explained with reference to homophobia. Edelman posits that the gay man is infinitely readable, and we might say that this is true to the exclusion of other subjectivities. The gay man must be read even where he is not present, a reading-over process that carries with it the potential not just to threaten straight men, as Edelman argues, but also, I would add, to erase trans and trans-gay experience. At what point in the novel are we sure that David is, indisputably, a man? We see David interpret his desire as homosexual and interpret homosexuals as women. But David is an interpretive failure. Though he is read by the zombie, the sailor, Jacques, and Giovanni, David is a terrible reader of himself. Turning now to two scenes of misinterpretation and to David's final, emblematic moment of self-misrecognition, I suggest that David and the reader need a trans-gay reading strategy for interpreting gender in Giovanni's Room—even if David ultimately neither identifies himself as transgender nor is identified as such by the reader.

Narratologically, Giovanni's Room uses the abjection of transgenderism, evinced in the phantom figure of the transgender specter, to shore up its message that neither gay nor straight identifications can empower David. In other words, a queer privileging of the failure of categories to speak truth to desire rests on a willingness to render and use the potentially transgender agent as a non-subject, an "unreal" category. What is needed is an understanding of trans subjectivity grounded in personhood rather than deadly figuration. "The truth is I'm no mystery," Leslie Feinberg flatly attests.[51] Quoting Naomi Scheman's "Queering the Center by Centering the Queer," Jacob Hale similarly points out the obvious: "Transsexual lives are lived, thus livable."[52] Hale goes on to suggest that trans representations must not exist devoid of reference to trans lives, experiences, and embodiments. I am arguing that the narrative of Giovanni's Room, warped as it is by David's impoverished imagination, not only erases trans lives but does so quite literally by disfiguring and then killing off the transgender "threat."

Baldwin's narrative mechanism is not subtle. He articulates a dehumanized subject position for gender variants by participating in a version of what Namaste calls the "staging of transgendered subjects."[53] In fact, as David levels his gaze at Guillaume's patrons one evening, the bar operates as a stage, one on par with a cage at the zoo. In that cage, the potentially transgender subject becomes, horribly, a shit-eating monkey.

> There was a boy who worked all day, it was said, in the post office, who came out at night wearing makeup and earrings and with his heavy blond hair piled high. Sometimes he actually wore a skirt and high heels. He usually stood alone unless Guillaume walked over to tease him. People said that he was very nice, but I confess that his utter grotesqueness made me uneasy; perhaps in the same way that the sight of monkeys eating their own excrement turns some people's stomachs. They might not mind so much if the monkey did not—so grotesquely—resemble human beings. (27)

The "boy" in this passage, standing alone in the spotlight created by Guillaume's emcee-like teasing, exists as though on stage for David's spectatorship. As the metaphor shifts to that of a cage, however, David, the gender-appropriate male onlooker, remains and is simultaneously re-created as human in relation to the "monkey" that threatens him with identification. Namaste claims that trans staging in gay bars, in that it "excludes transgendered people even as it includes us,"[54] operates as a means by which "gay male identity establishes itself as something prior to performance."[55] In this case, that exclusion works through a false human/non-human distinction to simultaneously display and invisibilize the trans subject. I wonder, though, precisely what identity is given priority in David's case as he speculates on the caged and dehumanized transwoman. The gay bar in which David inevitably locates himself contains a much more diverse set of sex/gender practices than can be accounted for by the gay male/transgender dichotomy imagined by Namaste. David, for instance, is trying to confirm his phantasmatic heterosexual masculinity. Giovanni is trying to earn a meager living by relying on precisely the trappings of masculinity that David and many of the patrons admire. Guillaume is trying to earn a handsome living by hiring and staging—though behind the bar—the angelic masculinity of Giovanni. Surely some of the patrons, including gay ones, are learning about and even learning how to become transgendered subjects. Inevitably, gay bars represent spaces that not only divide gay and trans but also make possible and encourage investigations across sexuality and gender. If transgenderism is staged, as it always is from our first-person narrator's transphobic perspective, it is also modeled, if modeled from a staged distance.

In thinking about the trans possibilities in *Giovanni's Room*, it is worth pausing for a moment to consider the particular context in which the novel was produced, so as to better understand the social relations that are inscribed in the text. Georges Sidéris describes the atmosphere of the Saint-Germain-des-Prés quarter of Paris, the setting of much of *Giovanni's Room*, as "the principal setting for male homosexual life in Paris" during the 1950s.[56] Baldwin lived primarily in Paris from 1948 to 1957, the year after *Giovanni's Room* was published. He was, without doubt, familiar with *le quartier*. Yet why did he choose to depict Saint-Germain-des-Prés rather than another Parisian neighborhood where gay life was visible and even vibrant? Saint-Germain-des-Prés had, according to Sidéris, "a special place in the homosexual geography and sociability of the period,"[57] for it contained a unique blend of artists and existentialist philosophers; homosexual cafés, bars, and restaurants; and an active street scene that provided plentiful cruising opportunities. Sidéris cites an October 1952 edition of the homosexual French newspaper *Futur*: "Saint-Germain-des-Prés, capital of non-conformity, [is] the only place in Paris where you can amuse yourself according to your tastes."[58] Perhaps the most characteristic "taste" of this particular quarter of Paris was a taste not simply of gay men for gay men but of gay men for gender variance. "[T]he quarter," writes Sidéris, "was famous above all for its *folles*, who were not specific to it but who stood out by their effeminate mannerisms, their swishing walk, their elegant clothes, sometimes their facial makeup, and especially their mannered way of speaking, often punctuated with piercing shrieks, which distinguished them from other homosexuals."[59]

The distinctive openness of gay life in Saint-Germain-des-Prés was largely a response to the pressures of overarching social norms, gender prescriptions chief among them. Predictably, agents of social enforcement pushed back. By the 1970s, the transgressive atmosphere of the neighborhood had been changed by homophobic laws passed in the name of "decency."[60] But it was not only dominant culture that worked to eradicate "the scourge" of *les folles*. "Homophile" culture, characterized by its insistence on gay male virility and the assimilation it could provide, was well organized through a variety of memberships (including, in the United States, the Mattachine Society). Representatives of the homophile movement attempted to minimize the presence of *les folles*, to blame them for social animosity toward homosexual men, and to pathologize them for their strident effeminacy.[61] Sidéris thus identifies an important dichotomy within Parisian gay life: the homophiles versus the "effeminates." At no point does he identify the "effeminates" using the language of transgender, as that language was not fully part of the socio-linguistic conditions of post-war Paris.[62] Indeed, he refers to the effeminates' "distinctive and authentic homosexual identity that challenged a normalizing society."[63] But the homosexual dichotomy that emerged most urgently in Saint-Germain-des-Prés clearly broke along lines of gender, and it is that dichotomy that Baldwin found so useful for dramatizing David's dilemma in *Giovanni's Room*. James Campbell argues that "Baldwin has scant interest in serving up a picture of the gay scene in St.-Germain. Although there are one or two vignettes featuring screeching queens—*les folles*—their appearance provokes disgust rather than desire. . . . Such descriptions are there in order to set in relief the purity of purpose of Giovanni and . . . David."[64] I suggest that, distinguished by its "degeneracy," Saint-Germain-des-Prés offers the ideal and even necessary setting for the novel because it casts difference between the pure and profane of gender as always threatening to collapse. If various homosexual identities were being realized and contested in this context, this was done, to a significant extent, in ways that expanded the insistent possibilities for gendered existence. One can even surmise that it was precisely the threat of gay-trans crossover that galvanized the homophile movement to attempt to shore up the imperiled masculinity of homosexuality. Within the reality of gender non-conformity, variance, and rebellion that indisputably marks the Saint-Germain-des-Prés of the period, can we not posit a nascent and perhaps elaborate mode of transgender-gay male sociality? If there was quite possibly, in the figure of the blond boy from the post office, a future "ex-GI turned blonde beauty," what other gay-trans formations were occurring?

Baldwin, perhaps inseparable from David in this respect, can only envision the person who transitions gender as threatening beast, not beauty. This is nowhere so evident as in Guillaume's murder scene, in which Baldwin elaborates on the trope of transgender mortification by literalizing the death of the gender non-normative individual. As reported in the French press, the known facts of the "terrific scandal" are few but straightforward. The destitute immigrant Giovanni has strangled Guillaume, who, whatever else he may be, is a French citizen and symbolic patriarch from a well-known family. David rejects the motive, reported in all the Paris newspapers, of a botched robbery attempt. In place of such speculation, David meticulously reconstructs the events of the murder as he imagines them to have happened. That wholly imagined recounting of what was "too black for the newsprint to carry and too deep for Giovanni to tell" (153) emerges, however, not simply from David's belief that the French have demonized the man he loves as a foreigner-criminal but that they have made of Guillaume a national hero. In an argument with Hella, David rails against the hypocrisy of the French press ensuring that Guillaume's name will become "fantastically entangled with French history, French honor, and French glory, and very nearly . . . a symbol of French manhood." "But listen," David counters, "he was just a disgusting old fairy. That's *all* he was! . . . Isn't there some point in telling the truth?" (150).

That "truth" compels David to imagine another one, and he believes that he alone knows this deeper truth: "I may have been the only man in Paris who knew that [Giovanni] had not meant to do it, who could read *why* he had done it beneath the details printed in the newspapers" (153). David's rereading of Guillaume's death stems not from a belief in Giovanni's innocence but from a confidence that "Giovanni certainly did not *mean* to do it" (156; my emphasis). Relieving Giovanni of intentionality, David points the finger of blame elsewhere. As his detailed fantasy of the murder reveals, the truth for David is that Guillaume, a "silly old queen," has participated in his own death. David thus recasts the murder as a murder-suicide by suggesting that Guillaume has reneged on a sex-for-work bargain struck with Giovanni, driving the Italian into a blind rage. That imagined provocation to violence, however, operates as a false front for the deeper logic that governs David's retelling of the event. An analysis of David's reconstruction of the murder reveals that what truly motivates and justifies Giovanni's murder of Guillaume was the murderous truth of Guillaume's gender nonconformity.

David begins to reconstruct the night—and reorient blame—by imagining that "[i]t must have been a great evening for the bar when Giovanni swaggered in alone. I could hear the conversation." As Giovanni approaches his former employer in hopes of being rehired, Guillaume's homo-femininity violently offends, even "hits" him: "Guillaume's face, voice, manner, smell, hit him; . . . the smile with which he responds to Guillaume almost causes him to vomit" (154). The vomitous Guillaume tells Giovanni to return after the bar closes. He then directs him to his quarters above the bar, where Giovanni finds himself "surrounded by Guillaume's silks, colors, perfumes." Guillaume, "precipitate, flabby, moist," appears in his "theatrical dressing gown" and, becoming one with his feminine accoutrements, "seems to surround [Giovanni] like the sea itself," until the now helpless Giovanni "feels himself going under, is overcome, and Guillaume has his will" (155).

This scene of conquest of the masculine foreigner by the feminine Parisian happens, remember, in what David imagines to be his singularly insightful imagination. "I think that if this had not happened," David ventures, "Giovanni would not have killed him." But what is "this" in David's mind? On the one hand, "this" stands for unpaid sex. David believes Guillaume to have broken his promise and refused to rehire Giovanni: "For, with his pleasure taken, and while Giovanni still lies suffocating, Guillaume becomes a business man once more and, walking up and down, gives excellent reasons why Giovanni cannot work for him anymore" (155–56). But there is more here than a deal gone wrong. The price Giovanni has paid goes far beyond sex. David pictures Guillaume being so delighted with himself—"he has scarcely ever gotten so much for so little before"—that he "begins to prance about the room." There can be only one response: "[N]ow it was Giovanni's turn to be delighted."

[Giovanni] grabbed him, he struck him. And with that touch, and with each blow, the intolerable weight at the bottom of his heart began to lift. . . . The room was overturned, the fabrics were shredded, the odor of perfume was thick. Guillaume struggled to get out of the room, but Giovanni followed him everywhere: now it was Guillaume's turn to be surrounded. And perhaps at the very moment Guillaume thought he had broken free, when he had reached the door perhaps, Giovanni lunged after him and caught him by the sash of the dressing gown and wrapped the sash around his neck. Then he simply held on, sobbing, becoming lighter every moment as Guillaume grew heavier, tightening the sash and cursing. Then Guillaume fell. And Giovanni fell—back into the room, the streets, the world, into the presence and the shadow of death. (156–57)

Given his class status as a foreigner, Giovanni's body becomes his last resource and resort. Guillaume uses his position—not only as business owner, but also as arbiter of national propriety—to cheat Giovanni out of what his masculine body was meant to purchase for him. When Guillaume fails to live up to his end of the bargain, however, we see that Giovanni strikes a new deal. Crucially, the quid pro quo of this new deal, the price to be extracted from Guillaume, responds not merely to unpaid sex but to unpaid sex with this kind of person. To be fucked by a "silly old queen," by a perfumed, prancing man in silk robes—*this* justifies murder. Giovanni literally kills Guillaume with the symbol of his gender transgression, the sash to his dressing gown. In David's dangerous imagination, this end seems fitting, as though Guillaume's hyperfemininity has sealed his fate, as though to be gender variant is to don the instruments of one's own inevitable demise. No longer metaphorical specters of death, gender non-conforming individuals explicitly invite death on themselves.

In addition, we must remember that underwriting David's fantasy of Guillaume's gender nonconformity is a different gender narrative. The "truth" that Guillaume is a "disgusting old fairy" operates so powerfully on David, perhaps, because the "fairy" can simultaneously lay claim to a masculine identity. Though David fantastically effeminizes him, Guillaume unmistakably represents the masculine authority of the law, not only because his legal standing as a French citizen trumps Giovanni's status as foreign worker, but because, given Guillaume's family name, the police are forced to cooperate with him by giving advance notice of their raids on his bar. Most unimaginable to David, Guillaume becomes, in death, the very "symbol of French manhood." It is, then, Guillaume's irreconcilable status as boy-girl that galvanizes David's need to justify Giovanni's act of murder by reimagining it.

The question of why Giovanni murders Guillaume thus has two very different answers. On the one hand, Guillaume has reneged on a deal. Guillaume's action has a material consequence, and perhaps the murder can even be said to be justified in this sense. But on the other hand, what permits Giovanni to kill Guillaume, makes him murderable, and actually justifies the murder in David's imagination is not the act of reneging on the deal. Rather, the murder is a consequence of a transphobic threshold of personhood. Guillaume is the victim of transphobic violence, punished by—quite literally as a function of—his gender transgression and not simply his homosexuality. Further, more dramatically, the point at which personhood can be denied, the point at which a person becomes murderable, is arbitrarily, immeasurably low for those who fail to obey the rules of gender, and this is true whether they make good on their promises or not.

I have used Guillaume's murder scene to suggest that transgender analyses—in this case, one attuned to the deadly implications of a transphobic imagination—can offer important insights into the narrative logic of an alternately "classic" gay and "exemplary" queer novel. I want to pursue that idea further in a discussion of the final scene of *Giovanni's Room*, a scene that seems to purposefully withhold or evade meaning. A bookend to the opening scene of the novel, in which David considers his thin white reflection in a darkened window on the night preceding Giovanni's execution, the final scene stages yet another confrontation between David and his now "dull and white and dry" body, as reflected in a large bedroom mirror just before dawn. The scene progresses according to a dual, entwined narrative in which David both imagines Giovanni being led to the guillotine and also searches out his own fate on this last night of their lives "together." That fate crystallizes in a corporeal mystery, the pull of a strangely resolute yet uninterpretable body: "The body in the mirror forces me to turn and face it. And I look at my body, which is under sentence of death. It is lean, hard, and cold, the incarnation of a mystery. And I do not know what moves in this body, what this body is searching. It is trapped in my mirror as it is trapped in time and it hurries toward revelation" (168).

The most important point to make is that a certain "recalcitrance of bodily matter"[65] emerges at the end of *Giovanni's Room*. In that the novel stages its final, dramatic moment as a confrontation with corporeality, it stands as a body-insistent text. That materiality is complicated by the fact that, though David recognizes it as "his" body, he largely dissociates "the" body in the mirror. In part, that dissociation reflects sympathy with the doomed and absent body of Giovanni, who will soon be "thrown forward on his face in darkness." David perceives his body, like Giovanni's, as "under sentence of death," and thus he identifies with his lover's metaphysical condition. As Giovanni's "journey begins," David senses that his own body "hurries toward revelation." But this mirror scene also reflects the larger theme of self-ignorance and, specifically, the problem, identified by Mae Henderson, of "self difference—or the 'otherness' of the self."[66] Henderson argues that the specular/spatial logic that governs *Giovanni's Room* traps David within his own illusory reflection in this final moment of the novel. If David is to rescue his manhood, "his false mirror image must be destroyed."[67] Henderson brilliantly links David's predicament and potential salvation to Baldwin's own authorial strategy of "racial drag," in which he "produces a highly mediated reverse passing narrative in which he appropriates whiteness as a way of exploring the contours of his own sexuality." Notes Henderson, "In other words, Baldwin's literary masquerade, and racial imposture, enables the author to examine internal aspects of the complex self by occupying a position of radical otherness."[68] While the term "racial drag" stands open to critique for deploying a gendered term to indicate a racialized transition, it has the great advantage of implying that Baldwin's use of narrative "whiteface" initiates and compels the powerfully normative associations, including gendered ones, that offer David both privilege and torment. This stabilizing dynamic implicit in "racial drag" becomes clear if we remember that drag, rather than being typified by spectacular performance, better describes the "mundane" ways that gender is done.[69] The figuration of white manhood thus not only grants Baldwin "a certain self-distancing"[70] but also helps him to construct an "other" narrative about the price of normalcy. Indeed, in some ways, through that self-distancing in the writing of *Giovanni's Room*, Baldwin achieves a "radical otherness" that David never will.

Ultimately, though, the stability of white masculinity—which is, after all, David's double-edged American birthright—cannot hold. While Henderson suggests that David "must divest himself of conventional notions of masculinity before he can achieve self-realization,"[71] I propose an alternate reading that dramatizes a different mode of self-confrontation. I suggest that at the heart of this final scene operates a very specific kind of body questioning, located as a deep-seated anxiety of the sexed flesh. If David seems unsure of how to inhabit his body, whether his body is habitable, how it is bounded, and what it contains ("I do not know what moves in this body, what this body is searching"), this is largely because he finds himself, unavoidably at last, at odds with his "sex," including its racial meaning. Arrested by his inscrutable reflection, David laments, "I long to crack that mirror and be free. I look at my sex, my troubling sex, and wonder how it can be redeemed, how I can save it from the knife.... [T]he key to my salvation, which cannot save my body, is hidden in my flesh" (168). What interests me in this passage is the stubborn materiality of the body, shrouded as it is in Baldwin's characteristic invocation of religious mystery. For what is happening here but a fundamental failure on David's part to recognize, identify with, and own "his" body. David's anxiety is not, as it has been for much of the novel, related to a figurative or performative gender switch. Certainly David fears more than castration as he imagines a literal alteration of the sexed body.[72] Instead, we need to read this scene as a person's failure to recognize himself as unified with his reflected image. I therefore contend that both transsexual theory in particular and transgender theory more generally offer important critical lenses through which to view this scene and the larger work, for if problems of the sexed body define David's ultimate identity troubles, we might also ask whether that particular problematic has been there all along.

What relationship must David now forge with himself, trapped as he is in a state of "somatic non-ownership?"[73] I propose that what David lacks—and what remains underdeveloped without transgender and transsexual analyses—is a theory of gay male embodiment by which he might ground his various desires. The equally complementary and competing insights of Prosser and Halberstam have been particularly important in helping me to understand the need for a theory of gay corporeality, because the field of transsexual and transgender studies forcefully articulates the importance of attending to sexed embodiments, to gender as an embodied register of identity, and to the claim that the body is the "contingent ground of all our knowledge."[74] Once more, then, I want to stress the utility of trans critique for "non-trans" interpretations, while also blurring the line between what is a "properly" trans narrative. The "trans-gay" reading strategy I have proposed means to capture the potential of these ambiguities. I do not want to appropriate transgender experience for a purely textual queer reading practice; nor, conversely, do I want to dismiss the possibility of re-narrating David's experience as transgender or transsexual; nor do I want to delimit the scope or impact of trans critique, even in cases where homosexual desire is the operative and perhaps primary narrative consideration. Following Gayle Rubin, Prosser affirms that "the writing of transsexual history will surely depend upon performing retroactive readings of figures and texts that have been central to the lesbian and gay canon."[75] Significantly, those retroactive readings, informed by transsexual possibility, must be brought to bear on a diverse set of lesbian and gay texts and give new meaning to those texts even where transsexuality and transgender cannot ultimately be reinscribed. If there is surely no regular pattern by which narratives of homosexual desire and trans experience are imbricated, we must ask how they might sometimes nevertheless be meaningfully related.

The point of overlap I have currently identified in *Giovanni's Room* is the moment where the mysterious body becomes the site of non-identity for the gay man whose culture has produced out of his desire a profound sense of gender dysphoria. In David, that dysphoria seems to undercut, rather than enable, trans subjectivity, building, as it does, on the transphobic undercurrents that buoy up the homophobia in the novel. Yet in theorizing female masculinity, Halberstam writes that "it would not be accurate to make gender dysphoria the exclusive property of transsexual bodies or to surmise that the greater the gender dysphoria, the likelier a transsexual identification."[76] So while David's narrative of self-difference is not (yet) characterized by the "lengthy, formalized, and normally substantive transition"—a "correlated set of corporeal, psychic, and social changes"[77] that, according to Prosser, typifies transsexual narrative—his trans- and homophobia-induced gender dysphoria nevertheless causes him, unequivocally, body problems. In terms of the applicability of trans critique, does it matter that those problems are not "rooted" in the body or that David appears to come late to an explicit, felt sense of corporeal non-identity? If it is true that "[t]ranssexuality reveals the extent to which embodiment forms an essential base to subjectivity," can it also be true that the experience of embodiment is mystified and thus unrecognizable as "an essential base to subjectivity?" Perhaps the central metaphors of dirt- and soap-covered bodies, for example, need to be reread as *literal* states of embodied experience even as they are used, primarily, to *figure* the complementary failures of heterosexual and homosexual categories. David *feels* dirty as a gay man, and that feeling renders him not only unable to accept his homosexuality but, crucially, unable to *feel* the gay body overlaid with figurative-but-felt dirt. The transsexual insight that "embodiment is as much about feeling one inhabits material flesh as the flesh itself"[78] is therefore apropos, though the ways transsexuals and gay men feel or do not feel their bodies may drastically differ. How, then, does a gay man *feel* his body? How is gay male desire materialized as and on the body? What is "gay embodiment?"[79]

Like transsexuality, which is often characterized by a felt body image or experience that does not align with or feel like the apparent physical body, gay identity, I argue, is also typified by (though certainly not limited to) a felt body experience, that of the "felt desiring body." I am arguing that rather than merely positing a gay male body, gay identity raises questions about embodiment and specifically about how gay bodies feel. Gay identity suggests the corporeal manifestation of desire not in the facile sense that humans must have bodies but because it is in some respects akin to (and in many cases achieved by)[80] the corporeal recovery noted in transsexual autobiography. Prosser reports that in transsexual narratives, pre-operative transsexuals often report feeling a different body, sensing a "second skin" that is not coextensive with their tangible flesh yet that offers the true psychic/somatic interface for their experience of themselves in the world. Indeed, the pre-operative transsexual's "invisible" body image has such sentience, such material force, that Prosser postulates that "the transsexual's postreassignment body [might] be reconceived as already phantomized preassignment."[81] "Surgery," Prosser continues, "deploys the skin and tissues to materialize the transsexual body image with fleshly prostheses in the shape of the sentient ghost-body."[82]

Rather than describing a second skin, gay people often tell their stories by using the metaphors of "living a lie," of not being their "true selves," or of being "trapped in the closet." These figurations help many to narrate the experience of the ways homophobic culture impinges on their self-realization. Notably, self-difference in these formulations is not described in corporeal terms, nor is the problematic trope of the "wrong body," frequent in trans narratives, typical when gay people tell their stories. But this only highlights the degree to which metaphorical constructs such as the closet, helpful as they have been to those seeking language for their experiences, have inadvertently turned attention away from the materiality of gay identity.[83] Transsexual theory, by troubling the relationship between bodies, felt experience, and subjectivity, can be effective in turning our attention back to the idea that gay people do not just desire bodies; insofar as the body is an important locus of desire, our relationship to our bodies can determine our relationship to our desire.[84] Gay identity may require an interrogation of how and where we feel our desiring bodies.

The connection I have made to trans theory exposes, I hope, a fascinating point: it is not at all clear just how the bodies made available as gay relate to gay desires. Being gay may necessitate *a search* for a gay body, may require a journey toward gay embodiment precisely because homophobic and transphobic culture demands of gay people a certain non-ownership of the body. Gay people are given sentient metaphors, such as filth, that literally make them feel on their skin different than they ought to feel about their desires. They are given images of themselves, the "trans" specter chief among them, that attempt to prescribe the relationship between the material referent of the body and the possibilities for gendered experience. Coming out, as much as it might be said to affirm or solidify an identity, might actually thwart and therefore necessitate a search for embodied desire, much to the surprise of the gay individual who thinks—but may only ambiguously feel—that he already has a gay body.

With this idea of articulating a new relationship to gay bodies, I want to return to David's corporeal questioning in order to close this chapter. David does not know quite what to do with his body. Specifically, he does not know what to do about or what is to be done with his penis. Is it the source of masculinity or emasculation? Does his stare indicate a classically fetishistic over-investment of meaning in his genitals, or does he stare precisely because meaning cannot be fixed by/on the phallus? Or perhaps we need to ask different kinds of body questions. Does what David desires to do with his penis make him feel ownership of his body or feel improper toward and in it? Does the prospect of losing his penis to the knife operate in his imagination purely as a threat? Or is the dissonance David experiences at the level of the sexed body an indication either that he feels his gay male body elsewhere or that the body he feels elsewhere is not that of a gay male at all? How does it *feel*, at this moment, to be gay or not? These questions are not answered with certainty in the text. But I propose that, confronted by his body, David seems on the verge of initiating a transition from one kind of gay man to another. On the final page of the novel, he determines that his nakedness must be held "sacred" and, therefore, "scoured perpetually with the salt of my life" (169). This final, painful resolution to abrade the flesh, to both punish it and make it feel, seems either to escalate the effort to cleanse the body of homosexual desire or, conversely, to wear away the gay body that cannot feel, in the search for one that can.

CHAPTER 3

What Straight Men Need

Gay Love in *Another Country*

> If you believe the propaganda, it would seem that every time a fag or a dyke
> fingers a vagina or asshole is a demonstration of queer love and community.
>
> —ROBERT REID-PHARR, *BLACK GAY MAN: ESSAYS*

> Orientations are about the direction we take that puts some things and not
> others in our reach.
>
> —SARA AHMED, *QUEER PHENOMENOLOGY: ORIENTATIONS,
> OBJECTS, AND OTHERS*

Why do straight people have sex with gay people? The question is a queer
one, strange in that its rhetorical power to surprise and even unsettle comes
from the mundane facticity with which it asserts its underlying claim:
straight people have sex with gay people. The question does not simply
ask to be answered. Rather, it produces the need for an explanatory narrative, a substitute logic by which such straight-gay sex can make sense. In
a culture in which the homophobia-producing straight/gay binary holds
sway, straight people cannot *simply* have sex with gay people. There must be
something more to the story. Ironically, the reverse assertion, that *of course*
gay people have sex with straight people, seems naturally to contain its own
explanations. Straight people are "logically" understood to be the objects
of gay desire, idealization, recruitment, and predation. Indeed, narratives
of why gay people (want to) have sex with straight people abound. But in
the reverse case, excuse narratives (drunkenness, adolescent curiosity) and
closet narratives (the straight person is not so straight after all) provide eva-
sions rather than explanations. One model of bisexuality could account for
shifting sexual identifications, while another would suggest that everyone is
bisexual, but both models avoid the seemingly paradoxical question of why

straight and gay people have sex with each other *as* straight and gay people.[1] In a different way, the overarching narrative of postmodern queer theory makes sense of the question of straight-gay sex by deconstructing sexual identity and rendering the binary distinction incoherent. In the queer act of sex, "straights" are not having sex with "gays" at all. What narratives, though, might respond to the question of straight-gay sex in ways that are more nuanced, not purely deconstructive, and yet still believable—ways that even create new possibilities for belief?

James Baldwin's third novel, *Another Country* (1962), attempts to create just such a narrative. Baldwin offers a strange, imaginative, and perhaps fantastic answer to the question of why straight people have sex with gay people: because they need to. Because it is good for them. Because "gay sex"—a deeply problematic phrase that nevertheless proliferates in critical assessments of *Another Country*—offers straight people a revelatory, authenticating experience. While both straight men and women have sex with the novel's central gay male figure, Baldwin clearly posits the straight male situation as the more pressing concern. "Gay sex" and the love it expresses, Baldwin paradoxically dares to imagine, is what straight men need.

In Baldwin's expression of what *straight* men need, we have a sexualized version of his more recognizable artistic and cultural inquiry that asks what *white* people need to be told, need to hear, need to face up to in America, that is, what they need to know about themselves so that they may know their "other." The liberal white audience to whom *Another Country* appealed may have looked to Baldwin with precisely these race questions in mind, but the novel shocked—and therefore appealed all the more thoroughly—because it taught its race lesson as inextricable from its sexual lesson: what *straight white* men need. The precise nature of what David Gerstner calls Baldwin's "white seduction"—the complicated dynamic by which Baldwin "simultaneously eroticized while excoriating the seductive powers of whiteness"[2]—will be an active and open question for this chapter. But generally, such knotted relationships between sex and race were informed by Baldwin's long-held claim, reiterated in a late interview, that "the sexual question and the racial question have always been entwined."[3] A striking exploration of this connection between sex and race, "gay sex" in *Another Country* initiates in the straight white man (for he becomes Baldwin's primary, though not exclusive, test case) a kind of loving transformation that not only attempts to redraw conventional sexual boundaries but also prepares him to confront what is represented as the related yet more impenetrable border of interracial desire.

Rather than homosexuality functioning as some kind of solution to racial discord, *Another Country* implies that one crossing of lines of identity can motivate and enable another.[4] This chapter argues that although the novel offers a wide-ranging critique of American identity, it stakes its forward progress—that is, its narrative logic—on the claim that straight white maleness represents an impoverished and impoverishing cultural location, one that can be enriched by the love of a good gay man. The ambiguously queer "asshole" in Robert Reid-Pharr's epigraph to this chapter, lovingly touched as a "demonstration of queer love and community," is relocated onto the straight white man as a symbol of his unfulfilled racialized need.

If Baldwin was seduced by the needs of white straight men, his work also suggests that at the center of the national erotic landscape is a disavowed blackness. Reid-Pharr, in a chapter titled "Dinge," suggests that "even and especially in those most sacred moments of sexual normativity (white dominant male on white submissive female), the specter of the black beast is omnipresent."[5] Citing the work of critics who theorize blackness within whiteness,[6] Reid-Pharr participates in the project of analyzing "how blackness is indeed the always already lurking in the netherworld of white consciousness."[7] Thus he notes that Rufus, the central black male character in *Another Country*, exists as the "specter of the black beast," "the ghost who haunts even [his white friend] Vivaldo's most intimate interactions."[8] I am deeply indebted to Reid-Pharr, who demonstrates that only by keeping Rufus's race status and his raced experience in full view can we encounter whiteness as other than a transparency. Yet I diverge from Reid-Pharr's interpretation of *Another Country* in several meaningful ways, especially from his willingness to identify as "queer" the white (and, I argue, straight) man who relies on an omnipresent black male presence to (invisibly) mediate and thereby relieve him of his own racial knowledge. This can be done, I believe, only if the black specter is necessarily not recognized as the black *gay* specter in the novel. Behind the inscrutable Rufus, who sleeps with men and women, stands a more resolutely black gay character in the fleeting presence of the young southerner LeRoy, on whom (even Baldwin seems not to recognize) the novel's vision depends. I will argue that two problematic shifts occur to the extent that LeRoy recedes from view. First, "gay" identity in the novel comes to mean white gay male identity. Second, in the sexual liaisons between gay and straight made possible precisely thanks to shared whiteness, straight whiteness comes to mean "queer." "Queerness" is but another form of white erotic transparency, a failure to recognize the devastating immobility of straight white masculinity.

Stepping back for a moment, one can hardly overstate the radical nature of Baldwin's vision of a "different way to live and love."[9] In mapping anew the terrain of straight-gay sex, Baldwin makes good on what would become one of the promises of queer theory: to enumerate and problematize narratives of desire.[10] However, even as queer theory looks forward into an unknown, necessarily unknowable, knowledge-producing future, it always does so from what we might call an identifiable present in which identity categories function for better as well as for worse. So, for example, while the late queer theorist Eve Kosofsky Sedgwick advocates, in *Touching Feeling: Affect, Pedagogy, Performativity*, for a version of future-looking queer theory, she nevertheless also necessarily invokes the presence of gay men. This move typifies her inquiry in her other seminal queer theory texts, *Between Men*, *Epistemology of the Closet*, and *Tendencies*, as well. On the one hand, Sedgwick keeps a vigilant eye on the homophobic pressures that continue to produce a demonized gay minority and that undermine the universalizing queer logic toward which her work surely tends. On the other hand, Sedgwick writes precisely for a positively imagined—and thus restabilized—gay community. In her retrospective preface to the 1992 republication of *Between Men*, Sedgwick reflects a version of this queer interplay between gay male presence and absence: "There's a way in which the author of this book seems not quite to have been able to believe in the reality of the gay male communities toward whose readership the book so palpably yearns. The yearning makes the incredulity."[11] Sedgwick's essay from *Tendencies*, "Queer and Now" (reprinted as the opening chapter of the latest state-of-the-field anthology, *The Routledge Queer Studies Reader*, from which I quote), deepens the integrity of the author's relationships with gay men in light of her breast cancer diagnosis:

> Probably my own most formative influence from a quite early age has been a viscerally intense, highly speculative (not to say inventive) cross-identification with gay men and gay male cultures as I inferred, imagined, and later came to know them. It wouldn't have required quite so over-determined a trajectory, though, for almost any forty-year-old facing a protracted, life-threatening illness in 1991 to realize that the people with whom she had perhaps most in common, and from whom she might well have most to learn, are people living with AIDS, AIDS activists,

and others whose lives had been profoundly reorganized by AIDS in the course of the 1980s."[12]

If Sedgwick can be taken as representative, queer theory simultaneously—often unintentionally, and perhaps characteristically—deconstructs but also relies on and reconstructs gay identity as part and parcel of its critical project. Queer theory needs and even affectively yearns for a gay referent.

This long-standing and still-productive tension frames my reading of *Another Country*, the queerness of which relies on entwined problematic representations of gay identity. An antihomophobic reading of *Another Country* must attend carefully to the narrative function of the gay man in facilitating straight-gay sex. More specifically, it must critically examine the use of the gay man and "gay sex" as mechanisms by which straight people transcend sexual and racial differences, for as the gay man bears the weight of others' personal insights and revelations, he does so with his body and at his own expense. Although it may appear to hold a privileged place in the novel, given that "the homosexual connection magically produces 'a healing transformation' in racial terms as well [as sexual terms],"[13] homosexuality is, in effect, unevenly exchanged or traded on in the interest of straight sexual liberation and racial reconciliation. The nature of this exchange becomes most disturbing when the social gains that result from the "liberatory" powers of homosexuality—powers embodied in the character of gay white southerner Eric Jones and ghosted in the figure of gay black LeRoy—are shown, paradoxically, to reinscribe heteronormative sexuality. In that gay trade-off, homosexuality is both used and also figuratively "used up," changed into a concept evacuated of positive content, made a self-defeating means to an ostensibly queer end. In fact, "redemptive" homosexuality represents the foremost of the novel's many forms of prostitution, not primarily because it is offered up in service of racial integration, but because it concomitantly stabilizes and privileges straight identity. Moreover and bizarrely, that straightening out is accomplished through straight-gay sexual couplings that would appear to unsettle straight (and, to a lesser extent, gay) identities. From this critical perspective, the novel is deceptively "queer."

In a famously homophobic attack that nonetheless provides an unexpected touchstone for this chapter, Eldridge Cleaver also identified a connection between sexual exploration and racial identity in Baldwin. Characterizing the central black male figure in *Another Country* as a "pathetic wretch who indulged in the white man's pastime of committing suicide, who

let a white bisexual homosexual fuck him in the ass,"[14] Cleaver fell in line
with one black nationalist discourse that pitted African American masculinity against queer sexuality.[15] Signifying off of and diffusing Cleaver's accusation, I want to suggest that Baldwin is not so much a "race traitor" as a "gay
trader" in *Another Country*, constructing a fantasy not of black destruction
but of homosexual sacrifice disguised as revolutionary love. The gay trade
of the novel occurs when heteronormalizing questions of gender and race
are worked out on the "loving" body of the gay man. Not surprisingly, then,
I characterize the gay trade of *Another Country* as an essentially bad deal
for the homosexual man, who, circulated as the instrument of racial and
sexual exploration for straight people, gives much more than he receives,
both physically and emotionally. The price of enlightenment in the novel, I
argue, is paid in a special way by the gay man, whose revelatory sexuality is
predicated on an unproblematized sexual accessibility that evokes not only
gay prostitution but a larger sellout of homosexuality itself.

My argument, I am acutely aware, runs counter to Baldwin's intentions,
which were to expose the uselessness and, indeed, danger of suffocating
sexual identity categories, rather than to reuse them in even more dangerous ways. *Another Country* remains perhaps the best example of Baldwin's
universalizing poetic, his attempt to act as witness to our flawed but common humanity and to articulate the fundamental but not reciprocal interde-
pendence that exists within difference. Nevertheless, while Baldwin's artistic
impulse was queer, the narrative strategy that I am calling the "gay trade" disrupts that queer vision. In contrast to most recent critical work on *Another
Country*, I contend that sexual identity categories function quite normatively
in the novel, even, in a perversely ironic echoing of Cleaver, to the point of
whitewashing homosexuality by creating of the black gay man an ontological impossibility. My own intention is not to criticize Baldwin bluntly but,
rather, to suggest the nearly insurmountable difficulty of the narrative dilemma he faced: how to craft his universalizing message about the sexual
and racial identities into a believable narrative without, as Reid-Pharr has
noted is also true at times of the black man in Baldwin's work, relying on a
gay scapegoat.[16]

As I trace what I will gently call Baldwin's narrative "failure," I also want
to draw attention to the difficulty that queer theory has had in grappling
with a text like *Another Country*, a problem that crystallizes in the way that
critically queer interpretations of the novel, reluctant to read straight-gay
sex through the eyes of a resolutely gay male character, privilege the novel's

"queerness," as though queerness harbored some kind of inherently positive content. Reid-Pharr pointedly attests that the naive transparency associated with white privilege—white people's ability to exist outside their white bodies in the act of sex so as not to acknowledge what they think as they fuck—extends to (white) queer privilege as well. If, argues Reid-Pharr, we recognize that "[w]e do not escape race and racism when we fuck" and that "[o]n the contrary, this fantasy of escape is precisely that which marks the sexual act as deeply implicated in the ideological processes by which difference is constructed and maintained,"[17] we must also confront an idea that is "more difficult to accept": that "the sexual act, at least as it is performed between queers—and yes, I am nominating Vivaldo [the novel's central white male character] as queer—is not necessarily a good, expansive, and liberatory thing, a place in which individuals exist for a moment outside themselves such that new possibilities are at once imagined and actualized."[18] While I will disagree about naming Vivaldo as "queer"—arguing, instead, that his straight privilege mirrors and buttresses his white privilege—I join Reid-Pharr in his underlying queer critique, a critique that is not oppositional to but, rather, deeply invested in queer theoretical reworkings of difference. Ultimately, I ask whether certain queer theories reinscribe Baldwin's "failed" narrative, encouraging a critical/analytical gay trade by subverting gay interpretive positions in favor of impossibly positive queer ones.

A FAILED LOVE SCENE

The pressing question of straight white male need in *Another Country* surfaces after the suicide of Rufus Scott, a talented African American musician. Rufus's experience of being an expendable commodity in the white man's world references the African American slave trade and also echoes with the threat of a modern-day lynching: "How I hate them—all those white sons of bitches out there. They're trying to kill me. . . . They got the world on a string, man, the miserable white cock suckers, and they tying that string around my neck, they killing *me*."[19] Tortured by the knowledge that the black man's extinction is the price white America willingly pays for its survival, Rufus jumps from the George Washington Bridge.[20] Rufus's suicide forces Vivaldo Moore, Rufus's best friend, to face his own racial guilt, as he wonders how, given the historical inertia of racist violence, he (and, by extension, other white men) can recuperate and recover—indeed, love—the black man in America. Vivaldo's belated need to love Rufus will govern the remainder of the novel.

In a remarkable scene of what I want to describe as hetero-raced paralysis, the Irish-Italian Vivaldo recalls having been unable to reach out to and potentially save his best friend.

> [T]he last time I saw Rufus, before he disappeared, . . . I looked at him, he was lying on his side. . . . Well, when he looked at me, just before he closed his eyes and turned on his side away from me, all curled up, I had the weirdest feeling that he wanted me to take him in my arms. And not for sex, though maybe sex would have happened. I had the feeling that he wanted someone to hold him, to hold him, and that, that night, it had to be a man. . . . I lay on my back and I didn't touch him and I didn't sleep. . . . I still wonder, what would have happened if I'd taken him in my arms, if I'd held him, if I hadn't been—afraid. I was afraid that he wouldn't understand that it was—only love. Only love. But, oh, Lord, when he died, I thought that maybe I could have saved him if I'd just reached out that quarter of an inch between us on that bed, and held him. (342–43)

I want to make several related points about how Baldwin constructs the impasse described in this scene. The passage reflects, foremost, a deeply racialized encounter marked by a debt, to use one of Baldwin's chief metaphors, that can never be fully paid. Tuhkanen notes that "the question of economy is never a simple one for Baldwin. Paying the 'price of the ticket' never rids us of all our debts; in a sense the notion that debt is fully cancelable is characteristic of the economy of protest novels, which seek to redeem us . . . by binding . . . history into neat, consumable units of fiction."[21] Indeed, Baldwin had already famously derided such fiction in his early essay "Everybody's Protest Novel" (1949). For Baldwin, "the price of the ticket" for living in America is that we must live with our race debts even as we seek to redress them. Vivaldo, however, cannot negotiate that exchange, for he surely fears that Rufus will interpret his touch as a sign of a white man's pity for his black friend. He knows, for instance, that Rufus has been living on the streets "peddl[ing] his ass" (42) to white men in order to eat. Vivaldo's touch, then, would be charged by the same sexualized energy that has come to mean precisely racial disempowerment, not "only love," for Rufus. The scene thus functions as a microcosm for a larger social dynamic by which racial inequality, whether through white pity or white sexual appropriation, circulates in the novel.

If Vivaldo cannot bring himself to reach across the gulf of racial differ- ence, neither can he negotiate the overlapping terrain of gendered intimacy. He intuits that only a man can hold Rufus and that, in fact, Rufus wants to be held by a man, yet he fears that an act of male-male union will be misinterpreted as something other than "only love." It would seem at first glance that Vivaldo is worried that his making a move *toward* Rufus will be misunderstood as his making a move *on* Rufus. While Vivaldo seems oddly unfazed by the potential for sex to occur—"maybe sex would have happened"—he cannot imagine how to engage his black friend in a loving, physical, potentially sexual embrace that might be defined against homosex- uality, against the "gay love" that such an embrace would most immediately, even definitionally, call to mind. But if Baldwin is careful not to represent Vivaldo's desire to take Rufus in his arms and "only love" him as homosexual, it strikes this reader as somewhat odd that Vivaldo would later turn to a homosexual, Eric, to learn exactly that lesson of how to reach out to and love a man. Gay love is thus both problem and solution, ostensibly confusing the issue of male-male intimacy by threatening to define Vivaldo's intentions as homosexual and therefore needing to be undercut by the caveat "only love," but also offering to guide Vivaldo toward a greater understanding of the love between raced men that he has such difficulty articulating and enacting. Vivaldo avoids homosexual identification as he struggles for some kind of racial reconciliation with Rufus, but, as I will demonstrate further on, only the gay man and the love he alone seems capable of embodying can prepare the straight white man to face, at last, the challenges of loving across lines of race.

A second reading of Vivaldo's apparent indifference to the possibility of sex with Rufus suggests a different kind of familiarity that, rather than sig- nifying homosexuality or bisexuality, seems to effect a designification of the male-male sex act. In fact, a "queer" current of sexual liberalism runs through Vivaldo's relationship with Rufus. Discussing their troubles with women, Rufus asks Vivaldo, "Have you ever wished you were queer?"—as though homosexuality, a synonym for "queer" in this context, would provide a tidy escape when a woman "was eating you up" (51). Vivaldo helplessly replies, "I used to think maybe I was [queer]. Hell, I think I even *wished* I was. But I'm not. So I'm stuck." Rufus then picks up the exchange:

"So you been all up and down that street, too."

"We've all been up the same streets. There aren't a hell of a lot of streets. Only, we've been taught to lie so much, about so many things, that we hardly ever know *where* we are." (52)

Here, Vivaldo in particular reveals an ostensibly queer-friendly brand of heterosexuality heavily coated with liberal intent. But only from the position of straight white male privilege in which he is "stuck" can Vivaldo assert his open-mindedness: he would not mind being "queer." His position proves not only sexist, with the man-eating woman representing the problem, but heterosexist, with gay male life supposedly affording an escape from straight troubles. Paradoxically, Vivaldo's "wish" to be "queer," buttressed by his later claim that he is "condemned to women," positions him as "stuck" indeed, immobilized by what should be understood as a false relation to sexual identity. Using a metaphor of urban geography, Vivaldo depicts the streets for expressing sexuality as few and the sexual landscape as fairly small and undifferentiated. But rather than persuasively depicting a socio-sexual common ground, this metaphor actually reveals that for Vivaldo—and for Vivaldo alone—the stakes of exploring new sexual avenues are remarkably low. Only because he operates from a place of straight white male privilege can the streets function as queer contact zones. While Vivaldo at one point refers to his "time with boys" (315) and recalls a fantasy of touching a boy named Stevie, the more telling episode of Vivaldo's "boy time" unfolds when he remembers how he and his buddies from Brooklyn once used, beat, and left for dead a gay boy they had picked up on one of these supposedly queer streets.

I am arguing that Vivaldo's failure to "only love" Rufus reflects his naive relation to white privilege and his disingenuous relation to straight privilege. One has the impulse, perhaps, to attempt the impossible and parse out the degree to which Vivaldo's hetero-raced paralysis is straight and the degree to which it is white. Resisting that impulse, a postmodern strain of queer theory and queer cultural studies has recently been productively deployed to read Baldwin's third novel as a commentary on the means by which myths of racial difference and sexual difference might be reciprocally deconstructed,[22] thereby reinforcing the destabilizing, queer-making potential of Baldwin's social vision.[23] Just as important, critics have argued that while readers cannot possibly disarticulate race and sexuality, they must nevertheless attend to the particulars of different but overlapping oppressions, lest one becomes an interpretive shortcut for the other.[24] According to William Cohen, "[t]he universalizing maneuver whereby [the homosexual man's] consciousness of gay oppression comes to stand in for all other modes of subjugation not only obscures the specificity of power relations structured by sexuality but elides the different and often contradictory concerns of people who feel themselves, as Baldwin might say, to be outsiders."[25] While *Another Country* attempts to initiate a healing between black and white and ostensibly does the same for gay and straight, and while its larger crossing over is between race and sexuality themselves, the social fabric created by various threads of oppression in *Another Country* does not unravel evenly. A central refrain of this chapter is that the black gay man, situated at the narrative crux where identities ostensibly break down and "healing" begins, represents a particular crisis of representation within the novel.

If the power of Baldwin's message about the absolute necessity and supreme difficulty of racial reconciliation diverts attention away from the questionable uses to which both white and black gay men's body are put in the novel, it very effectively exposes, by contrast, the misuses of black women's bodies as they are prostituted to white men, especially to the "liberal" Vivaldo. The most critical task for Vivaldo, if he is to "save" Rufus, is to trade in his liberal white fantasy that "suffering doesn't have a color" and that one can simply "step out of this nightmare" of American race relations (417). Yet Vivaldo's "liberal, even revolutionary sentiments" (133) butt up against his sense of imperiled white masculinity. Sex with black female prostitutes in Harlem, where "he had merely dropped his load and marked the spot with silver" (132), represents Vivaldo's attempt to forge his masculinity in a place where the danger "was more real, more open, than danger was downtown." Consequently, Vivaldo feels that "having chosen to run these dangers, [he] was snatching his manhood from the lukewarm waters of mediocrity and testing it in the fire" (132). When, in an attempt to get closer to the absent Rufus, Vivaldo enters into a relationship with Rufus's sister Ida, he positions her not only as racial proxy, a stand-in for her brother, but as sexual proxy, another one of the uptown prostitutes the white man has made a habit of visiting.

Ida, who prides herself on "knowing the score," understands the tricky and, indeed, deadly race and gender dynamics at play in her relationship with Vivaldo. She therefore rejects the liberalism of the white man's claim that he loves her and her dead brother: "[H]ow can you talk about love when you don't want to know what's happening. . . . How can you say you loved Rufus when there is so much about him you didn't want to know? How can I believe you love me?" (324–25). In Ida's experience, people, both black and white, make the cheap trade. They pay with their money or with their bodies rather than entering into the more difficult and perhaps impossible exchange by which blacks and whites might actually attempt to know each other. She tells Vivaldo, who insists that he wants to spend the rest of his life finding out about her, that he is not truly willing to do so. "And, listen," Ida concedes, "I don't blame you for not being willing. I'm not willing, nobody's willing. Nobody's willing to pay their dues" (325). The price, she knows, would be too high. Throughout the novel, Vivaldo listens to the blues, but in his liberal innocence, he does not truly hear; Ida, however, sings the blues as the song of experience. She therefore sees Vivaldo's attempt to recover Rufus (and redeem himself) as a white liberal fantasy that blacks, who know the score, cannot afford to share.

Yet in their last scene, Ida and Vivaldo do share a breakthrough, perhaps beginning to pay off their race debts. Confessing her opportunistic affair with an influential white music producer, Ida begins to tell Vivaldo something of her connection to her brother, of their mutual lost innocence, of their experience as African Americans living in a white world. Vivaldo, shedding his liberal skin, feels, in turn, that Ida "was not locking him out now; he felt, rather, that he was being locked in. He listened, seeing, or trying to see, what she saw, and feeling something of what she felt" (415). When Ida breaks down sobbing on the floor, Vivaldo's "heart [begins] to beat with a newer, stonier anguish, which destroyed the distance called pity and placed him, very nearly, in her body, beside that table, on the dirty floor . . . , her sobs seeming to make his belly sore" (426). The scene ends with Ida "stroking his innocence out of him" (431). At the novel's close, then, Vivaldo seems willing to trade his white innocence as he attempts to participate more genuinely in Ida's African American experience, and Ida, in turn, appears willing to accept the legitimacy of that cross-racial exploration, as, in sharp relief to Vivaldo's paralysis with Rufus, their black and white body barriers seem almost literally to dissolve.

In stark contrast to Vivaldo's final scene with Ida, in which Baldwin portrays racial intersubjectivity as a long and painful endeavor, the sexual encounter between Vivaldo and the gay man Eric makes straight/gay difference into a hurdle quickly leapt. Whereas Ida "strok[es] the innocence out of" Vivaldo, Eric returns Vivaldo "back to his innocence" (386), suggesting utopic closure as opposed to an agonizing beginning. Unlike sex with Ida, sex with Eric catalyzes in Vivaldo not the type of mystification seen above but a revelation, one that translates not as sexual redefinition but as a precursor to a hoped-for racial integration. Baldwin's secretary and biographer David Leeming tracks this same movement: "Finally, Vivaldo's brief affair with Eric is a metaphor for the shedding of the kind of innocence that prevents him from knowing Ida. Since Eric had once made love with Rufus, Vivaldo's night with Eric was for Vivaldo a love act, by proxy, with Rufus."[26] In claiming that "Eric . . . helps [Vivaldo] past gender and sexual orientation" and that "[h]e is then 'positioned' for a fully human relationship with Ida," James Dievler also marks this too-easy slippage past sex to the foundational issue of race.[27] Ultimately, the stakes involved with exploring new streets are much lower in sexual excursions than in racial ones.

The critique I am offering here does not stem from a disagreement with the claim that knowing one's racial other—and thereby, Baldwin would say, knowing oneself—is remarkably difficult and painful. Rather, I am bothered by the way the gay male body becomes utterly available as part of that "queer" process, for why should it make sense that Eric would serve in the capacity he is made to? Why should we not question the representation of the gay man as the relatively unproblematic sexual partner of straight men? Baldwin explicitly thematizes prostitution when other characters' bodies are traded on—Rufus, Ida, and Eric's French boyfriend, Yves, all prostitute themselves—but Eric's relationship with Vivaldo receives no such treatment. Indeed, in Eric's case, as I will more thoroughly demonstrate below, gay male sexual and emotional accessibility is privileged and appreciated, naturalized and narrated with neither commentary nor the irony that would encourage critical distance. Interestingly, the resulting interpretive silence makes for strange bedfellows. Under various readings of Eric's ability to conjure a kind of sexual healing for Vivaldo operates a powerful and dangerous intersection of gay and queer cultural fantasies. On the one hand is the fantasy of the gay man's wish to have sex with "the" (read "any") straight man, whether to be validated as a man by the straight man's masculine authority or to be validated as a woman in contrast to that authority. On the other hand is the fantasy of perverse queer desire that tends to privilege sexual border crossings per se. The two fantasies converge such that the same kind of faulty logic that might have been—but is pointedly not—used to naturalize the exchange of a woman, Ida, between white men precisely is used to naturalize the exchange of the homosexual man, Eric, between straight men in Another

Country. The gay man willfully serves the needs of straight men, he does not think to refuse straight male sexual advances, and ultimately, despite what he may or may not say, he wants it. And the reader is encouraged to want it for him. Eric is not given the chance to reject the conflation of his homosexuality with sexual availability, largely because that availability allows Vivaldo to transcend sexual and then racial categories—to become, in a word, queer.

If I have made a case above for denuding gay heroism as gay prostitution, the racial ends of which are used to justify the sexually appropriative means, I want to continue by redoubling my focus on the ways that those means are made invisible, for they are not erased by race alone. Rather, there is another justification that hides the misuse of the gay man, one rooted in Baldwin's most privileged term, "love," and the notion that "love is refused at one's peril."[28] Of Eric's role in the novel's search for love, Leeming writes that "[o]n the level of parable . . . , *Another Country* has at its center the observing artist-mediator played by Eric, who preaches and practices a lesson of acceptance and love among a group of American who are 'victims' of the incoherence of American life, who must find their own identity before they can love and be whole."[29] In other words, as Eric gives not only his body but, more important for Baldwin and for the novel, his heart, love transcends and overshadows the sex act. This love, I argue below, is a specifically gay love. Yet as the troublesome dynamic of sexual availability defers to the pacifying glow of love, the gift of gay love, rather than being ironized by the fact that it is anchored in a dubious sexual trade, is naturalized as an option for the heterosexual man in need. Gay love to the rescue.

THE STRAIGHT USES OF GAY LOVE

If, as I argued in chapter 2, homosexual categorization represents deadly paralysis in *Giovanni's Room*, a markedly gay love would seem to offer the potential for liberatory destabilization in *Another Country*, with Eric, the out gay man, representing the anti-David. Eric would seem to embody a category-busting, deconstructive potential: by crossing lines that mark off sexual taboos, we can also forge bonds across racial lines.[30] Told as a flashback, the initial instance of that dual crossover comes when Eric's adolescent homoerotic desire for his friend LeRoy releases him from the racist grip of his native Alabama. He pleads with LeRoy, "You're not a nigger, not for me, you're LeRoy, you're my friend, and I love you." LeRoy's reply, "You a nice boy, Eric, but you don't know the score" (205–6), will later be echoed in the sentiments of Ida. LeRoy exhibits greater empathy than Ida, though, presumably because he understands the interracial dynamic of the situation through his own homosexual desire for the white boy. Indeed, the gay love shared between the two youths takes on a revelatory function, as, lying by the stream, LeRoy

> worked in Eric an eternal, a healing transformation. Many years were to pass before [Eric] could begin to accept what he, that day, in those arms, with the stream whispering in his ear, discovered; and yet that day was the beginning of his life as a man. What had always been hidden was to him, that day, revealed and it did not matter that, fifteen years later, he sat in an armchair, overlooking a foreign sea, still struggling to find the grace which would allow him to bear that revelation. For the meaning of revelation is that what is revealed is true, and must be borne.

As Eric learns to bear and comes to embody the "meaning of revelation," LeRoy—and black gay male sexuality—disappears from view.[31] LeRoy's disappearance is not mere precedent for Rufus's erasure later in the novel. It not only establishes a pattern of black male abjection and death, though it does this as well; more important, the trajectory from LeRoy to Rufus traces an ontological shift, a change in what it is possible to be as a black man in America. Specifically, if LeRoy is a black gay youth, Rufus can never "be" a black gay man. That identity, as I will conclude, represents an impossible subject position in *Another Country*. My point for the moment, though, is that thanks to LeRoy, Eric has learned the lesson that vexes his straight counterpart Vivaldo: how to love the black man and thereby be revealed as a man. Crucially, if white gay Eric is able to "love" Vivaldo, this is only because another gay person, the black adolescent LeRoy, has prepared him for that later preparatory moment.

Mimicking the encounter between LeRoy and Eric, the sexual union of Eric and Vivaldo is represented primarily as a loving and revelatory exchange. After a night of drinking, Vivaldo passes out in Eric's bed, and Eric falls asleep beside him. They awaken to the "monstrous endeavor" of bringing to fruition something "long desired" by both. "[T]hank God it was too late [to stop]," thinks Vivaldo (383). Having failed to initiate his own loving moment with Rufus, Vivaldo thus inevitably turns to Eric for his love lesson. Eric's importance to Vivaldo, much like Ida's, lies in his ability to artificially re-create a sexual union between the straight white man and his dead friend, for Eric and Rufus have been sexual partners as well. Vivaldo's mind races during sex with Eric.

> Rufus had certainly thrashed and throbbed, feeling himself mount higher, as Vivaldo thrashed and throbbed and mounted now. *Rufus. Rufus.* Had it been like this for him? And he wanted to ask Eric, What was it like for Rufus? What was it like for him? . . . Had he murmured at last, in a strange voice, as he now heard himself murmur, *Oh, Eric. Eric.* (386)

What was it like to experience this as Rufus did, Vivaldo wants to know. What was it like for the black man to be loved? Vivaldo's questions re-establish his desire to share in Rufus's experience, to achieve a level of racial intersubjectivity previously denied him. His call to Eric thus operates as an act of racial ventriloquism by which Vivaldo attempts to unite his voice with Rufus's.

Afterward, confident that "there was a man in the world who loved him," Vivaldo realizes that "[h]e loved Eric: it was a great revelation." Vivaldo begins the following exchange:

> "I love you, Eric, I always will, I hope you know that." He was astonished to hear how his voice shook. "Do you love me? Tell me that you do."
>
> "You know I do," said Eric. . . . "I love you very much, I'd do anything for you. You must have known it, no? somewhere, for a very long time. Because I must have loved you for a very long time."
>
> "Is that true? I didn't *know* I knew it."
>
> "I didn't know it, either," Eric said. He smiled. "What a funny day this is. It begins with revelations."
>
> "They're opening up," said Vivaldo, "all those books in heaven." (387)

The hyperbole of Eric's claim, that the act of sex with Vivaldo is somehow akin to divine revelation, invokes the concept of "love" in problematic ways. First, it reveals the extent to which Baldwin will go to distinguish loving male-male sexual relations from male sex acts that are otherwise motivated. Eric and Vivaldo supposedly transcend the purely physical, rising above the cheap trade of male sex made by closeted men, "that ignorant army. They were husbands, they were fathers, gangsters, football players, rovers; and they were everywhere. . . . [Their need] could only be satisfied in the shameful, the punishing dark, and quickly, with flight and aversion as the issue of the act" (211). Distinguishing male-male sex as redemptive when it is loving, Baldwin portrays "ignorant" male-male sex as the darkest act of sexual betrayal. Sex acts between men thus stand at the poles of sexual liberation and confinement. Whereas female-male relationships in the novel are marked, in the end, by compromise, male-male unions, operating at the extremes, are impossibly situated as idyllic or doomed.

Vivaldo and Eric, reveling in the revelation of their mutual love for each other, clearly fall into the former category. But just what does this revelation reveal, particularly about Vivaldo? What does his newfound love, one that takes shape through sexual union with a gay man, say about him? It would appear that Vivaldo has at last found the "only love" he so desired to share with Rufus. But why, in that case, is he not afraid that Eric, too, will misinterpret that love as homosexual? What does this hypocrisy expose?

Here we find the second and more troubling point about the coupling of Vivaldo and Eric. Unlike the anxiety-producing near miss with Rufus, the encounter with Eric, as Vivaldo well knows, cannot possibly call into question his heterosexual identity. Contrary to Vivaldo's declaration, he does not and cannot reciprocate Eric's gay love. Instead, in response to his overwhelming need, the straight man can only receive. On waking, Vivaldo quickly understands that "Eric really loved him and would be proud to give Vivaldo anything Vivaldo needed" (383). Eric proceeds to offer himself up to Vivaldo as a disciple or servant: "Eric bowed and kissed Vivaldo on the belly button, half-hidden in the violent, gypsy hair. This was in honor of Vivaldo, of Vivaldo's body and Vivaldo's need" (383–84). Honored in the act of sex with a gay man, the straight white man and his need are the focus of the exchange. Even though it is the straight man who "surrender[s] to the luxury, the flaming torpor of passivity," as he whispers in Eric's ear "a muffled, urgent plea" (385), it is the gay man whose peril increases. In taking the (supposedly) dominant role of the "giver of the gift" (385), Eric diminishes himself, bowing, kneeling, giving, serving. His love is, quite literally, a selfless love, an act of giving himself up so that Vivaldo can feel "fantastically protected, liberated" (387). Although Vivaldo does not view Eric as "the inferior male of less importance than the crumpled, cast-off handkerchief" (384), as he had his previous male sex partners, he nevertheless realizes that, as was the case in those sexual excursions, the stakes of this sexual exchange are very different for Eric and himself. Eric gives his love as a man "condemned to men"— to borrow Vivaldo's words—thus giving something that, as Vivaldo is aware, puts the gay man at great risk. The sexual encounter is, in fact, underwritten partly by the fact that "Eric had risked too much" not to continue (384). What propels Eric—gay love—is therefore also the source of his danger: his love will be unreturned and is, indeed, unreturnable.

In *Insult and the Making of the Gay Self*, Didier Eribon identifies a "structure of inferiorization" at work in the creation of homosexual identity. For Eribon, the concept of "the insult" encapsulates all the "processes of 'subjection'" by which a homosexual is made to be gay.[32] Through a critically reflective process of self-reinvention, or "resubjectification," however, the gay man reappropriates and transforms his identity, essentially making himself over as gay in response to the violence by which society has made him gay.[33] Eribon can help us to understand not only the construction of the gay man's identity but also his capacity to love as a response to inferiorization and insult. In the scene quoted above, rather than exhibiting a revelatory or transcendental love, Eric demonstrates a particularly gay love, one created by the way he understands himself in relation to his straight male partner, who is himself constructed as the subject by whom and against whom the gay man has long been inferiorized. Unlike Vivaldo, Eric brings to the male-male sex act "all those intensely lived experiences" that coalesce around "homosexual acts," "around their very possibility, around the impulses that lead to them, around fantasies that have been nourished by images and models perceived since childhood, and even around the fear of being recognized as one of those people [he] know[s] are likely to be called a 'faggot.'"[34] With such a special relationship to the male-male sex act, a relationship moored by fantasy but also fear, how can Eric also not have a special relationship to the love he expresses in that act? More pointedly, can the gift of gay love given to a straight man be anything but the expression of yet another homophobic insult?

The important question becomes, does the gay love Eric gives reflect his subjectification by insult or a resubjectification in response to the inferiorization that constructs him as gay? I fail to see evidence of a conscious or even unconscious reinvention of the gay man by the gay man in the scene quoted above. In fact, Eric's coming to consciousness copies, rather than rewrites, the script of the gay man serving, to use the metaphor suggested by Vivaldo, as cumrag for the straight man, despite the reversal of insertive positions and the thin veneer of Vivaldo's "love" that helps to gloss over this fact. Missing is the endangered sense of self that one would expect the "reinvented" gay man to ascertain and defend against when asked by the straight man to give him the gift of love. Missing is Eric's deep knowledge—a learning that surely borders on intuition—that Vivaldo has abused gay boys in the past (as, indeed, he has). Eric shows no signs of inner conflict, no sense of gay jeopardy. In fact, he seems wholly satisfied with his liaison with Vivaldo, and that satisfaction notably does not emerge in terms of the gay man's conquest of his culturally valued other. Eric is, simply, satisfied, his gift requiring a divestment of himself in honor of Vivaldo and in service of the revelation Vivaldo must experience in order to return to Ida. In this uniquely homosexual exchange, an evacuative trade-off that only the gay man is capable of making, we should not read a transcendental gay love but, rather, a heteronormative reabsorption of a very culturally bound gay love. In short, Eric gives love as the straight man's gay man, as a subjected subject of desire.

Kevin Ohi also offers an important critique of transcendence in *Another Country*, arguing that seemingly redemptive moments in the novel function so as to "unsettl[e] any subjective 'revelation.'"[35] For Ohi, however, Eric's "thwarted revelation" stems from a more generalizable "epistemological disadvantage," one demonstrated both in the narrative and in the Jamesian opacity of Baldwin's language. Eric and the others do not achieve self-knowledge in supposedly revelatory encounters but, instead, come face to face with the impossibility inherent in the project of identity: "The unveiling of a self in Baldwin usually reveals only its own process of unveiling, revealing not a positive 'content' around which a coherent identity might coalesce, but a traumatic kernel we might conceptualize as a 'crypt.'"[36] Liberation becomes less a utopic vision than code for the struggle for greater self-awareness amid a "traumatic center" of sadness that is the American condition.[37] While Ohi's reading of Baldwin deftly undermines liberal/progressive interpretive teleologies, I think it does so by reading from within Baldwin's ideological wheelhouse. My argument, like Ohi's, is that Baldwin evacuates gay identity of content, but I contend that he does so only by relying narratologically on specific social-sexual experiences and histories that give gay identity meaning. If revelation is thwarted in the novel (and I agree that it is), this is not because an utter lack of self-knowledge defines Eric's "epistemological disadvantage" but, rather, because the self-knowledge Eric has is actively unknown, covered over by a heteronormative divestment of the gay self.

Accordingly, the assertion that Baldwin introduces "loving gay male sex"[38] into straight-gay male relations makes the playing field on which sexuality exists as a lived experience deceptively level for gay and straight characters. Vivaldo does not enter into loving gay male sexual relations, because the stakes that partly define those relations as homosexual do not apply to him. He neither works to creatively redefine himself as gay nor is made to be gay through a failure to do so. Indeed, Vivaldo, by virtue of the fact that Eric is made to be gay through the unquestioned and unquestionable heterosexual appropriation of his gay love, is made to be straight. Put another way, Vivaldo loves Eric from the position of the straight man having sex, albeit "lovingly" instead of violently, with the gay man. To argue that "homosexuality . . . is normalized in *Another Country*" and that "it offers itself up as a relatively unproblematized possibility to anyone (at least to any male)" is both to hit and miss the mark.[39] Homosexuality is indeed "relatively unproblematized" compared to race, but what is normalized is not homosexuality but a brand of heterosexuality achieved through male-male sex—hardly an unproblematic revision and, indeed, an evacuation of the sex act in which much of gay male identity is intimately invested. Vivaldo, I protest, is fucking straight.

I mean this literally. In fucking Eric, Vivaldo engages in a performative act that not only reflects but also constructs a straight identity. "Straight" does not merely describe Vivaldo in an ontological sense but connotes an enactment (it is what he does when having sex with Eric) made possible by virtue of a particular kind of straight privilege. Sara Ahmed's insights in *Queer Phenomenology: Orientations, Objects, Others* are helpful in understanding the intractability of Vivaldo's straightness and, by extension, the theoretical problems with queering straight characters. Grounding her analysis in phenomenology, which "emphasizes the importance of lived experience, the intentionality of consciousness, the significance of nearness or what is ready to hand, and the role of repeated and habitual actions in shaping bodies and worlds,"[40] Ahmed argues that we might once again privilege the term "sexual orientation" rather than "sexuality" or "sexual identity." Indeed, she takes seriously questions about what it means to be *oriented* sexually. By working at the intersection of queer studies and phenomenology, Ahmed recasts the notion of "sexual orientation" in part as a matter of one's spatial orientation toward or away from possible love objects.

If we presume that sexuality is crucial to bodily orientation, to how we inhabit spaces, then the differences between how we are oriented sexually are not only a matter of "which" objects we are oriented toward, but also how we extend through our bodies into the world. Sexuality would

not be seen as determined only by object choice, but as involving differences in one's very relation to the world—that is, in how one "faces" the
world or is directed toward it. Or, rather, we could say that orientations
toward sexual objects affect other things that we do, such that different
orientations, different ways of directing one's desires, mean inhabiting
different worlds.[41]

Citing Judith Butler on how sexual orientations are performatively
shaped and produced rather than random or coincidental, Ahmed further
proposes that "the 'nearness' of love objects is not casual: we do not just find
objects there, like that."[42] Instead, "[w]hat bodies 'tend to do' are effects of
histories rather than being originary."[43] Sexual orientation must be thought
not simply in terms of the object toward which one tends but also in terms
of its conditions of emergence and in terms of the socio-spatial conditions
of one's own approach to an object. The shaping of the sexual possibility, or
sexual orientation, thus reflects "intertwining histories of arrival."[44]

Not surprisingly, given its enormous power in Western culture, compulsory heterosexuality dramatically shapes the ability of bodies to come
into contact and to appear in the field of erotic possibility. The given history
of sexual orientation is thus the history of what Ahmed calls "the straight
line," an orienting force that privileges the heterosexual couple as a "social
gift" and facilitates that couple's extension into space while also, recursively,
being shaped by that couple's presence. In a section of *Queer Phenomenology*
entitled "Becoming Straight," Ahmed continues to move the discussion far
afield from an interiorized identity and toward a field of possibility: "Heterosexuality is not then simply 'in' objects, as if 'it' could be a property of
objects, and it is not simply about love objects or about the delimitation of
'who' is available to love, although such objects do matter. . . . Rather, heterosexuality would be an effect of how objects gather to clear a ground, of how
objects are arranged to create a background."[45] As ground is cleared by body
histories, life sequences, and accumulated habitations of space, the heterosexual extends in such a way as to create the impression of a straight line, a
well-ordered life, one that, if successful, will extend the heterosexual straight
into the next generation.

By contrast, queer bodies, objects, and desires are those that deviate
from the straight line, that are "off line," that are on a slant, that exist "at an
oblique angle to what coheres" along the straight line.[46] Perceiving an object's
queer orientation to the straight line can thus disorient the well-ordered,

straight-oriented viewer. Yet, because "the work of ordinary perception . . . straightens up anything queer or oblique,"[47] the relationship between that which is "on line" and that which is "off line" is often "fleeting." More often, "[q]ueer objects, which do not allow the subject to approximate the form of the heterosexual couple, may not even get near enough to 'come into view' as possible objects to be directed toward."[48]

While Ahmed posits a fleeting relationship between heterosexual and queer orientations, especially as queer bodies tend not to (or "fail" to adequately) inhabit the charmed space cleared by "straight tendencies" for the heterosexual couple, I want to posit a more proximate but no less vexed and no more visible relationship between straight and queer orientations. If queer bodies deviate from the accumulated history that creates the straight line (so that often they literally do not come into view), might it not also be true that they sometimes either deviate or are made to deviate in such a way as to intersect the straight line, to crisscross it at various non-random points and precisely for certain straight perspectives? What if, to extend Ahmed, becoming straight requires encountering queer objects along the very line and in the very space cleared for and by heterosexuality as a way of all the more rigorously straightening the line, of keeping it straight? Put another way, what if tracing the straight line by connecting the dots of objects given to us by heterosexual culture reveals queer dots coinciding with that line, the queer objects littering the path of straightness like so much roadkill— unrecognizable, twisted, queered indeed? What if people become straight not only by turning away from queerness but by requiring that queers continually contort themselves by turning back toward and crossing over the straight line? What if the history of how heterosexuals arrive depends on the fleeting availability of queer objects "as things to 'do things' with?"[49] If "queer" has resounded as part of a liberatory social and intellectual drumbeat, have we ignored the ways queers have continued to be not liberated but, in new and painful ways, bent out of shape by and for the sake of compulsory heterosexuality?

I find Ahmed so useful for my own inquiry into *Another Country* because the book is staked on the very problematic of characters' intertwining "histories of arrival," particularly the raced, gendered, and sexualized backgrounds that put some bodies in touch and others out of touch, that bring some bodies into view and shift others out of view. If Ahmed's queer phenomenology suggests that bodies, as love objects, might be rethought as (the histories of) things that are or are not within reach, and if, as I have just suggested, the visibility of queer love objects might be inversely proportional to their proximity to straightness such that the nearer the queer love object is to the straight line the more *invisible* it necessarily becomes due to the paradoxical straight need for queers to be here and to *not* be here, then what does it mean for Vivaldo to be sexually oriented? What does his "successful" reaching out to Eric mean about how their histories, according to Baldwin, can intertwine? What does Vivaldo's failure to reach out to and touch Rufus mean? What objects are reachable for Vivaldo, and why?

Conveniently, Baldwin gives us a handy locus of comparison, the bed. Recall that Vivaldo shelters Rufus in his bed one night but that he cannot reach across the quarter of an inch between them to hold Rufus and "only love" him. Faced with Rufus's back, Vivaldo is confronted with a bodily horizon, an edge that operates as an absolute limit. We can now understand Vivaldo's inability to love (and potentially have sex with) Rufus as a function of his straight white male orientation: he is oriented in such a way—which is to say, his tendencies toward certain objects have accumulated in such a way—as to make impossible the extension of himself into space that would result in the breach of the distance between himself and Rufus. In this scene, Vivaldo arrives, once again, in the space of white male heterosexuality, making him unable to reach across what would seem to be an utterly penetrable divide. How, and in such a small bed indeed, could he *not* hold Rufus? As I have suggested, Baldwin turns to Ida and Eric to explore this question along racial and sexual lines, respectively.

The question now becomes, in the next bed, Eric's bed, does Vivaldo's sexual orientation change? If we take sexual orientation as a matter of phenomenology, it does not. Rather, the gay man's bed in *Another Country* (and wider culture) becomes one more of those spaces oriented around the straight body that allows that body to extend straight into space. Heterosexual orientation can require that gay objects be placed precisely in straight paths and that gay objects are made available anything but casually or randomly. In *Another Country*, straight people encounter gay men's bodies on purpose, intersecting the "history of the coming to speech of gay people" and interrupting the processes by which gay men "reformulate" themselves.[50] Instead of a queer realignment or an act of what Ahmed characterizes as queer slipping away, the "plot point" at which Vivaldo closes the space between himself and Eric actually re-establishes the impression of the straight line. Thanks to his straight orientation (the ways he extends into space vis-à-vis other bodies), Vivaldo does not give up the possibility of sex with non-heterosexual love objects, as heterosexuality would seem to require; in fact, his orientation constructs and insists on that possibility. Further, it is through this straight demand, rather than in spite of it, that Vivaldo enacts the impossibility of him ever mistaking himself for the gay man with whom he has sex.

That Eric's journey as a gay man has prepared him for this moment in which he can love, by serving the needs of, the straight man would be disturbing enough alone. Synthesizing Eribon's and Ahmed's arguments, we might even say that Eric's own bed becomes, in this moment, a place of pure phenomenological gay insult, the ultimate heteronormative straight space. Even more troubling, though, Eric's insulting exchange is masked by the transformative, healing power of his love, gay love thus dissolving into universal love that anyone, gay or straight, can experience. The value that Baldwin held so dear, love, thus erases the history of the gay individual—especially the black gay man, as I will demonstrate shortly—who bears the burden of revelation in the novel. Only by forgetting that gay love has a history (of subjectification as well as spatial orientation) can the affair between Vivaldo and Eric in *Another Country* become purely symbolic, "a metaphorical rendering of Vivaldo's transcendence beyond a categorical approach to identity."[51]

This move—from the literal (contextual, historical, experientially informed) enactment of male-male sexual love to the symbolic (ahistorical, "queer") representation of transcendent love—places the loving homosexual in a dangerous position. When male-male sexual love becomes the switch point for liberal humanist visions of social progress, attention to the motives and emotions of the homosexual man recedes and is replaced with a focus on the straight man's liberation. Rather than reading Eric in terms of his strategic role as a revelation figure who offers other characters "a different way to live and love," we might, instead, read him in the way that seemed obvious in reading Rufus, as an object of symbolic exchange. If, as Terry Rowden has suggested, Rufus actually represents not black men but, rather, "the kind of black male that Baldwin needs to serve his ideological purposes,"[52] Eric can and should be read with the same critical distance. Just as America trades on the life of gay and straight black men in the novel, the novel trades on/in the sexual love of black and white gay men. The wants and the needs of the gay man, left behind in the search for a more universal (now seen to be heteronormative) love, must be taken into account.

If *Another Country* encourages the reader to forget that gay love has a past, it also prohibits the possibility that gay love has a future. In an admission astonishing in its undisguised manipulation of the gay man, Vivaldo makes clear that Eric's love can never be enacted again and, impossibly, that it also must be given endlessly and forever. Immediately after sex, Vivaldo warns Eric, "It may never happen again." He later admits, "I'm sort of hiding in your bed now, hiding even in your arms maybe. . . . But I don't, really, dig you the way I guess you must dig me. You know? . . . So what can we really do for each other except—just love each other and be each other's witness?" (395–96). While, as a queer scholar, I find compelling Robert Reid-Pharr's idea, raised in a different context, that "the transcendent is not fixed but always fleeting, even peculiar,"[53] I find it peculiar beyond all patience that Vivaldo would at once flee from this moment while simultaneously demanding Eric's lifelong devotion: "I want you to love me all my life" (397). Thus recruited into a bizarre witness protection program, the gay man is integral, needed, yet hidden away as an ever-absent presence for straight male orientation. In this version of love, Vivaldo has his cake and eats it too, while starving Eric gets the cavity.

Although Vivaldo provides the primary test case for sexual and racial exploration in the novel, Eric's revelatory sexual power extends to less central characters as well. Dievler humorously writes, "In the simple sense that he sleeps with almost all the other characters in the novel, Eric is a significant character."[54] Excepting Rufus for the moment, Eric has sex not only with Vivaldo and Yves[55] but also with Cass Silenski, mother of two and disenchanted wife of author Richard Salinski, another of the novel's prostitutes, who has sold out his dream of writing important fiction in order to produce valueless but lucrative mystery novels. But if sexual flux affords characters insight into other conflicts within their lives (primarily racial, but, in Cass's case, also gendered) the terms of these sexual explorations for the individuals involved vary dramatically.

The heteronormative uses to which homosexuality is put are blatantly revealed in Eric and Cass's affair, "an encounter [that] almost parodically dramatizes an oedipal model of heterosexual desire."[56] When Cass realizes she has no faith in or respect for her husband's writing, she looks to Eric to make her feel something real, something authentic. She says to Eric, after she confesses to her husband and ends the affair, "That was you you gave me for a little while. It was really you" (407). A sexual relationship with a gay man (infantilized though he is) is meant to show the importance of freeing desire from the constraints of convention and makes Cass feel once more like a "real" woman. But again, why does she need Eric? Why does she not, for instance, become a writer herself (like one of the women writers with whom Baldwin was familiar) as part of her search for authenticity? Because Eric's centrality to his friends' liberation—mirrored by his centrality to a scene from his latest movie in which his character operates as a force of calm, magnetic gravity in an uproarious sea of friends at a café—requires that they encounter and literally move through him. Cass's character is therefore sacrificed by the narrative of her own (gay-inspired) liberation. The depth that Rufus had earlier seen in her, his sense that "she knew things he had never imagined a girl like Cass could know" (78), goes unexplored, her own promise unfulfilled. Like Vivaldo's affair with Eric, Cass's brush with "authenticity" rings of heteronormative sexual tourism. She returns to her husband, Richard, who she knows will not sue for divorce, because he "hasn't got the courage to name [Eric] as correspondent" (407). The homosexual thus secures the heterosexual relationship in two ways: Cass has had the "real" experience she wanted and can now more honestly relate to her husband, and Richard, who cannot face the public shame of admitting to having been cuckolded by a gay man, is powerless to seek a divorce. Although Eric has less to lose in his affair with Cass, for "he had never loved her" (404), Cass, not Eric, ends the relationship. Sexual exploration with a gay man is short lived. Cass, like Vivaldo, quickly reasserts her heterosexuality, never doubting the transitory nature of her "queer" sexual encounters with Eric.

By forging a theory of healing love on the gay man's body, Baldwin both prescribes (rather than destabilizes) homosexual identity and simultaneously erases it through straight people's heteronormative return to race and gender matters. A further paradox emerges in the relationship between homosexuality and male-male sex in the novel: as Baldwin makes clear through other instances of prostitution, male-male sex acts are not particular to homosexuality—sodomy is not represented as an exclusively gay sex act—yet it is precisely and exclusively through male-male sex that the homosexual bestows his revelation. Male-male sex is therefore not gay yet also quintessentially gay. The act bespeaks an absence of sexual labels that depends, ironically, on the abundant homosexual experience that facilitates the discovery of a suddenly universalizable love. If we focus on this end, we can certainly argue that Baldwin advocates "a postcategorical, poststructural concept of sexuality that we might call 'postsexuality,'" achieved through "sex that is itself taking place beyond the socially constructed senses of sexuality that have dominated the twentieth century."[57] But the specific means by which Baldwin accomplishes this deconstruction of sexuality exact very different prices from straight and gay "lovers," the price of gay love—one is tempted to say *real* gay love—itself.

The boldly assimilationist sexual project of *Another Country*, like less dramatic efforts at the assimilation of homosexuals, thus ultimately participates in what Leo Bersani has called the "de-gaying" process underway on a variety of fronts. This is so not simply because any man might have sex with any other man in the world of the novel ("gay sex" loses meaning) but because any man might share something much more intimate: gay male love. Gay love is constitutive of homosexual identity in the novel yet is also always under erasure, given up as a gift to the needy straight man who has not learned to love men on his own. In this way, Eric is made to be gay—same-sex desire being the root of his revelatory intersubjectivity— even while he is divested of the interiority that Bersani identifies as a crucial "breeding ground" for "redrawing [one's] own [gay] boundaries" and thus resisting being made the target of America's homophobic need for both the homosexual's presence and his annihilation.[58]

CONCLUSION: IMPOSSIBLE STORIES

I have taken a largely critical view of Baldwin's compromise, this "gay trade" by which the gay man serves as plot device and point of exchange for heterosexual liberation and is thus made to appear salvational. I have therefore fallen in line with a critic who once said, "James Baldwin's novel *Another Country* has, as the cliché says, something for everyone—in this instance, something offensive for everyone."[59] But what were Baldwin's options? The notion that a heterosexual might need a homosexual represented a radical idea in the 1950s and early 1960s, when Baldwin was writing *Another Country*. Outside the capitalist niches of personal style and home decor, it is a radical idea still today. Compared to other notable works of fiction dealing with relationships between gay and straight males, *Another Country* breaks new ground by reversing the theme of the gay man's obsession with and rejection by the straight man. I intend to offer here, then, less a damning critique of Baldwin than a new strategy for examining the "radical" or "revolutionary" role of the gay man in Baldwin's novel.

Is there not, underlying Baldwin's overlapping fantasies of sexual and racial cohesion, a deeper conflict, a more complicated version of the tension with which this chapter began? As the homosexual helps to make the white man's reconciliation with the black man possible, are raced masculinity and homosexuality envisioned so that one exists at the price of the other? If the black man is sacrificed to white America, must the homosexual and homosexuality be symbolically sacrificed in order to repay the white man's debt? And is there not a more fundamental sacrifice—that of the black gay man?

The black gay man becomes extinct, an impossibility in the novel. We catch a brief glimpse of his vanishing figure in LeRoy, Eric's childhood friend who emerges refigured as Rufus, having fully learned the impossibility of his black gay existence. But the black gay man has been sacrificed in his youth. To call Rufus a black gay man may be true in some essentialist way, but the reader can never really know, given the warped creature Baldwin gives us in the grown man Rufus. By that point, Rufus's desire, his social status, his very meaning has been overwritten by the American "race problem." Just as we cannot know Joe Christmas's racial identity in Faulkner's *Light in August*, we cannot know Rufus's sexual identity; and just as the former's race status is obscured by sexual indecipherability in the text, the latter's sexual status is obfuscated by the powerful meaning of his race. A great tragedy of the novel is that if Rufus is gay, we cannot know it, because he is made to be so symbolically black. Rufus's race dramatically overdetermines the texture of his social relations so that even his sexual relationship with Eric fails to mark him as gay. "[B]ecause it is Rufus's status as a black man and not his sexual identity, whatever it may be, that makes him essentially unacceptable and places him outside of the positive community that Baldwin is conceptualizing in *Another Country*," argues Rowden, "whether Rufus can best be coded as homosexual, heterosexual, or bisexual is finally unimportant." Rowden thereby suggests that the more central problem of the novel is "how ambivalent was Baldwin's relationship not only to the sexuality of the black man, but to the simple fact of the existence of black men in society."[60] When Leeming calls Rufus "an instrument of history" who "is too broken to accept love or to give it,"[61] we see that perhaps Rufus functions more like Bigger Thomas in Richard Wright's *Native Son* than Baldwin would have liked to admit. Feeling emasculated by whiteness, Rufus seeks to bolster his threatened black manhood by exerting sexual power over a white person, subordinating considerations of sexuality to raced masculinity. Although Rufus "had despised Eric's manhood by treating him as a woman, by telling him how inferior he was to a woman, by treating him as nothing more than a hideous sexual deformity," he does not so much punish him for his homosexuality as for his whiteness, for, thinking of his ex-girlfriend, Leona, he recognizes that "Leona had not been a deformity. And he had used against her the very epithets he had used against Eric, and in the very same way" (46). Sedgwick contributes to an understanding of the complicated relationships expressed here when she observes that "a variety of forms of oppression intertwine systematically with each other. . . . [A] person who is disabled through one set of oppressions may *by the same positioning* be enabled through others."[62]

With the black gay man an impossibility, Rufus defaults, at least in relation to Vivaldo, to straight. Consequently, the absent but structurally integral story created by the failure of Vivaldo and Rufus to consummate their straight relationship through sex, counterintuitive as that sounds, represents the void Vivaldo attempts to fill through sex with Eric. Indeed, (white) straight-gay male sex tries to reproduce or mimic the abstraction that is straight black-white male sex in the novel. The (white) gay man, in this scenario, must be gay in order for the sex to happen in the first place, but he must also occupy the role of the absent (black) straight man for the union to come to full fruition and meet its true mark. Incredibly, the gay man is forced into an imitation of straightness, a coercion reminiscent of the closet, through sex with a straight man.

Cleaver's accusation that *Another Country* reflects Baldwin's racial death wish as a black man now seems not only homophobic but exactly backward. The man that Baldwin fantasizes and perhaps theorizes in *Another Country*, the man he has the most urgent hopes for, is not a "white bisexual homosexual," as Cleaver would have it, but a white heterosexual, as Baldwin would have it—that is, as the kind of straight man Baldwin wishes him to be. Though I have already argued, in chapter 1 of this study, that Baldwin does not write strictly autobiographically, Leeming, Baldwin's cherished friend, observed that Baldwin "was drawn not to other homosexuals but to men who were sometimes willing to act homosexually, temporarily, in response to a need for money and shelter or to what can only be called his personal magnetism and persuasiveness. The nature and length of the given relationship always depended on how much the lover resented or was psychologically unnerved by playing a homosexual role or by being controlled by that magnetism."[63] What Baldwin wishes Vivaldo to be can therefore be linked to the author's own erotic investment, returned yet not fully returned, in Lucien Happersberger, who was, according to Baldwin, "the love of my life."[64] Yet in *Another Country*, Baldwin does not want Vivaldo *for* Eric as he wanted Lucien for himself. The erotic attentions of the white straight man, routed through the homosexual, have another object as their aim. To adapt David Gerstner's term, Vivaldo is a more complex figure of Baldwin's "white seduction" than if he were merely a stand-in for Happersberger. Gerstner's primary concern is the way that "the cinematic" is deployed as a process of aesthetic negotiation by queer black artists responding to the seductions of queer white culture. The inventive result for these artists, Baldwin among them, was an "erotic commingling" or "[q]ueer pollination of artificial boundaries" such as black/white and gay/straight so as to "giv[e] fresh life to the relations between black men."[65] Ultimately for Gerstner, "[i]f black culture is seduced by the white order of things in Baldwin's work, it is so to the extent that their relationship is persistently destabilized—at once turned inside-out and then outside-in again. It is re/disfigured."[66] As seduced by white culture as Baldwin undeniably (and, à la Gerstner, productively) was, the fascinating seduction he dares to—but cannot fully—imagine in *Another Country* is between white and black straight men. Working outward from the novel, we see that in Baldwin's queer imaginary, straight white men (distilled into Vivaldo) must seduce and be seduced by the straight black Cleaver, not the gay black Baldwin.

For is straight male-male sex between black and white men not what Baldwin is really after here? But how to have these men come together lovingly, sexually, in a revelatory experience, without one of them being gay? That story seems to be nowhere in modern literature. This absent story becomes, for Baldwin, a—perhaps *the*—question of race. But the goal of racial union is not compelling enough, in a racist, sexist, heteronormative society, to legitimate sex between straight black and white men. Re-shaped as all the other relationships and identities in the novel may be, that relationship is never "re/disfigured." So Baldwin's novel insists—indeed, must insist—that a gay man occupy one of the straight male positions as men come together to work toward racial union. To put it another way, the gay man takes the pressure off of the straight men, who would otherwise be forced to come together, lovingly, on their own. Of course, they do not, and even in the Baldwin's brilliant queer imagination, they cannot. Straight male-male sexual love remains an abstraction, unformulated, *queerer than it is possible to say*.[67] Baldwin thus makes a virtue of necessity: the plot cannot work without the tumbler that falls into place like the missing piece of Vivaldo's novel—the accessible gay white male body. So, very much in LeRoy's absence, Eric becomes the hero.

Had Rufus and Vivaldo come together, perhaps Baldwin would have identified a more liberatory sexual act. Perhaps, too, Baldwin's vision of proliferating sexual possibilities might seem more believable, and his characters might seem truly free of sexual categories. But the failure of straight men to have sex with each other indicates an underlying immobility in the novel, a heternormative stasis in which women and black/gay men are prostituted, the first explicitly and the last implicitly, to the straight white man, who is therefore ever more securely positioned, for all of his sexual and racial experimentation, in the seat of privilege.

CHAPTER 4

Papas' Baby

Impossible Paternity in *Going to Meet the Man*

> In any case, this country, in toto, from Atlanta to Boston, to Texas, to California, is not so much a vicious racial caldron—many, if not most countries, are that— as a paranoid color wheel. . . . And, however we confront or fail to confront this most crucial truth concerning our history—American history—everybody pays for it and everybody knows it. The only way not to know it is to retreat into the Southern madness: indeed, the inability to face this most particular and specific truth is the Southern madness. But, as someone told me, long ago, *The spirit of the South is the spirit of America.*
>
> —JAMES BALDWIN, *THE EVIDENCE OF THINGS NOT SEEN*

> One's genesis is multiple not unitary.
>
> —JOHN BRENKMAN, *STRAIGHT MALE MODERN:*
> *A CULTURAL CRITIQUE OF PSYCHOANALYSIS*

Near the end of his life, James Baldwin wrote, in the introduction to his collected essays, *The Price of the Ticket,* that "white people are not white: part of the price of the white ticket is to delude themselves into believing that they are. . . . America is not, and never can be, white."[1] Marlon Ross thus distinguishes Baldwin from W. E. B. Dubois: "For Baldwin, it is not 'the strange meaning of being black' that is the 'problem of the Twentieth Century,' nor even 'the problem of the color line.' Baldwin makes the central problem of the twentieth century the strange meaning of being white, as a structure of felt experience that motivates and is motivated by other denials."[2]

This chapter examines the paradoxicality of being white in Baldwin's 1965 collection of short stories, *Going to Meet the Man,* arguing that "The Rockpile," "The Man Child," and "Going to Meet the Man"—the three stories original to the collection—act as recursive and interlocking texts that urgently demand comparative analysis, bound together as they are by their cumulative power to defamiliarize, to make strange, whiteness. That strangeness is, indeed, an estrangement, for these stories powerfully cleave "white" fathers from "white" sons as they reveal the secret obscured by the price of the white ticket: that whiteness cannot be reproduced. Nowhere in his fiction does Baldwin more compellingly evoke the white father's anxiety about reproducing race and thereby sustaining the white paternal order. Nowhere does Baldwin so poignantly show the white man's denial—so hidden and so costly—to be his own impossible paternity.

As my chapter title implies, I am indebted in my critical approach to Hortense Spillers's ever-suggestive 1987 essay "Mama's Baby, Papa's Maybe: An American Grammar Book." Raising the issues of paternal presence and absence with which I will be concerned, Spillers argues that in African American slavery, "a dual fatherhood is set in motion, comprised of the African father's *banished* name and body and the captor father's mocking presence." "In this play of paradox," Spillers continues, "only the female stands *in the flesh*, both mother and mother-dispossessed."[3] The two fathers, in sharp contrast to the literal flesh of the mother, become figurative, disembodied entities. This is true for different reasons. The absence of the African or African American father, long a national motif, was guaranteed, on the one hand, by the law that denied him the privilege of patrimony—his name was banished—and, on the other hand, by the likelihood of his physical separation through sale or death from his biological offspring. The captor father, likewise, was only a "mocking presence," an absence that stems from a certain rhetorical exclusion made possible under the system of American slavery. Spillers explains that "[t]he denied genetic link [between the master and his slave child] becomes the chief strategy of an undenied ownership, as if the interrogation into the father's identity—the blank space where his proper name will fit—were answered by the fact, de jure of a material possession."[4] Ironically, the master could not be both father and owner (though, of course, he often was), and the ability to deny fatherhood was predicated precisely on the master's identity as property owner. Thus the presence of the master/father was "mocking": the more present the master, the more absent the father.

I want to foreground two ideas about paternal possibilities implicit in Spillers's critique of gender and race relations stemming from the African American slave trade. The first is that we take seriously the idea that fatherhood, broadly, is a pliable and deeply contested construct marked by bifurcations, disavowals, and strange investments that produce a variety of forms of paternal agency. Therefore, in the context of raced masculinity in

America, fatherhood must, by extension, always be understood figuratively, even when literal patrimony is not in question. It is in this interplay of the literal and the figurative, in the tension between the biological and the so-cially legislated, that the role of the raced father is mystified. One of the goals of this chapter is to follow the lead of thinkers such as Robert Reid-Pharr by contributing to the increasingly nuanced conversation between critical race studies and queer intellectual culture. Like Reid-Pharr, whose writing seeks to "demonstrate the essentially permeable and thus impure nature of all American identities" by acknowledging and investigating erotic "perversi-ties,"[5] I seek here to trouble white paternity so as to dramatize the failure of normative biological narratives of reproduction to grapple with this crisis of race making. The "confusions of consanguinity"[6] that Spillers identifies as fertile ground for an investigation of how the African American female in captivity was (de)gendered will therefore be expanded to include liter-ally impossible but figuratively compelling paternal relations, particularly those paternal relations that demand the eroticized presence of the black man in the white father's bed as part of a father fantasy intent on producing white sons. Ironically, with the absent black father a fixture in the cultural imaginary, Baldwin locates him where no one else had looked: at the heart of white paternity.

I argue that a dual, interracial fatherhood emerges from that unnerving reconciliation and that the price of that union is unthinkable, yet utterly present, for the white man. Ultimately the progeny of a white father divided within himself by his erotic dependence on the black man, the son produced by this two-fathered struggle for racial purity (papas' baby, mama's maybe, so to speak),[7] is not only erotically "illegitimate" but, despite his fathers' in-tentions, racially ambiguous. In Baldwin's figural race logic, the paternal at-tempt to indelibly inscribe race ultimately generates a state of racelessness.

BLACK FATHER BLOOD: REPRODUCING
RACE IN "THE ROCKPILE"

While my primary aim here is to reevaluate the racial integrity and erotic in-vestments of the white father in *Going to Meet the Man*,[8] that paternal figure comes fully into view only against the backdrop of black fatherhood in "The Rockpile." Baldwin opens the collection by emphasizing how property rights have been inimical to the black man's paternal rights in America and how, in response, "black blood" has become a singularly flexible signifier of black paternity. Like Baldwin's first novel, *Go Tell It on the Mountain*, "The Rockpile" is set in the Harlem apartment of Gabriel and Elizabeth Grimes.[9] The urban rockpile that looms outside the Grimes's apartment window symbolizes the hard and unusable land of a disinherited black people, a fact thrown into sharp relief by the lush and fertile fields handed down from white father to white son in "The Man Child." A disputed plot on which the neighborhood boys ceaselessly struggle in an ironic, because unwinnable, game of King of the Mountain, the rockpile functions foremost as a reminder of impossible ownership and racial disenfranchisement. The black boys cannot inherit the rockpile, for their fathers do not own it.

Without property or material entitlements, the black father, Gabriel, must look elsewhere for manifestation of his posterity. When his son Roy is injured while play-fighting on the rockpile, Gabriel sees in his son's blood the symbol of his paternal legacy, raced as that legacy is by the erasure of property rights. Examining the cut above his son's eye, Gabriel comforts Roy: "You don't want to cry. You's Daddy's little man. Tell your Daddy what happened. . . . Don't cry. Daddy ain't going to hurt you, he just wants to see this bandage, see what they've done to his little man."[10] Roy's blood provokes in Gabriel a possessive reaction; neatly responding to the racial threat to black fatherhood, Gabriel's invocation of "his little man" collapses the roles of paternal and proprietary "caretaker."

At the center of this paternal reclamation, blood functions as the substance through which race is made transitive from black father to black son. Crucially, however, Roy's blood is equivalent to and an irreplaceable marker of Gabriel's paternity not because of a biological or genetic link but because black paternity in the story cannot be concretized as property, that is, through the investment of property with paternal meaning. In other words, racial inheritance attaches to the black son's blood not through faulty metaphors of race science but through a privileged interiority that compensates for an exterior disenfranchisement. Indeed, the father-son blood bond in "The Rockpile" is de-biologized by the weight of history, of what it means to be a black father in America.

Significantly, however, Gabriel locates the threat to his paternal legacy not on the rockpile amid the gangs of warring boys or within the larger context of white-on-black racism but, translating racial vulnerability into gender advantage, within his own house. In wanting to "see what *they've* done to his little man," Gabriel refers primarily to Elizabeth and John, the sinful wife and her bastard son from a previous relationship, whose blood holds no value for Gabriel. First blaming Elizabeth for her carelessness, Gabriel then turns on John, threatening to "take a strap" (18) to him for not being forthcoming about his failure to watch over his brother and protect him from harm. As Elizabeth and "Johnnie" become the true enemy, we see that the father's concern for "his" son's physical condition belies an underlying anxiety about maternal influences. Not only is the maternal bond between Elizabeth and "her" son foregrounded and juxtaposed to the proprietary paternal bond between Gabriel and Roy, but John also serves as his mother's surrogate, sharing her maternal duties. Although their maternal positioning protects them, to some extent, from Gabriel's anger (Elizabeth and John hand the baby Ruth back and forth, almost as a shield, during the argument with Gabriel), it also represents the threat against which Gabriel rages.

Though Roy's injury is no more than a flesh wound, the "hieroglyphics of the flesh" at work here—the phrase is Spillers's[11]—are made readable as a crucial gendering of the blood that flows from that wound. Gabriel does not simply define paternity narrowly, as a matter of biology, in his rejection of John and protection of Roy. Rather, he exhibits a particular confusion of consanguinity by employing an exclusionary, masculinist logic that debiologizes the parental connection between Elizabeth and Roy—but also, oddly enough, between Roy and himself—and instead invests the blood moment at the heart of the story with the singularly paternal meaning. As the father becomes sole protector of "his little man," Roy's blood, supposedly shed at the hands of a maternal enemy represented by Elizabeth and John, becomes entirely Gabriel's own. The son's blood therefore represents a purely masculine inheritance, a gendered bond that eclipses the logic of biological reproduction. This non-biological brand of paternal reproduction has, as I will later show, important implications for relations between black and white males elsewhere in Baldwin.

The exclusion of the black mother from the father-son blood bond suggests that a corollary blood logic accompanies the well-known "one-drop rule," a racist mathematic in which blood, based on the presence or absence of even one drop of "black blood," is represented as either wholly white or wholly black and whereby no mixed-race identity is possible. The "blackness" of the father-son blood also makes it exclusively masculine as part of what might be called its "property value"; the value of the blood is specifically tied to the black father's proprietary interests as a black man. The black man's blood thus signifies not only as "black blood" but as the more suggestive "black father blood." The effect of that hypercondensed paternal bond is that blood becomes a strikingly "fluid" signifier, its meaning far outrunning the thing itself, even when blood is also an utterly literal marker of African American suffering and death. "Paternity," by extension, becomes a similarly flexible familial relation.

WHITEWASHING: REPRODUCING RACE IN "THE MAN CHILD"

If the paternal crisis in "The Rockpile" is notable for a black father's turning inward, quite literally, in an effort to establish what might be called his proprietary masculinity, "The Man Child" reverses that perspective by looking outward through a white father's eyes at the endless fields and pastures that represent the masculine legacy that he will one day pass on to his son, the young protagonist Eric. The plot of the story is straightforward: Eric, an only child and sole heir to his father's property, is strangled by a childless, propertyless family friend, Jamie. But unlike the realistic narrative of "The Rockpile," "The Man Child" draws on mythic conventions, its vast scope and murderous finale suggesting an allegorical reading of both the white father-son bond and the white interloper who ultimately breaks that bond. In the figure of Jamie, Baldwin both inverts patriarchal desire and whitewashes the racial landscape, and he does so in order to insist that threats to white paternity are all the more dangerous because they are hidden by and within heteronormative whiteness itself.

"The Man Child" presents a sweeping picture of white male ownership in its endless display of land and sky, a perspective that originates at the farmhouse of young Eric and his parents and then arcs out past the yard's encircling stone wall to the fields and barns and finally to the far-off cow pastures and beyond. In this short work, Baldwin twice gives the reader a tour of the extensive property young Eric will one day inherit from his father. First, in a rite of initiation, Eric's father, whom Baldwin does not name, reveals to his eight-year-old son his destiny as landowner. Walking together, father and son stand high above the land they survey: "Then they walked till they came to the steep slope which led to the railroad tracks, down, down, far below them, where a small train seemed to be passing forever through the countryside, smoke, like the very definition of idleness, blowing out of the chimney stack of the toy locomotive" (59). The perspective, elevated and

dominant, is deceiving in its diminution of the train and the aggrandize-
ment of man and man child. Rather than presenting the men as small or
insignificant in comparison to the greatness of the land, Baldwin reverses
the scale, emphasizing the comprehensive authority of the white landowner
over his possessions. Master of all he sees and owner of all he touches, Eric
stands at the very center of a world that has always been his own, from
"[t]he day you were born," his father tells him (59).

The second tour, on which Eric explores the far reaches of his land alone,
culminates appropriately with a vision of the centripetal force that accrues
around the privileged white heir.

> Eric pretended that he was his father and was walking through the fields
> as he had seen his father walk, looking it all over calmly, pleased, know-
> ing that everything he saw belonged to him. And he stopped and pee'd as
> he had seen his father do, standing wide-legged and heavy in the middle
> of the fields; he pretended at the same time to be smoking and talking as
> he had seen his father do. Then, having watered the ground, he walked
> on, and all the earth, for that moment, in Eric's eyes, seemed to be cel-
> ebrating Eric. (64)

Imitating the father, the son engages in a phallic display of authority over
the land that confirms and celebrates his proprietary masculinity. The seemingly endless property rises to meet Eric as though part of an uninterrupted
male ego, one that is specifically raced when read against formations of manhood in "The Rockpile." White masculinity, unlike black masculinity, extends
outward into the land itself in Eric's symbolic act of watering the ground,
an act of fertilization that emphasizes the connection between the farmer
and the father, property and white paternity. If Eric understands, however,
that he is pretending, forging a bond with his father by playacting, white
paternity ignores its own performativity—and, thus, its vulnerability—as it
naturalizes its entitlements.

Indeed, to Eric's father, the son's destiny as landowner is so seamlessly
connected to his appropriation of phallic power that it becomes cotermi-
nous with his destiny as progenitor. Eric's father thus explains Eric's position
as property owner by prescribing the reproductive role the boy will play.

> "When I get to be a real old man," said his father . . . "you're going to
> have to take care of all this [land]. When I die it's going to be yours." He

paused and stopped; Eric looked up at him. "When you get to be a big man, like your Papa, you're going to get married and have children. And all this is going to be theirs."

"And when *they* get married?" Eric prompted.

"All this will belong to *their* children," his father said.

"Forever?" cried Eric.

"Forever," said his father.

Not quite sure of his position in the unending lineage imagined by his father, Eric inquires further into his new role.

"Will I?" asked Eric.

"Will you what?" asked his father.

"Will I get married and have a little boy?"

His father seemed for a moment both amused and checked. He looked down at Eric with a strange, slow smile. "Of course you will," he said at last. "Of course you will." And he held out his arms. "Come," he said, "climb up. I'll ride you on my shoulders home."

So Eric rode on his father's shoulders through the wide green fields which belonged to him, into the yard which held the house which would hear the first cries of his children. (60)

Eric's naive and narcissistic question "Will I get married and have a little boy?" exposes an interesting set of connections. Foremost, we see the heteronormalizing function of property rights in the story. "Taking care of the land" means both making the land productive and becoming reproductive oneself—indeed, "forever" reproducing oneself, as Eric's prediction of "little *boy*" implies. Eric's father apparently takes that association for granted, and thus he is surprised when Eric asks the question. But the father's response, his "strange, slow smile," followed by the protective measure of carrying Eric home on his shoulders, suggests that perhaps the heteronormative end of which he assures his son is not as inevitable as his repeated "Of course" in reply might indicate.

For the smile of Eric's father hides a fear of reproductive failure. Baldwin thematizes that failure in two separate but related ways: the literal inability to reproduce children and the symbolic inability to reproduce whiteness. This dual threat to the hetero-reproductive, racially "pure" paternal legacy stands at the center of "The Man Child." Already Eric's father has buried two miscarried children and so is well aware of the fragile nature of the idyllic family story he tells Eric. Furthermore, after these miscarriages, Eric's mother has become infertile, leaving Eric as the precarious link to future generations of white sons and landowners. The mother's inability to conceive other children then initiates her withdrawal: "shrunk[en] within herself, away from them all, even, in a kind of storm of love and helplessness, away from Eric" (62), the barren mother is effectively elided from the family romance. A similar dynamic plays out in each of the three stories analyzed here: Elizabeth is marginalized by the over-protective father in "The Rockpile," and Grace becomes a mere instrument on which Jessie plays out his homoerotically and racially charged fears of remaining childless in "Going to Meet the Man." Ironically, these mothers are displaced or subordinated by men intent on securing their own paternal positions in the procreative order, a father fantasy that is dependent—but blindly so—on the women it erases. Not surprisingly, the father-son bonds in these stories become more urgent and more tenuous as the mothers vanish and as the project of generation becomes an increasingly all-male affair.

The "strange, slow smile" of Eric's father also attempts to cover over a less visible threat to the paternal legacy in "The Man Child," one that arises from within and invisibly imperils white fatherhood. That threat is embodied in Jamie, the best friend and lifelong companion of Eric's father and a constant presence in Eric's life. Of the men's history, Baldwin tells us that "[t]hey had been destructing [the local tavern] long before Eric had kicked in his mother's belly, for Eric's father and Jamie had grown up together, gone to war together, and survived together—never, apparently, while life ran, were they to be divided" (49). Indivisible, the two men have, over time, become strangely united by their polar differences rather than their similarities. Jamie's wife has run away, he is childless, and he has lost his farm, which Eric's father has purchased. Like Eric's father, Jamie was once young, propertied, and "inevitably" reproductive, but without an heir, his name will be lost to future generations. A paradox, Jamie represents a nearly unthinkable end point, a failure of the white paternal legacy to reproduce itself.

When, at the end of the story, Jamie suddenly strangles little Eric in the barn, Baldwin dramatically literalizes Jamie's role as interloper in the white family romance. I suggest that, both like and unlike what we might call his "life partner," the murderous Jamie symbolizes whiteness divided from itself, a fissure in the white paternal order. That disruption is, I argue below, both sexually and racially coded so that Jamie intervenes into the dual narrative of unquestioned heteronormativity and unblemished whiteness that anchors the reproductive fantasy passed on to Eric by his father. Standing for the threat of inverted desire and racial betrayal, Jamie not only literally murders Eric but symbolically destroys the heteronormative white myth of racial purity.

Jamie's positioning as "invert" within the story is at first more obvious than his role as racial enigma (which is only fully revealed through the comparative analysis of "Going to Meet the Man" that will follow). In an unnamed way, Jamie's relationship to Eric's father seems to have given rise to his failure as husband, father, and landowner, for his connection to his best friend runs deeper and, more precisely, longer than it should. Eric's father chides, *"Jamie, Jamie, pumkin-eater, had a wife and couldn't keep her!"* (52), but it is not at all clear that Jamie wanted to keep her. Rather, when Eric's father criticizes his bachelor friend for sitting around and moping about "things that are over and dead and finished, things that can't *ever* begin again, that can't ever be the same again" (55), the "things" in question do not seem to include married life. Jamie's wife had been, it is suggested, a prostitute, with whom, according to Eric's father, Jamie had acted more "poetical" (54) than husbandly, preferring to roam the woods alone or drink with his male companion. Rather, the main "thing" that is "over and dead" seems to be Jamie's claim on the man who is now claimed, as his namelessness suggests, solely by his role as father. According to that father, Jamie has "thought about it too long" to start a new family. But just what has Jamie been thinking about that has kept him a bachelor?

Teased that he is too old to start a family, and with his sexual capacities therefore in question, Jamie responds, "I'm not old. I can still do all the things we used to do." Leaning toward Eric's mother with a threatening grin, Jamie offers to substantiate his past intimacies, specifically those that also involve Eric's father: "I haven't ever told you, have I, about the things we used to do?" In quick response to Jamie's implication that the men share ambiguously sexual secrets, Eric's father responds with a threat of his own: "He wouldn't tell you . . . , he knows what I'd do to him if he did" (52). Whatever the two men used to do in their youth, Eric's father has left it behind and warns that Jamie should do the same, calling him a "dreamer." The fanciful descriptions of Jamie as "poetical" and a "dreamer" compare poorly to the masculine characterization that Jamie provides of Eric's father: "I know you're the giant-killer, the hunter, the lover—the real old Adam, that's you. I know you're going to cover the earth. I know the world depends on men like you" (55). Distinguished here from his hetero-reproductive friend and, although he is the elder of the two men, later criticized for not being "as old as he should be" (58), Jamie occupies the role of a man caught in a state of arrested development, a state in which his erotic energies continue to be focused on the things he and his male companion once did rather than on the procreative things he might be doing with a wife. In classically Freudian terms, Jamie demonstrates "feelings of inversion and fixation of libido on a person of the same sex,"[12] symptoms that supposedly reveal stunted sexual development.

If Jamie is positioned as an "invert," however, his inversion must be understood in terms of his relation to the white paternal order and as an outmoded descriptor of his sexual development. His desires run counter to those of his "normal" friend not only in terms of romantic inclination but, more important, in terms of proprietary interest. Simply put, Jamie loves the wrong thing—the friend, not the father; the man, not the land—and that love places him outside the procreative and proprietary order that defines white manhood in "The Man Child." Foil to "the giant-killer, the hunter, the lover—the real old Adam," Jamie symbolizes an inversion of and a crisis within appropriative—that is, hetero-reproductive and white—fatherhood. Degout thus concludes that "[little Eric's] slaughter at the hands of Jamie itself signals a 'transcendental future'—the demise of the system of patriarchal indoctrination symbolized by the narrative of inheritance that he accepts but which dies with him."[13]

While "the implication is that the homoerotic urge—or rather, the inability to either affirm or acknowledge it—is, at least in part, what undermines the white male hegemony,"[14] it need not follow that Jamie murders Eric primarily because his love "is not returned adequately [by Eric's father]."[15] Rather, Jamie's importance as an "invert" lies in the fact that he helps to invert, to turn inside out, the hetero-reproductive paternal legacy that creates the illusion of stability in the text. Though Jamie rejects both land and son, that rejection comes from an insider's point of view, from the position of what might be called the paternal other. Jamie therefore does not represent an agent of unrequited love—an explicitly sexual invert—so much as his love for Eric's father is used to symbolize a non-normative or inappropriate desire at the heart of the paternal order and, therefore, a structural duplicity within white fatherhood. In other words, Baldwin uses Jamie not only to symbolize a threat to the white paternal legacy but to present that threat as existing within the father figure himself.

Indeed, the peril Jamie represents is structured by the very proximity to white patriarchy that his resemblance to Eric's father grants him. Although Jamie "lived alone in a wooden house . . . , Eric's mother kept his clothes clean and Jamie always ate at Eric's house" (50). The result is nearly unfettered access to little Eric. The father's notable absence in the final scene—in which Jamie strangles Eric in the barn while, from the house, his mother calls the boy to supper—reveals a shift in the family triad. With Eric's father elsewhere, Jamie emerges as a paternal shadow figure—quite literally out of the shadow of the patriarch. Importantly, he does not simply assume the father's authority or position. Trapped in the barn, Eric first desperately attempts to bribe Jamie with the land and the posterity that ownership bestows. "[Y]ou can have the land and you can live forever!", cries Eric. He then tempts Jamie with the even greater promise of fatherhood, pleading that "if you kill my father I can be your little boy and we can have it all!" (66). But Eric's betrayal of his father's proprietary interest does nothing to dissuade Jamie. In fact, it helps to confirm Jamie as the shadow father rather than a usurper of white patriarchy. Eric's self-serving attempt to realign his filial bond by refiguring Jamie as the father is thus futile, for his pleas appeal to normative patriarchal desires that hold no purchase for Jamie, a man whose inward desires for male companionship rather than a male heir run counter to the hetero-reproductive paternal desires that his outward appearance should, in the world of "The Man Child," dictate. Breaking Eric's neck, Jamie resolves that "[t]his land will belong to no one" (66).

Jamie's violent rejection of the material signifiers, both land and son, that not only confer status but also, when compared with "The Rockpile," represent a specifically white paternal legacy, also position him as racial outsider. On this point, the story remains deceptively silent, its characters so overwhelmingly white that racial otherness passes without notice. Yet within the larger argument of this essay, Jamie's racial liminality marks an interpretive flash point for understanding the crisis of white paternity in *Going to Meet the Man*. The racial other who co-exists invisibly at the very heart of whiteness, who nightly shares a table with his lifelong companion, becomes the ultimate threat to white paternity.

More than racial outsider, Jamie is a race trader. The ultimate concern of this chapter will be to explain the importance of the unexpected and deadly intervention into the production of white masculinity that Jamie's brutal and breathtaking murder of little Eric represents. If Jamie's jealousy of his best friend's reproductive capabilities represents an obvious but, ultimately,

unsatisfying answer to the question of why he kills Eric, the more compelling explanation lies in the assertion that Jamie represents the symbolic, invisible, and murderous infiltration of otherness, masked by sameness, into
the reproductive legacy to which Eric ought to be heir.

Only by turning to "Going to Meet the Man," a story that more directly
examines the complex racial workings of American paternity, can we understand the full implications of Jamie's prophesy that "[t]his land will belong to
no one" and, indeed, his identity as paternal other. My reading of "Going to
Meet the Man," a story in which the black man's body is viciously internalized by the white man as part of a racist fantasy of reproduction, will allow
me to return to and expand my claims about "The Man Child" in order to
posit a more general confluence of racial and erotic inversions by which the
black father is forcibly compelled to exist within the reproduction narrative
of the white patriarchal order. Revealing the production of whiteness to be
marked by the distinct appropriations of black male bodies, in addition to
female bodies generally, I will suggest that an invisible and disturbing fantasy of interracial homoerotic male union underlies the heterosexual reproduction of "race."

HOMOEROTIC FATHER-WISHES IN "GOING TO MEET THE MAN"

If "The Rockpile" and "The Man Child" are, as I have argued, stories about
the crisis of reproducing raced masculinity, whether by transfer of blood
or property from father to son, "Going to Meet the Man" complicates this
theme by depicting black and white men as intimately entwined in a destructive yet curiously productive paternal struggle, one that I will characterize as homo-productive. Creative, if not precisely procreative, this nameless
male coupling produces, as the residue of its disturbing homoerotic union,
native sons who are, to redeploy one of Baldwin's own identifications, "bas-
tards of the West," by which identification I mean to suggest that the role of
the unwilling black man within the white paternal struggle continually goes
unrecognized and disclaimed. In other words, I want to set alongside the
literal, hetero-reproductive tradition of denied white fatherhood and black
fatherhood both during and after slavery a parallel homo-productive tradition, figurative but no less real, of denied black and white paternal relations.

The catalyst for the plot of "Going to Meet the Man" is an episode of white male impotence. Jesse, a deputy sheriff, lies in bed staring at the "frail sanctuary" of his wife, Grace, unable to perform. Even though "[e]xcitement filled him just like a toothache . . . , it refused to enter his flesh." In an attempt to cure himself of his sexual paralysis, Jesse conjures up the image of one of the many black women on whom he has forced himself using the authority of his sheriff's badge, but the memory "was more like pain; instead of forcing him to act, it made action impossible" (198). What eventually makes action possible for Jesse is the recollection of two events, one from earlier that day and one from his childhood, both of which involve the violent eroticization of black men. In the first instance, Jesse has severely beaten a black prisoner, kicking him and shocking him with a cattle prod while simultaneously sexualizing him. Jesse remembers thinking that "*this ain't no nigger, this is a goddamn bull*" (202) and then, in a surprising and frightening response to his stereotypical rendering of the "black stud," becoming erect: "to his bewilderment, his horror, beneath his fingers, he felt himself violently stiffen—with no warning at all" (204). Yet Jesse seems only dimly aware that his violent enactments of power over the black man are deeply homoerotic. His recollection as he lies in bed hoping to reproduce that earlier erection is an apparently unconscious move: "'What a funny time,' he said, 'to be thinking about a thing like that'" (201). Early in the story, then, Baldwin portrays Jesse as not fully able to connect his memories of erotic violations of the black man to his quest for arousal in bed with his wife.

But Jesse's second memory, which stretches back to his boyhood on the day his parents take him to witness his first lynching, confirms that the first reflection was no mere coincidence. Jesse remembers his father lifting him onto his shoulders, as though to "carr[y] him through a mighty test" (217). From this position, the young Jesse had watched as a man, who held a gleaming knife in one hand, "cradled" and "caressed" "the nigger's privates" with the other. The exposed black penis, "the largest thing he had ever seen till then, and the blackest," was then cut away, and "the blood came roaring down" (216). Having found suitable erotic stimuli in these memories, the adult Jesse's body responds.

> Something bubbled up in him, his nature again returned to him. He thought of the boy in the cell; he thought of the man in the fire; he thought of the knife and grabbed himself and stroked himself and a terrible sound, something between a high laugh and a howl, came out of him and dragged his sleeping wife up on one elbow. . . . He thought of the morning and grabbed her. (217–18)

Here Jesse undergoes a change, manifest in his ability to perform sexually, so that "Going to Meet the Man" ends with the successful completion of his heterosexual mission. But his vocal outburst, an eruption of the subconscious other, simultaneously disrupts that mission by revealing that Jesse is not quite "man enough" to get the job done alone. Dependent and divided, Jesse owes his nocturnal "success" neither wholly to himself nor to his wife but to the black men—including the protestor he had beaten earlier that day—who inhabit his waking dreams.

> He thought of the morning and grabbed her, laughing and crying, crying and laughing, and he whispered, as he stroked her, as he took her, "Come on, sugar, I'm going to do you like a nigger, just like a nigger, come on, sugar, and love me just like you'd love a nigger." (218)

The fascinating resolution to Jesse's failure to perform—the internalization and impersonation of the black man—encourages a revision of the traditional Freudian explanation of impotence, the "refusal of the executive organs of sexuality to carry out the sexual act . . . , although a strong psychical inclination to carry it out is present."[16] Freud locates the source of male inhibition within the female sexual object whom the male in some way associates with his mother or sister. The male "sufferer" sometimes reports, according to Freud, "that he has a feeling of an obstacle inside him, the sensation of a counter-will which successfully interferes with his conscious intention."[17] But Jesse's sexual inabilities seem strikingly disconnected from female sex objects; neither his wife nor the black women who fail to arouse him appear precisely as unconscious sexual blocks.

Instead, white male impotence seems more closely associated with the black men who appear in Jesse's nocturnal reveries not as sexually victimized objects but as sexual accomplices or partners. Demonstrating the plasticity of male-male desire, Jesse does not fantasize about having sex with the black man so much as he desires to have sex along with or as the black man. In his discussion of internalization elsewhere in Baldwin, Lee Edelman writes that "Baldwin calls attention . . . to the complex exchange of inside and outside, self and other, that inheres in castration as the historic form in which white 'racial' hatred found its grotesquely distinctive expression."[18] Jesse's plea to Grace to "love me just like you'd love a nigger" thus maps forbidden heterosexual desire onto the white woman, but it does so primarily to secure and excuse the white man's own homoerotic internalization of and dependence on his black male counterpart. The problem, in short, has little to do with

Jesse's choice of sexual object at all, so that repressed homosexuality becomes an imprecise (though, I should say, entirely possible) interpretation of Jesse's impotence. The libidinal dynamic at play in "Going to Meet the Man" is homoerotic in a way not fully accounted for by homosexual attraction. In Jesse's case, the internalized black man does not act as obstacle or "counterwill" that blocks arousal; instead, the blockage is found not in the presence of the black man but, indeed, in his absence. The interference, contra Freud, is located not in a sexual object burdened with a surplus meaning leftover from the man's relationship with his mother or sister but, rather, in a psychic lack, a debilitating racial void.

Such voids have been widely interpreted as stemming from white male anxiety about inferior sexual capacities. In his classic study of racism, historian Winthrop D. Jordan notes that, in white cultures, the "concept of the Negro's aggressive sexuality was reinforced by what was thought to be an anatomical peculiarity of the Negro male. He was said to possess an especially large penis."[19] White fascination with the black penis bore itself out, according to Jordan, in the birth of the white male's growing sense of sexual inadequacy during the colonial slave-owning period: "[W]hite men anxious over their own sexual inadequacy were touched by a racking fear and jealousy. Perhaps the Negro better performed his nocturnal offices than the white man. Perhaps, indeed, the white man's woman really wanted the Negro more than she wanted him."[20] Baldwin, of course, thoroughly recognized the black man's status as "walking phallic symbol."[21] According to Trudier Harris, "James Baldwin has long argued that the prevailing metaphor for understanding the white man's need to suppress the black man is that attached to sexual prowess. . . . [T]he white man becomes a victim of his culture's imagination, . . . acting out his fear of sexual competition from the black man."[22] I suggest, however, that perhaps the white man's insecurity about penis size and sexual performance does not tell the whole story of his bedroom anxieties. Does another, related worry perhaps stand behind these?

If the black man has been hypersexualized, he has also been portrayed as part of a hyperreproductive black coupling—"pumping out kids . . . every damn five minutes," in Jesse's racist estimation (200). Significantly, Jesse and Grace are childless. As the narrative ends and Jesse "labor[s] harder than he ever had before" (218), that labor seems almost desperately procreative. Steven Weisenberger, characterizing "Going to Meet the Man" as a story about how "white supremacist terror reproduces itself," argues that "this apparently childless, Negrophobic man will fulfill the destiny implied in his biblically significant name and, at this monstrous moment and in his white supremacist view, become the providentially understood 'root' of a racially 'pure' people."[23] In other words, at stake for Jesse on this night are both fatherhood and, inseparably, whiteness. Yet given the specifics of this "pregnant" moment, one wonders just how "pure" Jesse's offspring will be. One wonders whether, in fact, the fantasized black man conjured up in the white man's bed is imagined as bringing more than his erection, more than the endowment with which he has been burdened in the white erotic imaginary.

I suggest that Jesse's incorporation of the black man does not so much reflect masculine insecurity in terms of a sexual lack as it reveals the white man's paternal paranoia. Jesse's erotic fantasy is a wish constructed out of paternal desire, a father-wish. Given that Grace, asleep beside her growling husband, operates on the periphery of this paternal struggle, the father-wish that binds together the sadistic white man and the black man of his tortured dreams is structured as a homoerotic fantasy, depending most fundamentally on male-male sexual liaison. In *Between Men*, Sedgwick reminds her readers that "the status of women, and the whole question of arrangements between genders, is deeply and inescapably inscribed in the structure even of relationships that seem to exclude women—even in male homosocial/homosexual relationships."[24] In turning my attention away from women, especially in discussions of reproduction that require female bodies and thus demand feminist analysis, I have had to willfully and sometimes skeptically set aside Sedgwick's well-reasoned advice. I do this for several reasons. I take as a premise that white paternal privilege is built on the bodies of women. Indeed, it is precisely my argument that the logic of "reproduction" fixes our attention, unthinkingly, on the female-male couple. In shifting attention away from "necessary" women, I mean to expose the critical blindness that itself reproduces the privileged biological duo as central to the reproduction of race, as though race were biologically reproduced. In short, the very requirement of the female-male dyad to narratives of reproduction itself promotes a kind of forgetfulness that race is constructed rather than born. That we accept as "fact" the idea that the circumstances of racial construction "demand," first and foremost, biological reproduction suggests the degree to which we continue to look to and in the body for "race."

What, then, are the implications of the white man's unwitting need to force the black man into the marital bed in order to reproduce and thereby secure his own paternal position? One might begin to answer this question by noting how odd it is that the white marriage bed would be the site at which the black man is invested with paternal presence, when he has traditionally been viewed either as an unwelcome perpetrator bent on violating white women or, more interestingly here, as a paternal absence in the black marriage bed. From the famous Moynihan report of 1965 to the October 1995 Million Man March, the notion of the missing black father has become a cultural commonplace. Excessively sexual and reproductive yet insufficiently paternal, the black man is thus caught between two apparently contradictory stereotypes, one hypermasculine and the other emasculating. Deeply problematic as well, Jesse's incorporation of the black man into his father-wish plays out as a form of enforced paternity reminiscent of the reproductive uses to which slaves were once put, throwing into doubt the presence of the black father as opposed to the black stud.

The justifications, however, for suggesting that the black man is conjured as a strangely paternal presence in Jesse's father-wish are several. As I have argued, Jesse is not fully conscious of his reliance on the black man's figurative participation in the white reproductive effort. Consequently, he cannot fully control the fantasy he evokes, as evidenced by the "terrible sound, something between a high laugh and a howl" (217) that erupts from him as he begins his father labor at the story's close. In fact, Jesse's manipulation of the black man's body in the prison cell stands in direct contrast to his powerlessness to fulfill his father-wish alone by manipulating his own body without fantasizing about the black man.

The homo-productive interracial union between men is, to be sure, a strikingly unbalanced affair in "Going to Meet the Man," even though the torture of the black man operates as the unacknowledged and disavowed erotic stimulus for the white man's heterosexual reproductive efforts. While Jesse clearly occupies the more visible position of power, however, the black man's role in the white man's paternal fantasy is crucial, even if we cannot attribute to the black man any volitional paternal agency. As a requisite presence within the white man's paternal fantasy —that is, as fantasy—the black man plays a key reproductive role, for Jesse unwittingly creates out of the black man a fantasy father by invoking him as part of the racist paternal project of white reproduction. Even as a young boy at the lynching, Jesse had been aware that the black man's eroticized body would be "a great secret which would be the key to his life forever" (217). Yet the grown man does not know—cannot afford to know—the truth of that secret or the need that demands such secrecy. Jesse's need stands in stark contrast to the needs of the black man in the jail cell, who, even as a boy, Jesse suddenly recalls, had said to him, "I don't want nothing you got, white man" (204). The irony of Jesse's racist deployment of the black man within his father-wish is obvious. Jesse uses the black man to become reproductive, but the real goal of that act—to reproduce whiteness—is impossible due to the very methods of production, for to produce whiteness, Jesse incorporates blackness. The "truth" of that symbolic interracial union, the "possibility" of Jesse's co-paternity, the "verity" of the ambiguously raced son that such fathers must produce—these are evidentiary hurdles that Baldwin can never surpass. Nevertheless, as I argued at the beginning of this chapter, "Going to Meet the Man" insists, as Baldwin did relentlessly in his fiction and essays, that raced paternity is marked by precisely such impossible relations.

THE BLACK FATHER AS EUNUCH: AGAINST FEMINIZATION, BEYOND HOMOSEXUALITY

Perhaps surprisingly, Jesse's homoerotic paternal desires draw attention away from, rather than toward, the mythic black penis that has been central to the hypersexualization of black men. William Pinar argues that in the act of lynching, which he takes to be an "imprinting episode" of racial violence in America, "the black man's phallus is the object around which the sequence of desiring events is structured."[25] Diverting our eyes from the black penis would therefore seem to be especially difficult when discussing castration scenes that almost paradigmatically expose both that penis and the erotic racial energies that coalesce, mob-like, around it. Baldwin's own display of the lynched man, as seen through the eyes of young Jesse, places the "the nigger's privates" at the center of the racial violence. But "privates" are constituted by more than the penis, of course. Hidden behind the penis, quite literally, are the black man's testicles, symbol of reproductive power and potency. In *Castration: An Abbreviated History of Western Manhood*, Gary Taylor exposes this interesting blindness.

> The psychoanalytic reading of castration keeps insisting that we stare at the penis. But castration need have nothing to do with the penis. Freud's theory (which Lacan recapitulates) would have us read "the lack of a penis" as a consequence of "castration." But *castration does not necessarily or*

even normally remove the penis. Castration—what medical dictionaries more precisely define as "bilateral orchiectomy"—is the removal of the testicles, not the penis.[26]

The black penis, it might be said, has eclipsed and even erased the black testes in castration narratives. My turn away from focusing on the penis in this discussion may strike the student of racist castration as odd, for the focus of analyses of the white man's castration of the black man has been almost solely on the penis (despite Baldwin's use of "privates"). Consequently, physical inadequacy, as opposed to reproductive capacity, has stood as the point of contention, with the primary questions being whose penis is bigger and whose is better. But we might also ask what has become of the testicles, the forgotten—or repressed—reproductive organs. The question of castration refocuses attention, as I believe Baldwin does, on the issue of generation and paternity.

Although it would seem to signify an end point rather than reproductive possibility, castration, as I will discuss it here, participates in a narrative of reproduction. While it provides the climax in the death ritual of lynching in "Going to Meet the Man," cutting away the black man's reproductive organs as part of the racist blood rite of lynching is a deeply layered act, one that attempts to enact a symbolic end within an end. Seen as an anti-reproductive measure rather than (or in addition to) psycho-sexual retribution, castration becomes a death before death, figuratively killing the procreative black father just prior to the black's man's death. Castration in this sense of a double end point differs from many historical uses of castration, ones that exclusively sought to deny males the capacity to reproduce. Citing the eunuch as his prime example, Taylor reveals the productive uses to which castrated men have at times been put. "The English word for eunuch derives from [an] ancient Greek word" that is a compound of two other words, one meaning "bed," especially "marriage bed," and the other meaning "to hold, keep guard." "Eunuchs were guardians of the marriage bed," continues Taylor, and "[t]hey were qualified for that social function by being disqualified from a biological one."[27]

No longer reproductive themselves, eunuchs participated nonetheless in the reproductive efforts of husband and wife by watching over the marriage bed in order to maintain the propriety of the acts performed there. They conferred paternal confidence on the husband, relieving him of the anxiety of uncertain paternity. In this sense, the eunuch was both reproductive end point and conduit for or guarantor of paternity. Positioned in such a way, the eunuch, though emasculated, could sometimes gain enormous patriarchal power, for "[a]lthough the power of eunuchs began in the bedchamber," Taylor argues, "it soon extended to the rest of the palace, and then the rest of the empire."[28]

I suggest that the black man in Jesse's waking dream/nightmare is transformed through castration into guardian of the white marriage bed, his reproductive incapacity bringing to fruition Jesse's reproductive potential. But this move, ironically, expands, rather than eliminates, the black man's reproductive powers within the white fantasy of racial reproduction. Jesse's father-wish does not, after all, require the presence of the stereotypical black "stud" who will serve as mere sexual proxy. Nor is the matter as simple as Jesse getting off by fantasizing about the tortured black male body. Rather, when Jesse conjures the beaten black prisoner who screams "as the prod hit his testicles" (202), when he remembers the lynched black man whose privates have been slashed away, the necessity of those recollections must be read within the context of Jesse's greatest fear: not that he is sexually inferior or even that he is literally impotent, but that he is racially impotent—unable to take his place within the racist tradition passed on by generations of white fathers through the creation of white sons.

Jesse restlessly ponders the race war that he and the other white townsmen are fighting, in terms of religious and social responsibility.

> He tried to be a good person and treat everybody right: it wasn't his fault if the niggers had taken it into their heads to fight against God and go against the rules laid down in the Bible for everyone to read! . . . He was only doing his duty: protecting white people from the niggers and the niggers from themselves. And there were still lots of good niggers around—he had to remember that. . . . They would thank him when this was over. (204–5)

Strikingly, Baldwin portrays the racist sheriff operating with a sense of moral agency, his principles deriving from the white supremacist tradition to which he blindly clings. Considering the "good niggers," Jesse smiles. "They hadn't all gone crazy. This trouble would pass" (205). But despite such attempts to comfort himself, Jesse darkly realizes that "[e]ach day, each night, he felt worn out, aching, with their smell in his nostrils and filling his lungs, as though he were drowning—drowning in niggers; and it was all to be done again when he awoke. It would never end." He fears that the struggle to maintain the ways of the past is already lost. His role models, "[m]en much older than he, who had been responsible for law and order much longer than he, were now much quieter than they had been." Among his friends, Jesse feels that "they had lost, probably forever, their old and easy connection with each other. They were forced to depend on each other more and, at the same time, to trust each other less" (207). When Joel Williamson remarks, in his groundbreaking *New People: Miscegenation and Mulattoes in the United States*, on the "racial dream world [that Whites] . . . fought tenaciously to preserve," he describes the past to which Jesse tries to cling and the future he so desperately hopes to re-create.[29]

Jesse therefore imagines—must imagine—in his bed a figure that will ensure the success of his racially reproductive labors: the black eunuch. Rather than a traditional eunuch, who acts as the guardian of female chastity (which would be another ironic role for him), the black eunuch, a figment of the white racist imagination and central to Jesse's father-wish, guards against the white man's failure to engage in the reproductive act that is meant to, above all, produce whiteness. He confers masculine confidence and paternal potential. An even greater irony is that, ultimately, the black eunuch is re-paid for this function by being re-masculated, positioned in the role of progenitor. Jesse, having been aroused by the memories of the castrated black man, goes on to impersonate the fully functional black man in the act of sex: "I'm going to do you like a nigger." As the black man is remade—made whole again both in and as the white man's body—castration gets translated into procreation. The black man, no longer merely a servant to Jesse's paternal fantasy, takes a privileged place in the white father's bed, his power extending unseen into the kingdom of white patriarchy.

It is important to note that the primarily male reproductive effort seen in "Going to Meet the Man" refuses to rely on a feminization or sex change for its logical resolution. This is true even when considering the act of castration that brings the men together. Robyn Wiegman notes that "empowerment based on maleness" is frequently "quite violently deferred": "In the case of the black male, who occupies an empowered 'masculine' and disempowered 'racial' positioning, this deferral has often taken the form of explicit feminizations in the disciplinary activity of castration that has accompanied lynching."[30] Wiegman continues, however, by suggesting that the feminization of the black man has become something of a critical shortcut. She points to the "masculine sameness" that "governs the black male's contradictory position in the cultural symbolic and underlies the various representational attempts to align him with the feminine." Rather than "exchang[e] potential claims for patriarchal inclusion for a structurally passive or literally castrated realm of sexual objectification and denigration,"[31] Wiegman implicitly challenges readers of raced masculinity to create interpretive strategies that hold open the possibility of black masculinity within castration narratives without deferring to the feminine position (or, likewise, to myth of the black stud) for explanation.

In the context of raced father struggles in "Going to Meet the Man," the castration of the black man is mocked by the recuperation of the black eunuch into the father's labor of reproduction. In fact, Jesse's fantasy of white fatherhood depends on the presence of the regenerated eunuch, the black male "father." In recasting the black man as participant in the procreative act along with the white man, Baldwin forces a reconsideration of how race is produced, for the focus on paternal doubling in Jesse—it takes both the black and white man to create the white father—maintains sex sameness despite racial difference, thereby resisting heteronormative closure. Following Wiegman, rather than regendering or resexing the black man (or the white man) in accordance with the heteronormative paradigm of biological procreation, one might instead follow a homo-cognitive practice, one that maintains a focus on sameness and the tensions it creates and that effectively—and, it seems to me, more simply—revises the use of the normative reproduction metaphor to include two men operating *as men* in a disturbing paternal coupling. In other words, rather than interpreting the multiple and multidirected emasculations driven by race within a frame of binary gender difference, it is possible to posit the existence of two men bound together in the act of racial production. Susan Gubar's understanding of the black man positioned as a "penis-not-a-phallus," which is one way of theorizing multiple masculinities,[32] might thus be expanded when considering raced paternity; when he occupies the role of invisible progenitor in the white man's bed, the black man edges toward a homo-productive role from which he can less easily be recuperated into a heteronormative narrative. In this way, the homoerotic refuses to be subsumed within the logic of the heteronormative, enabling a re-evaluation of the product of the violent male-male union.

At stake in this discussion—or one of the stakes—is the possibility of refiguring black/white male castration narratives beyond the norm of heterosexual gender difference or homosexual gender sameness, the fields on which interracial masculinities have lately been contested. This has become particularly true in the critical literature that frequently interprets the castrating impulse as nearly synonymous with homosexual desire. For Pinar, lynching expresses the white man's "repressed, racialized homosexual desire." "Lynching was," he concludes, "in no small measure a mangled form of queer sex."[33] Both the promise of and the problem with such a "homosexualizing" reading of racist castration is that no clear threshold for determining sexuality exists. Just how "mangled" can sex be and still be considered sex? It is of particular relevance here to ask whether gay critical theory has reached the point at which "homosexuality" must be considered an end point or an explanation rather than a conduit for interpretation. Certainly Pinar ventures a broad generalization in arguing that white lynchers were repressed homosexuals and, furthermore, that these men wanted to occupy the position of the female as part of their homosexuality. I have already argued against the necessity of imposing a gender switch on homoerotic relations generally and on Jesse's desire for the black man in particular, especially as such a reading participates in the often unquestioned practice, even within gay studies and queer theory, of heteronormative narrativization. In any case, Jesse at no time seeks out the feminine position vis-à-vis the black man, and he does not place the black man in that role. Instead, Jesse desperately constructs a volatile reproductive space in which he identifies with the black man, thereby resisting a male/female duality. Rather than reading strongly against the characterization of lynching as a fundamentally homosexual act of aggression, I hope to read through or past homosexuality by setting the stakes of the male struggle in terms of homo-productivity. The importance of framing interracial male relations in the context of paternal struggle must be understood as part of a move beyond representations of those relations as implicitly heterosexual or homosexual.

As space opens up for imagining a model of homo-productive male relations, such two-father stories offer a loophole for reading interracial male-male "marriages." In Baldwin, Norman Mailer's hipster or "white negro," helpfully characterized by Gubar as the "proleptic offspring of . . . interracial fraternity" and a "figure of the Not-Yet-Born out of male-bonding,"[34] becomes not a pale symbol of a cultural love child produced by the white bohemian's and juvenile delinquent's ménage à trois with the Negro but, rather, the white-skinned child born of woman but produced by two men in a struggle for racial posterity—read purity—that is inevitably undercut by the very fact of the men's interracial union.

"THE STRANGE MEANING OF BEING WHITE"

If, as I have claimed, relations between black and white men in "Going to Meet the Man" become homo-productive, what is the product? Although Jesse's incorporation of the black man seems ripe with procreative potential, Baldwin does not expressly show the fruits of that labor. So who and where is this child of male miscegenation, and in what sense is he—again, the product is always a son in Baldwin—"real"? Unlike his corporeal alter ego—the legally raced child produced by the white man/master who denies him and the black woman/slave whose status defines him—the illegitimately raced son of the unwitting white man and the unwilling black man does not figure in the American story of mixed-race at all. He is clearly not a "biological fact." But racial identity in America has never been as simple as biological facts. Biology has been sometimes ignored in constructions of race (as when it was superseded by the legal discourse of ownership) and sometimes trotted out as the very science of race (as in the pseudo-scientific discourse of the "one-drop rule"). Though a woman must literalize and give body to the child produced by two men in the story under consideration, her biological role does not, as I have argued, necessarily position her structurally alongside the child's fathers. Standing, as Spillers surmises, "in the flesh," she becomes *only* flesh, taking on the role of surrogate and carrying a child she must ultimately give up to his fathers in a demonstration of the misogyny that grounds paternity throughout *Going to Meet the Man*. The mother therefore occupies a fascinating liminal position—the transfer point between the literal and the figurative, between reproduction and production, between man and race man. Jesse's paternal fantasy, in its psychic incorporation of the brutalized black male body and its physical transfer of that fantasy onto the body of the white woman, powerfully condenses racist and sexist ontologies into a single subject position.

Where, then, is the "white negro"? At first glance, we seem not to notice the offspring of interracial fatherhood, because his hetero-reproductive parents are "white" and because his own pale flesh and blond hair avoid racial scrutiny. Yet, unlike the relentless visual logic that sought, in the minute details of skin color and hair texture, evidence of an invisible blackness against which "true" whiteness would quite literally pale by comparison, Baldwin refuses to locate race fears in the flesh. While the overwhelming anxiety of many "white" Americans was, as sociologist Charles S. Johnson predicted, "a time when men would 'ask for the Negroes' and be told, 'There they go, clad in white men's skins,'"[35] Baldwin insists that the real fear, the fear that cannot be quelled, lies in the realization that race is metaphor and thus cannot be physically located at all. The fear and the truth for Baldwin, quoted at the beginning of this chapter, is that "white people are not white: part of the price of the white ticket is to delude themselves into believing that they are. . . . America is not, and never can be, white." The strange meaning of being white in *Going to Meet the Man*, its unreality or metaphorization, is that whiteness cannot be reproduced. Instead, reproduced are the sexist, racist, heteronormative anxieties that have come to structure and define patriarchal power in America. Strangely indeed, those anxieties take shape as and look exactly like, to ironically recast Williamson's title, "new" people.

Ultimately, in *Going to Meet the Man*, Baldwin envisions an unsustainable racial landscape in which generations of what might be called "race orphans" are born of a white father dependent on the presence of the black paternal other. In Baldwin's vision, the state of racelessness—what Faulkner called "the most tragic condition that an individual can have"[36]—becomes the unspoken and, indeed, disclaimed American condition in general. That denial has behind it not only a mentality of racial preservation but also the weight of heteronormative conceptions of racial production that overlook the potential for interracial male fatherhood. Dual paternity—the new American race relation revealed in *Going to Meet the Man*—becomes visible, though, once castration is viewed as a wedge for reading male homoeroticism as productive of racelessness as opposed to race. If *kes*, the Indo-European root of castration, means not only "to cut" but also "to cut off from," castration in America takes on the double meaning of physically mutilating the black man and, simultaneously, cutting off the white man from his own race, invisibly cleaving whiteness from itself. As part of castration narratives, we must scrutinize the fractures within "whiteness" and, therefore, its paradoxical meanings.

I return now to "The Man Child," the only all-white story other than *Giovanni's Room* in Baldwin's oeuvre, reiterating my earlier question: why does Jamie kill little Eric? I propose that in "whitewashing" "The Man Child," Baldwin creates an *allegory of whiteness* that represents precisely the race lesson that Jesse cannot bear to learn in "Going to Meet the Man," for it prophesies his darkest nightmare: the death of race. By constructing young Eric from "The Man Child" as the double to the young Jesse found in the lynching flashback in "Going to Meet the Man," Baldwin insists that Jesse's race war is lost—has always been lost. The parallels drawn between the boys are many. Both rest their heads in the laps of their mothers and then, later, ride on their fathers' shoulders into manhood, whether at the lynching or across the family fields. Both stare for a brief and terrifying moment into the eyes of death. Jesse looks into the lynched man's eyes for what "could not have been as long as a second," though "it seemed longer than a year" (216), while Eric looks into Jamie's, "eyes which no one had ever looked into" (62). Both Jesse and Eric beg for life. In, as I have argued, an implicitly procreative fantasy, Jesse, now grown, cries to his wife to "love me just like you'd love a nigger," just as Eric begs for new life as Jamie's little boy. Given these similarities, Eric's fate becomes a window onto Jesse's own. There will be no white heir to take Jesse's place, not because Jesse cannot reproduce, but because the product of his paternal union with the fantasized black man cannot be white.

We may also approach the question from the other direction. Jesse's internalization of the black man turned father reiterates the theme of invisible paternity in the collection and thus helps to unmask Jamie, the shadow father in "The Man Child," as the race traitor who commits racial infanticide. The allegory of the doomed white son, Eric, therefore plays out the race nightmare—an end to the raced order of things—that terrifies Jesse. Within the whitewashed world that seems to celebrate the man child, there exists a symbolic figure of racial peril, one that invisibly infiltrates and disrupts the endless white lineage through a rejection of white land and most dramatically, the white son. "This land will belong to no one," Jamie's final decree, echoes the rejection of whiteness offered in "Going to Meet the Man," "I don't want nothing you got, white man." Eric's death does not intimate Jesse's own end but, rather, takes on mythic proportions as the death of the Last White Son, so that Jesse is positioned as racial end point. Playing out the allegory of whiteness, Jesse stands at the end of white generation and generations, the last heir to a whiteness he cannot pass on. The allegory of whiteness that Baldwin creates is, in fact, an allegory of lost whiteness.

"In America we still live with the paradox that white is black," writes Williamson, concluding, "Occasionally people who are visibly white declare themselves black, and millions of Americans who are more European than African in their heritage insist, sometimes defiantly, upon their blackness. Our paradox is unique."[37] The kind of race change Williamson points to, the claim to blackness by white-skinned people, is bolstered by the discourse of "heritage" and "descent" that seems to signify "real" racial identity. The race change I have traced in Baldwin is even more paradoxical, for the claims to invisible blackness I make here can fall back on no such legitimizing, hetero-reproductive discourse. Reading "The Man Child" as a type of neo-passing narrative requires a drastic reorientation in thinking about how race is pro-duced. John Brenkman, in an extended critique of Freud's Oedipus complex, suggests that such striking revisions of heteronormative origin stories are available.

> "Where do I come from?" inevitably gets answered *from this woman,* but the answer never exhausts the question. One's genesis is multiple not unitary. . . . One's own birth is at once fact and metaphor, singular event and cluster of meanings. It is therefore not, as Freud first suggests, "an event that is not open to any doubt and cannot be repeated." The revi-sions of the question *where do I come from?* can easily contradict one another or take shape around completely different desires or anxieties.[38]

The anxiety surrounding the preservation of race in "The Rockpile," "The Man Child," and "Going to Meet the Man" revises the hetero-reproductive question "Where do I come from?" by answering, "From these two men."

Reading *Going to Meet the Man* as a neo-passing narrative in which homo-productive interracial male union produces racially ambiguous sons requires, suddenly, that we re-evaluate all "white" children, tracing their parentage back to their multiple fathers as well as their mothers and fa-thers. This approach moves race off the skin and out of the blood, where it has so long been located, and effectively redraws the hetero-reproductive, pseudo-biological "race map" to take into account the possibilities of homo-productivity. Ironically, in that raceless sons are the result, Baldwin's homo-*productive* male relations in *Going to Meet the Man* are *destructive* of race. "Blackness" becomes invisible in such passing narratives not due to the dilu-tion of skin color from dark to light but because skin color can never tell the tale of impossible paternity; the black "father" within the white father is always invisible. However, his invisibility should be taken not as an ab-sence but, rather, as the very mark of his potency. Being located nowhere along the white family tree, he is suddenly everywhere. Whiteness itself then becomes the mark of questionable paternity, in that only whiteness might have necessitated the reproductive aid of the black eunuch. The child of the white male paternal fantasy is so unimpeachably white that every "white" son becomes potentially mixed race, just as every child under slavery was potentially fathered by the white master. I thus return to and reiterate Marlon Ross, who reminds us "[h]ow relative a notion whiteness can be."[39] The originary act of homo-productivity becomes not only akin to but, indeed, the ideal metaphor for hetero-reproductive interracial union in its power to produce utter "confusions of consanguinity." It is the ideal metaphor for the great American "race sin" of miscegenation, and its product, the "white negro" son, is a symbol of the great American fear: racial ambiguity and, indeed, racelessness.

Conclusion

The Queer Imagination and the Gay Male Conundrum

[G]ay male sexuality is as prone as any other mode of sexual expression to contradictions not entirely reducible to bad social arrangements. By attributing the inevitable suffering and struggle for power between intimately related individuals to the nefarious influence of patriarchal culture, gay and lesbian activists have found a convenient if rather mean-spirited way of denying human distress. To admit that being a gay man or a lesbian involves a certain sexual specificity, and even to go so far as to wonder about the psychic structures and origins of that specificity, might implicate us in that distress by forcing us to see the gay take on what is politically unfixable in the human.

—LEO BERSANI, *HOMOS*

Part of the dilemma was how in the world, first of all, to treat a black woman . . . , how to deal with a black girl whom you knew you couldn't protect unless you were prepared to work all your life in the post office, unless you were prepared to make bargains I was temperamentally unfitted to make?

—JAMES BALDWIN, *A RAP ON RACE*

James Baldwin believed in things not seen. The evidence was everywhere. The writer's sense of belief was forged in his early experience of religious mystery. Indeed, the phrase "the evidence of things not seen" is drawn from St. Paul's Epistle to the Hebrews. Paul writes, "Now faith is the substance of things hoped for, the evidence of things not seen."[1] One cannot help but acknowledge the importance of the original vehicle for this message in Baldwin's life, religion, even when that message finds a new mode of transport in the queer imagination. In this book, I have argued that it is by virtue of his dazzling queer imaginative capacity that Baldwin substantiates in writing the nearly unimaginable truths simultaneously created by and submerged in the currents of race and sex. His exploration of half-glimpsed reality was sometimes desperate, often hopeful, and always dogged. Indeed, the author's underappreciated late work on the Atlanta child murders that takes as its title a portion of the preceding scripture might be read as nothing so much as Baldwin's most straightforward and literal indictment of the tampered-with evidence of American life, the racialized judicial system being the surreal but official context in which "proof" is determined, patterns of "reality" woven, and "truth" found. Challenging the official story (e.g., the "false question of integration" that "as we could all testify, simply by looking at the colors of our skins, had, long ago, been accomplished"),[2] Baldwin argued that what had first to be discovered by piecing together the evidence of life were the "hidden laws"–the "unspoken but profound assumptions on the part of the people"—that governed society.[3] For Baldwin, the writer's job was to expose the product of those laws, the "myth of America." Further, by recovering "a sense of the mysterious and inexorable limits of life, a sense, in a word, of tragedy," the artist had to create "a new sense of life's possibilities."[4] This book's primary thesis is that, in its endless examination of American sexual and racial laws that everywhere circumscribe life's possibilities, Baldwin's fiction recasts the evidence into a case for queer reality.

My use of the "queer imagination" has been, I hope, continually problematized throughout this book. The use of the singular "imagination" belies not only the multiplicity of the term "queer" but also (because "multiplicity," too, now seems to contain flatly positive connotations) the fact that "queer" can mark as many imaginative failures as successes. The queer imagination, as I have charted it here, represents a curiously sprawling creative map on which some mountains—but not others—can be moved, sometimes. I thus want to make the case for a critical framework that capitalizes on the unpredictable success of "queer" as a navigation system for liberatory thought and action. I call this framework the queer imagination, and it provides a theoretical tool for reading queer texts. Mapping the paradoxicality of the queer imagination enables me to argue ever more strongly for Baldwin's queer creativity as an aesthetic mode, but it also compels an analysis of the shifting borders of queer thought. This inquiry can thus be added to the list of other works that offer a critique of queerness from within queer studies.

I have been fascinated by what I have called, in chapter 3, Baldwin's queer "failures."[5] While giving much importance to the fact that all texts are historically situated cultural products, I have felt, time and again, that the boundedness of Baldwin's queer imagination suggests other delimiting factors. At times, Baldwin outruns many cultural constructions and ideologies that grip his historical context, even as his imagination seems reined in by others. The queer imagination fluctuates as it seeks to articulate the bounds that queerness tests, penetrates, and fails to penetrate. The power of Baldwin's queer imagination, the power of queer theory's multiperspectival approaches to his work, thus ceaselessly outrun recontainment in some—but only some—ways. Queerness does not, I am saying, represent a totality, a goal, a utopic vision. While we must always push queerness into the boundaries, we must also prepare ourselves for what we might call the shock of queer failure—as part of the same emancipatory project. If the contours of the queer imagination must be traced not only as a matter of what is, but also what is not possibly thought, what accounts for the complexities of queer formations?

A second impulse of this book, then, has been to think critically about the queer imagination, both Baldwin's and the larger speculative energy developed in queer intellectual culture and deployed in the academy. This critical bent allows for a discussion of the strange ruptured-ness of queer creative thought. As I argued earlier, because "queer" contains an underlying imperative (queer!), it operates as an insistent speech act, prompting the user to do what it says; that is, "queer" layers and indeed belabors its own deployment by demanding a state of "ever-queerness" that cannot be sustained. However, beyond the predictably ever-failing project of making queerness new lurk thornier failures and breaches. Can a queer imagination be misogynist? Can a racist erotic be queer? Can queer thinking produce heteronormativity and homophobia? The answer to all of these questions, as the individual chapters of this book have argued, is yes, and the implication is that a radical tension and a central paradox is characteristic—and perhaps even definitional—of the very term "queer." But how to further explain these ruptures?

I want to point briefly to one final explanatory framework that is evocative of the kind of paradox in which I have been interested. I do not mean to pursue a rigorous application of this paradigm, nor do I wish to suggest that it exhausts the possibilities for understanding queer imaginative ruptures. Rather, it is useful to me because it introduces a certain *unanswerability* into the question, and I want to install this unanswerability as a feature of queerness. I want to suggest that perhaps the queer imagination is replete with what Jonathan Lear, in his philosophical rendering of Freud's unconscious, calls "motivated irrationality."[6] Lear argues against interpreting the unconscious as a "second mind," a formulation that inherently attributes rationality to what he says is a dynamic characterized by a lack of intentionality and, more importantly, by an absence of reasoning. The unconscious is marked not only by hidden reasons for thought, action, and feeling—a second, secret mind set at odds with a conscious mind, though operating with a similarly rational coherence—but, even more crucially, by the disruption, the short-circuiting, of reasoning itself. Freud's "strange" and compelling claim, for Lear, is that "people can be motivated to be irrational."[7] From this perspective, we do not do things, unconsciously, *for* reasons. The mystery of the unconscious is not to be found in the hiddenness of our motivations and desires but in their imperviousness to rational explanation. I want to think of what I have called the "unqueer" undercurrent of the queer imagination as, at least in part, similarly unexplainable, driven not only by invisible anti-queer logics—though I want to preserve this definition as well—but by a strategic unreasonability. The queer imagination may well contain a hidden normative impulse, but it also may harbor a more unwieldy interruptive mechanism than normativity. We might not set queerness in simple opposition to normative thinking, might not only argue that we have normative unconscious reasons—unexamined privilege, for instance—for undermining queerness. The pressures of normativity, real as they are, might not disrupt queerness from this perspective; in fact, in their rational narrativization, norms may instead disrupt our understanding of irrational, non-narrativizable disruptions of queerness. In short, the queer imagination might be marked by stranger contradictions and surprises than normative reasoning can imagine but that help to construct a creative field of both unpredictable liberation and blindsiding limitation. The value, the meaning of queer creativity, therefore, cannot simply be asserted as a positivity at odds with a normative negativity (an unqueerness) but must, rather, be made tenuous through the elaboration of the irrationalities of queer paradox. For this reason, it makes great sense to claim Baldwin as queer, but only as part of a project of investigating those parts of his writing that *make no rational sense*.

"BALDWIN'S" UNREPRESENTABLE WOMEN

To reformulate the preceding question in one final way, the remainder of this conclusion will explore Baldwin's queer imaginative relationships (both representational and interpersonal) with women. Throughout this book, I

have dramatized the fact that while Baldwin sometimes seems to purposefully re-create and sustain queer paradoxes (e.g., men literally reproduce race
together), there are other times when his imagination seems itself queerly
circumscribed and thus unaware of its paradoxicality (e.g., straight male-
male sex remains longed for but unimaginable). The paradigmatic case here
is his failure to portray women authentically and, specifically, to incorporate
lesbian desire in his fiction. Why are lesbians unrepresented in and, indeed,
seemingly unrepresentable for Baldwin? This absence of representation occurs, strikingly, even though several of Baldwin's most important and very
public intellectual engagements were with feminists and lesbians, including
Lorraine Hansberry, Nikki Giovanni, Audre Lorde, and Margaret Mead.
He does not succeed in renegotiating a pervasive masculinist worldview,
even as he enters into lengthy and forthright dialogue with these feminist
women. The point is not merely that Baldwin was not feminist enough, a
concern raised by Joseph Beam in his short essay, "James Baldwin: Not a
Bad Legacy, Brother." The point is that he was not feminist (enough) even
though he well might have been given his sincere investment in dialogue
with feminists. Similarly, his failure to portray lesbians in his fiction is not
remarkable except that he engaged personally and publically with several of
the most important lesbian artists and thinkers of the twentieth century.
Asking how it was possible for Baldwin not to represent the very women
with whom he interacted so meaningfully and consistently outside of his fiction might seem rather backward, except that, while Baldwin went to pains
to create in his fiction wide and nuanced spectrums of sexuality, he never
portrayed a lesbian. Although it is difficult to grapple with the concept of
queer imaginative absence, such creative voids, or unqueer ruptures, must be
explained rather than naturalized.

The most extensive study of Baldwin's representations of women is
Trudier Harris's 1985 *Black Women in the Fiction of James Baldwin*. Harris sets the standard for thinking about Baldwin's women by initiating a
sustained conversation "designed to fill a gap in Baldwin scholarship"[8] and,
more generally, in the critical literature about black female fictional characters. Fair-minded throughout her book, Harris argues that while "Baldwin
has given more serious attention, over a long period of time and through
many more works, to portraits of black women,"[9] "no woman is ultimately
so acceptable to Baldwin that she is to be viewed as equal to the prominent
male characters."[10] In the consistency of his portrayals of women, Baldwin
compares favorably to other black male writers of his day, including Ralph

Ellison and Richard Wright, yet Harris sees a representational veil shrouding these depictions: "black women we see in Baldwin's fiction, then, are usually at least twice removed—by way of Baldwin and his narrators—and are sometimes distanced through other layers as well. . . . [T]hey are not free of the creator who continues to draw in their potential for growth on the short rein of possibility."[11] Ultimately, Harris argues that the question of black women in Baldwin's fiction "centers upon value—how much value black women have to the males in their lives and how much value they can see in themselves without the yardstick of masculine evaluation."[12] Women "lose interest"[13] for Baldwin, Harris concludes, precisely to the extent that they fail to measure up to, for, and even as men. Extending Harris, lesbian women "lose interest" for Baldwin because they are women who do not exist along the measure of male eroticism. "Interest" becomes the naturalized gatekeeper at the threshold of imagination to the extent that erotic interest goes unremarked.

Like Harris, David Ikard notes a general black male patriarchal orientation toward black women in *Breaking the Silence: Toward a Black Male Feminist Criticism*. Beginning that study with an analysis of Bigger Thomas' misogynist formulation of Bessie's postmortem self-sacrifice, Ikard draws Richard Wright into a common black masculinist ideological tradition with Amiri Baraka, who "reinforces the idea that black men's experiences of oppression are normative,"[14] as well as with Chester Himes. However, explicitly distancing himself from Harris's position, Ikard then contrasts the Baldwin of *Go Tell It on the Mountain* to these patriarchal black male writers, arguing that Baldwin "casts light on the process by which black men rationalize their domination of black women."[15] Ikard continues his reading of "black patriarchy and the dilemma of black women's complicity" by attempting to place Baldwin beyond the reach of two forms of "attack": "While [Baldwin's] maverick status on gender, race, and cultural issues came at a high social cost—making him an easy target for homophobic black nationalists like Cleaver and hard-line feminists like [Trudier] Harris—they helped pave the way for important and necessary investigations into black patriarchy."[16] Alternatively, I want to suggest that Baldwin's positioning as a black queer "maverick," which gives him a special perspective on sexual and gender norms, especially as they consolidate around race, might also be said to *particularize* his brand of raced sexism rather than to remove him from the its grip. For when Ikard argues that Baldwin "accounts for the ways that black women are oppressed as women within the patriarchal structure of black community,"[17] he

conceives of those women as necessarily heterosexual, as did Baldwin. Neither does Harris's study address this different gap in Baldwin scholarship,
namely, the failure to consider that when the author declines to represent
lesbians at all (and therefore declines to represent women authentically), he
does so *as* a queer black man. Harris does not fully consider—and, in fact,
explicitly rejects—the possibility that Baldwin's sexuality was important to
his literary treatment of women. She nevertheless implicitly raises the difficult question of how gay men value women in their lives according to their
own, perhaps different, yardstick of masculine valuation. I want to examine
here, more specifically, how that valuation relates to the absence of lesbian
representation in Baldwin's fiction.[18]

I suggest that Baldwin's search for masculine valuation as a black gay
man reflects a paradoxical kind of authorial interestedness in his fiction.
That localized and specific interestedness helps to determine, which is not
to say over-determine, his imaginative capacities. Harris resists this interpretive avenue.

There is also a tendency in a study like this to bring the author's personal
life to bear upon the discussion. In practically all of the lectures I gave on
the topic prior to the appearance of this book, someone in the audience
asked how I thought Baldwin's life-style explained his portrayal of black
women. I can only say here what I said again and again in those lectures;
too much of what Baldwin has written has been explained away, com-
mented upon, or otherwise treated in the context of his personal life, and
too many of his essays have been used to interpret the literature. I have
tried to resist that urge in this study, except for the elements of *Go Tell
It on the Mountain* that are factually tied to Baldwin's biography. Otherwise, I have tried to remain within the realm of the created works for
my discussions and to allow commentary to evolve from within the text
instead of superimposing external notions onto the text.[19]

Harris may be attempting here to distance herself from the homophobic
strains in black literary and political culture that used Baldwin's homosexuality against him as a "race man." She may also be trying to dispel belief in a
simplistic, stereotypical brand of gay male misogyny, one that I certainly am
not seeking to reestablish. But she draws back when I think we must push on
toward interpretations that consider Baldwin's "life-style." From the distance
of today, it feels intellectually unrewarding that Harris avoids precisely the

question that was on the minds of attendees at "practically all" of her lectures on the book. The women in the audience, from Harris's report, were already making connections between themselves and Baldwin the man, and they appear interested to know how and why a black gay man represented women and female eroticism as he did. I would venture that these women's interest stemmed from their need to articulate the relationship between black/ gay women and black/gay men and between feminism and the raced, patriarchal currents of gay male literature. In a telling observation that points toward the primacy of male eroticism in Baldwin, Harris writes that "[i]f a male must engage in a heterosexual relationship, then perhaps that in which [*Just Above My Head*'s] Hall is engaged with Ruth is most acceptable to him and to Baldwin. As we have seen earlier, for Baldwin, the bisexual males who engage in homosexual relationships perhaps have the most acceptable world."[20] If Harris is correct about the privileged place of male bisexuality in Baldwin's queer creative worldview, then it seems fair to suggest that the author's male-inflected erotic imagination *actively* proscribes representations of lesbians. Lesbians lost interest by virtue of their distance from "the most acceptable" erotic relations, those between men. We can now begin to define artistic self-interest beyond material conditions to include the eroticism that accords to one's queer specificity and that disconnects one from another's erotic specificity. In this instance, the queer imaginative paradox takes the shape of the cultural dilemma created out of this tension between gay men's affinity toward lesbians as queers and the libidinal impulse away from queers who are lesbians, framed against the backdrop of patriarchy and race that informs both that affinity and that disinterest. Are gay male writers interested in lesbians, enough to write about them?

Baldwin might have, precisely through his dialogues with some of the most intelligent and creative lesbians of the late twentieth century, shown a writerly interest in representing lesbians in his fiction. One might expect Baldwin's love object Norman Mailer, by way of contrast, not to have budged much from his stalwart masculinism in his 1971 town hall debate with feminists Germaine Greer, Diana Trilling, Jacqueline Ceballos, and Jill Johnston, as, in fact, he did not. One expects something different from Baldwin in his interactions with feminist lesbians. But Baldwin's queer imagination in these cases belies his own brand of masculinism, one that tries to account for women within his worldview while nevertheless erasing lesbian existence in his fiction. We might then revise Harris's comment that "bisexual males who engage in homosexual relationships perhaps have the most acceptable world," to suggest that while Baldwin's black gay male erotic uses the denominators of race and queerness to make engagements with lesbians possible, it nevertheless draws on the privileges of sexism in a way that enables the author to turn his attention more fully to writing about intimacies among men. Though I will explore the irrationalities of that proscription shortly, it would seem at first blush that in Baldwin's queer imagination lesbians don't exist for reasons.

CONVERSATION WITH AUDRE LORDE

Baldwin's 1984 conversation with Audre Lorde at Hampshire College, a portion of which was published in *Essence* magazine,[21] demonstrates the odd boundedness of his sprawling queer imagination with regard to lesbian representation. The printed excerpt, titled "Revolutionary Hope," highlights the attempt by Baldwin and Lorde, who were meeting for the first time, to negotiate the terrain of gender difference between black men and black women against the larger backdrop of American racism. Throughout the piece, there are many gestures of agreement born out of a shared sense of urgency and predicated on the hope for a revolution that, both speakers realize, is anything but assured. Lorde and Baldwin also mirror each other in their arguments that women's and men's experiences are different. Lorde argues that black women not only have been denied the America dream but have not even been written into the American nightmare. "Even worse than the nightmare is the blank," Lorde says, "[a]nd Black women are the blank. . . . Nobody was even studying me except as something to wipe out."[22] Baldwin, for his part, insists that the black man has a special signification or status in terms of racial and gender oppression. Rather than a blank, the black man is a marked man, a target of the state: "A Black man has a prick, they hack it off. A Black man is a nigger when he tries to be a model for his children and he tries to protect his women."[23]

The speakers' agreement about gender as difference quickly produces, however, a recurring tension in the conversation about where the revolution indicated in the title needs to occur. Baldwin and Lorde diverge when they try, as Baldwin says they must, "to locate where the danger is."[24] He orients the root of the oppression—and thus the danger—in the white Western world. Baldwin's macroscopic view, however, becomes a skewed optic that, by privileging the danger for black *men*, re-creates black women as the blank to which Lorde referred. Time and again, Baldwin reiterates a version of his question to Lorde: "But don't you realize that in this republic the only real crime is to be a Black man?" Lorde denies that formulation of oppression, arguing, "No, I don't realize that. I realize the only crime is to be Black, and that includes me too."[25] Lorde locates the danger not only across racial difference but also across gender difference, noting that black men and black women are both vulnerable but differently so. While she claims that "the boot is on both our necks," Lorde argues that black women's blood is flowing at the hands of black men. But "[m]y blood will not wash out your horror," she insists. In predicting the inevitability of black women "cleaving your head open with axes," Lorde warns that black men and boys must address their misogyny if a full-out intra-race gender war is to be avoided.[26] In response, Baldwin accuses Lorde of "blaming the Black man for the trap he's in," insisting that though his violent actions toward black women are his "responsibility," they are not his "fault." "[I]t's not him who is my enemy," Baldwin contends, "even when he beats up his grandmother. His grandmother has got to know."[27] While Baldwin seems to take Lorde's point about the potential for mutual destruction between black men and women, he cannot but see the black man (including himself) as the protector of "his" women and children, even when he violently transfers his pain onto their bodies.

We could argue, initially, that Baldwin is an odd spokesman for the black male protector of women, but the construction offers more than a passing metaphorical utility. Baldwin *was* a deeply devoted family man, helping to raise, care for, and protect his eight younger siblings before his expatriation and throughout his life. Moreover, he does not derive a cheap vicariousness from his use of that positioning, for he implies that all black men share a responsibility and a burden in that their very manhood is staked on a necessary relation of gender asymmetry with black women, a necessity created out of the racial power asymmetries that define their relationship to white men. For Baldwin, to be a black man is to (have to) protect black women from whiteness and especially from white men—but not from black men.

Critics have taken Baldwin to task for his commitment to this perspective. Dwight McBride rejects "[t]he logic implied by such thinking [for it] suggests that because whites constitute a hegemonic racial block in American society that oppresses black and other people of color, blacks can never be held wholly accountable for their own sociopolitical transgressions."[28] Further, he critiques the ways that "the black community" often becomes an exclusionary rhetorical-political device, meant, ironically, to reflect, create, and protect a comprehensive coherence. Absent from such narrow constructions of "black community" is any reference to or recognition of black lesbians and gay men.[29] McBride's deeper critique of black queers' corrective project of making themselves undeniably present within "the black community" is that they—and he cites Baldwin specifically—"claim the category of racial authenticity"[30] and thus fail to indict the ideological categories of race. In the case of Baldwin, we must, characteristically, split hairs. On the one hand, he does reinsert black queers into black community, but on the other hand, this is true only for black queer *men*. Black lesbians do not exist in his cultural imaginary. Bizarrely, black gay men are reintroduced into black community by taking on the rhetorically powerful role, adopted time and again by Baldwin, of protector of black women. Thus, even though Baldwin frequently does critique racial categories, he nevertheless tends to draw readily on masculinist black male privilege, thereby reflecting a specifically black gay male masculinism. Reinscribing hierarchized binaries of sex, Baldwin permits black gay men like himself to "step up" into the empowered role of protector/defender while black women—more pointedly, black lesbians and all black women on what Adrienne Rich identifies as the lesbian continuum of women-identified women—"step down" into the role of that which is to be protected/defended. This leaves no space for imagining either that black women might need to be protected from black men or that they might prefer to and be able to protect themselves and each other.[31]

Rather than argue for the obviousness of the contradictions of the black man's trap—in other words, rather than argue that Baldwin might have more readily adopted Lorde's perspective of the ways gender and race oppression doubles down, in particular ways, on black women as well as black men—I want to explore the reason that Baldwin is nearly blinded to those contradictions. While Baldwin's possessive pronouncements about "his woman" may be partly a power play left over from his desire to occupy a more central role in the often masculinist Black Power movements of the 1960s and 1970s, I think they point at least equally to the heterocentrism that is one of the inevitable results of a system of white patriarchal oppression. In Baldwin's case, the gay black man, like the straight black man, negotiates the demands of that system by both rejecting its racism and adopting its patriarchal imperative of compulsory heterosexuality, in word if not always in deed. In this trap, black women must not only be protected, but they must first be made "protectable." For a man to reject racism might seem to require the necessary erasure of unprotectable women, such as Lorde, whose message to Baldwin was that she did not need the kind of protection he insisted on offering. The failure in Baldwin's epigraph to this chapter is that he seems never to have understood how to deal with Lorde, "how to deal with [this] black girl whom you knew you couldn't protect." That is, in his fiction, Baldwin may have needed to create protectable women, even if he was not "temperamentally" fit to "protect" them in his life.

Absent in Baldwin's analytic, the blank that his analytic re-creates, is the presence that is literally present in front of him: the black lesbian. Near the end of the *Essence* piece, Lorde places the fact of lesbian existence directly in Baldwin's line of sight, replacing the male-female protective dyad with a picture of the lesbian couple that exists outside his field of vision. She suggests to Baldwin a model in which black women exist as the responsibility not of black men but of themselves and of each other. But this is to no avail. Though she literally embodies that absent presence, Lorde represents the unthinkable for Baldwin, someone outside of erotic relationship with black men and outside the reach of their heteronormative brand of protection.

DIALOGUE WITH NIKKI GIOVANNI

Baldwin's conversation with Lorde echoes, in many respects, his earlier discussion with poet Nikki Giovanni, published in 1973 as *James Baldwin/ Nikki Giovanni: A Dialogue*. While Giovanni was not out as queer in the same way Lorde was, she nevertheless helps to demonstrate Baldwin's paradoxical inability to imagine that which he directly engages. In the dialogue with Giovanni, Baldwin had already articulated the vision he would share with Lorde, that of a world in which the black man is the ever-degraded yet necessary center. He tells Giovanni that

> the situation of the black male is a microcosm of the situation of the Christian world. The price of being a black man in America—the price the black male has had to pay, is expected to pay, and which he has to outwit—is his sex. You know, a black man is forbidden by definition, since he's black, to assume the roles, burdens, duties and joys of being a man. In the same way that my child produced from your body did not belong to me but to the master and could be sold at any moment. This erodes a man's sexuality, and when you erode a man's sexuality you destroy his ability to love anyone, despite the fact that sex and love are not

the same thing. When a man's sexuality is gone, his possibility, his hope, of loving is also gone.[32]

What Baldwin does not and, I think, cannot imagine in his genealogy of black male sexual erosion is black female sexuality. The question of how "his" child came to be "produced" from the black woman's body seems to have little to do with her sex, her relationship to it, or her sexuality. Rather, the black man's innate ownership of the child and of the black woman's body that bears the child operates as the pressure point for Baldwin, the point of his own unique violation. At stake for Baldwin in the Christian drama is, most fundamentally, a proprietary black male sexuality, addressed in my discussion of "The Rockpile" in chapter 4 and here placed by Baldwin at the center of the Christian world's lovelessness. Both the price the black woman pays with her sex and who demands that price go unnamed.

Responding to Baldwin's description of how his father was made to be a "nigger" by white power, Giovanni pivots, as Lorde does, to gender dispari-ties. She admits, "I really don't understand it. I don't understand how a black man can be nothing in the streets and so fearful in his home, how he can be brutalized by some white person somewhere and then come home and treat me or Mother the same way that he was being treated."[33] For Baldwin, how-ever, the mistreatment of black women by black men provides commentary not primarily on black men's relationship with black women but on black men's situation vis-à-vis the racial disparity with white men. When Baldwin insists to Giovanni, as he will go on to do in his conversation with Lorde, that the black man is "not mistreating *you*" (my emphasis), he erases, in a single motion, the reality of black and lesbian women who see things differ-ently. This move occurs again after Baldwin, once more claiming Giovanni as "my wife or my woman," argues that if he is not allowed to be a man and take responsible for his own home, "it doesn't make any difference what you may think of me."[34]

Having already declared that "I'm not dealing with that,"[35] Giovanni pushes back again. Linking her resistance to the way "I've structured my life,"[36] she attempts to articulate (and here the meanings and motives of Baldwin's interruptions become most interesting) a lesbian feminist critique, even as she works with the heterosexual examples on which Baldwin re-lies.[37] "It does indeed make a difference what I think about it," she insists.[38] I believe she then attempts to explain her "lack" of understanding of the brutalizing black man with reference to her own socio-sexual positioning as a lesbian mother: "I mean, you take somebody like me. I'm not married, right? . . . I couldn't play my mother. . . . I just couldn't deal with her role. I would say, No, no, no, this won't work."[39] Baldwin misses her meaning, how-ever, making the purely historical argument that "since your mother played that role you haven't got to." In this vein, Baldwin implies that Giovanni "underestimate[s] the price paid for us,"[40] not realizing that her vision of gender equality might stem from the centrality of her sexuality in her life, even though he clearly conceives of black male sexuality as "the center" of his own life.

Undeniably, this exchange occurs at an intersection fraught with compli-cated power dynamics, the most obvious of which are raced and gendered. Moreover, an underlying queer paradox helps to structure this confronta-tion. Apparently, a black man is here arguing that he cannot be blamed for brutalizing a black woman because his (implicitly hetero) sexuality matters so much—"when you erode a man's sexuality you destroy his ability to love anyone." In actual fact, however, a black *gay* man is here arguing that he can-not be blamed for brutalizing a black *lesbian* woman, as though their sexuali-ties did not matter. In other words, for Baldwin's logic to make sense, the re-lationship between the black gay man and the black lesbian must be erased, made into a distorted copy of a heteronormative patriarchal black paradigm, which itself has already been made into a distorted copy of a heteronorma-tive patriarchal white paradigm. Baldwin fails to recognize that Giovanni, as a black lesbian single mother, has structured her life so as not to have to deal with the black (gay) man's brutalization of her and hers. In other words, rather than using the specificity of his own black gay male positioning to re-assess and rearticulate his relationship both to the racist, heterosexist larger culture and to the person sitting in front of him—someone, I should add, who explicitly offers him a model of how to do just that from a black lesbian perspective—Baldwin dislocates himself in such a way as to reveal his black gay male privilege but not reflect on it.

Perhaps Baldwin's most interesting performance as race man in his dia-logue with Giovanni comes by way of an anecdote he tells of almost getting married at the age of twenty-two. The story comes at a point in the discus-sion at which Baldwin is explaining the black man's misogynistic responses to his trap as irrational (though completely understandable) and thus un-dermining (while also agreeing with) Giovanni's "rational" argument that he should treat her better. The "several reasons" Baldwin gives for not having married are fascinating. He explains,

I threw my wedding rings in the river and split, decided I would have to leave. I didn't get married partly because I had no future. . . . I couldn't keep a job because I couldn't stand the people I was working for. Nobody could call me a nigger. So I split to Paris. Now I loved that girl and I wanted children, but I already had eight and they were all starving. And from my point of view it would have been an act of the most criminal irresponsibility to bring another mouth into the world which I could not feed.[41]

Giovanni tries to draw a distinction by suggesting that "those weren't your children." She continues, with subtlety, "One cannot, and I'm not knocking your life, but one cannot be responsible for what one has not produced." Baldwin can only offer, "I said we are not being rational."

Though Giovanni's comments might be read as letting Baldwin off the hook by shifting the burden of fatherly responsibility away from him, another meaning exists as well. In not "knocking" Baldwin's life, she must also mean his decision to run to Paris, to remain single, to love men. But by virtue of that decision and that life, Giovanni also refuses to allow Baldwin to step into the role of the straight black father or husband. She will not grant him the responsibility that he will nevertheless attempt to use against her when he cannot achieve it. Further, she will not allow him to speak, in this moment, as the kind of race man he is not. As I have suggested, Baldwin was very much a family man, and there is a great deal of depth in his simple declaration that "those are my brothers and sisters."[42] I do not believe that Giovanni is making light of those connections. Instead, I hear her speaking as a single queer mother, a place of responsibility that, in fact, Baldwin will not grant her even as he accesses it as a gay man. If she is dismissive of Baldwin's claims here, it might well be precisely because of the matrix of irrationalities created by Baldwin's story of a marital near miss. He first recounts his very real experiences of having racist employers, a story told at length in *Notes of a Native Son*, and then introduces his own imagined starving child and his starving brothers and sisters as reasons for not getting married, despite the fact that, he tells Giovanni, he "loved that girl." As "his" children become the reason for him not getting married, Baldwin becomes the resolutely single black father. When Giovanni pleads for rational expectations of the black man, she is perhaps making two pleas at once: for straight black men to be men without misogyny and for gay black men to be men without wives (or the children that take their protected place), akin to the way that she is a black lesbian without a husband. The deeper critique of black masculinism that is imminent in the feminist analysis offered by Giovanni and Lorde is a lesbian critique of black gay male privilege and, more broadly, of what I call the "gay male conundrum."[43]

THE GAY MALE CONUNDRUM

The gay male conundrum offers a perhaps prototypical instance of queer paradoxicality. It is created by the simultaneous positioning of gay men as queer with respect to dominant patriarchal culture, insofar as homosexuality is subordinated to the normative ideals of masculinist heterosexuality, and their positioning as normative with respect to queer subculture, insofar as (queer) women are subordinated to the cultural ideals of personhood, that is, (queer) men. As seen above, race can be deployed within the gay male conundrum in many conflicting and complementary ways. Baldwin's unquestionable concern for black women, for example, emerges most often through the construction of himself as a black man. He thus speaks of "his woman" in ways that appeal generally to the larger heterosexist patriarchal American culture and that simultaneously ingratiate him with members of the Black Power and Black Nationalism movements whose own brand of protective masculinism responded to the racist imperatives of that dominant white culture. This strategy places him in the seat of queer paradox that I am here calling the "gay male conundrum" and, more specifically, the "black gay male conundrum."

Lorraine Hansberry, Baldwin's dear friend and "sister," predicted the work of Giovanni and Lorde in their efforts to speak, however directly or obliquely, to the vexed positioning of the black gay male conundrum. Though there is no comparable published dialogue between Hansberry and Baldwin, the outlines of a such a dynamic can be reconstructed beginning with two letters Hansberry wrote to the *Ladder* (a publication of lesbian organization, the Daughters of Bilitis), in May and August of 1957. Hansberry begins her May letter by reflecting her understanding that the lesbian publication to which she was contributing was necessarily feminist. "Our problems, our experiences as women are profoundly unique as compared to the other half of the human race," she writes. Her gratitude for the *Ladder* (she opens her letter with "I'm glad as heck that you exist") thus comes from a shared experience that seeks to interject women's perspectives into urgent

women-centered conversations.[44] Yet at the same time that she argues that
women need their own publications, Hansberry is also broadly integrationist. She first eschews "any strict separatist notions, homo or hetero" of wom-
en's organization. Then, having parenthetically stated, "(I am a Negro)," she
advocates for the integration of lesbians into mainstream women's behavior
and dress based on her "cultural experience" of assimilating as a black women
into white cultural codes. She is clear to lay the blame for the "discomfort"
caused by butch lesbians and the "ill-dressed or illiterate Negro" at the feet
of the heterosexist and racist majority, but she nevertheless concedes "for the
moment" that when even "one's most enlightened (to use a hopeful term)
heterosexual friends" remain "disturb[ed]" by lesbian gender nonconformity,
assimilation into the norm is perhaps required.[45]

Crucially, as part of her integrationist vision, the twenty-seven-year-old
Hansberry foresees that lesbians would not only need to speak as women
and as feminists to each other but would need to speak back to and confront
men as well. Near the end of her longer, August letter, Hansberry turns
more fully to the feminist issue of confronting "male dominated culture" and,
I argue, the lesbian issue of confronting the gay male conundrum. Though
she does not explicitly mention it here, she has already positioned race as intersectional with gender. In the following passages, Hansberry again works
from the baseline of women's experience and then specifies at the level of homosexuality. She first writes, "I think it is about time that equipped women
began to take on some of the ethical questions which a male dominated culture has produced and dissect and analyze them quite to pieces in a serious
fashion. It is time that 'half the human race' had something to say about the
nature of its existence." That feminist/lesbian critique of patriarchy generally then leads into a more pointed lesbian/feminist focus that entwines homophobia and sexism: "In this kind of work there may be women to emerge
who will be able to formulate a new and possible concept that homosexual
persecution and condemnation has at its roots not only social ignorance,
but a philosophically active anti-feminist dogma. But that is but a kernel of
a speculative embryonic idea improperly introduced here."[46] The "speculative
embryonic idea" would find fuller formulation two decades later, to cite but
one important example, in the "Black Feminist Statement" of the Combahee
River Collective.[47]

For his part, in "Lorraine Hansberry at the Summit," Baldwin records
the kind of powerful act of speaking back that Hansberry had called for and
then accomplished. The remembrance details how the thirty-three-year-

old playwright stood at the vortex of the famous 1963 meeting of black and white civil rights leaders with Attorney General Robert F. Kennedy. Despite the clarity and eloquence of Hansberry's remarks, Kennedy refused to hear. Baldwin writes,

> The meeting ended with Lorraine standing up. She said, in response to Jerome [Smith's] statement concerning the perpetual demolition faced every hour of every day by black men, who pay a price literally unspeakable for attempting to protect their women, their children, their homes, or their lives, "That is all true, but I am not worried about black men—who have done splendidly, it seems to me, all things considered." Then, she paused and looked at Bobby Kennedy, who, perhaps for the first time, looked at her. "But I am very worried," she said, "about the state of the civilization which produced that photograph of the white cop standing on that Negro woman's neck in Birmingham." Then, she smiled. And I am glad that she was not smiling at me.[48]

Baldwin positions Hansberry as transcendent. He remembers her standing, though he knows she was seated ("she towered, that child, from a sitting position"),[49] and he attributes to her a final, withering smile, one he was happy to avoid. Baldwin believes that Hansberry was not speaking to him in that moment, that her penetrating gaze did not include him. But might it be otherwise, especially if the woman with the boot on her neck represents the absolute failure of (at least some of) the men in the room to imagine the stakes of American racism and sexism for black lesbians?

A point easily lost in a reading of Hansberry's letters is that the men Hansberry sought to speak back to as a black lesbian feminist were, inevitably, black and gay as well as straight and white men. The critique she levels at Kennedy contains, not far from its center, a critique of black gender relations. It certainly contains a critique of Baldwin's claim, in his interview with Lorde, that "the only real crime" in America was "to be a Black man." Further, bubbling just under the surface of Hansberry's August contribution to the *Ladder* is the largely unexamined tension created when sexist homophobia emerges as gay male ideology. While she connects the price that homosexuals (both men and women) pay *as homosexuals* to the costs of sexism toward women, Hansberry's "rhetoric of intersectionality"[50] compels an inquiry into the complex gender differential between gay men and lesbians and, as it pertains here, between gay men and lesbians of color.[51]

WHY LESBIANS?

The feature of the gay male conundrum that I am interested in here is the way that Baldwin engages with and attempts to make use of black lesbians (or, in Margaret Mead's case, a lesbian who shares Baldwin's devotion to the analysis of race). I suggest that Baldwin does so in deeply personal ways *as* a black gay man. There were inevitably professional considerations at play. The dialogue with Nikki Giovanni was motivated partly by Baldwin's desire to stay relevant at a time when his critical and popular success had waned. His attempt to write a novel with a female protagonist in the 1974 *If Beale Street Could Talk* might be read, in this light, as a gay male writer's "gimmick," more self-interested than woman-centered. This sounds uncharitable, but I do not mean the term "self-interested" to identify here any singular, mercantile motivation. Undoubtedly, Baldwin was terribly concerned with matters of career and success.[52] At a point when his literary reputation was flagging,[53] the temptation to find a "gimmick"—the word is Baldwin's, used to describe how a young black boy in Harlem must find something to "start him on his way"[54]—must surely have been strong. Despite the fact that queer poet June Jordan faulted *If Beale Street Could Talk* for its unconvincing portrayals of women in her review for the *Village Voice*, for the struggling black gay male author writing in an age of black masculinism, women held a certain queer appeal.

One wonders, though, why Baldwin seemed compelled to turn to lesbians in turning to women, especially when he could not imaginatively render or feel implicated in the boot on their necks. This question helps to elucidate Baldwin's place within the gay male conundrum, insofar as he was apparently concerned with yet inattentive to lesbians and lesbian desire. Clearly, it cannot be argued that sex was not on the speakers' agendas in his dialogues with women. Likewise, sexuality was omnipresent, if encoded or unspoken. I would go even further: Baldwin, *as* a gay man, engaged with these women *as* lesbians, and they engaged with him *as* a gay man. This is nearly to say "because" they were lesbians, which would seem reasonable. But by "as lesbians" I intend a more nuanced meaning: that is, in the context of their being lesbian, or in the context of the speakers being queer. Such a context could be very useful to Baldwin, whose attempts to be a family man might have been buttressed, precisely (and not ironically) by his status as "family" in the queer context of the dialogues. A certain protectiveness by lesbians might have been (rightly, it turns out) assumed by Baldwin, enabling him to inhabit the guise of being their protector. Such an assumption or reliance on his part would have been both naive and cunning, for while the women resist his sexism, they do not fully expose its paradoxical orientation. As "the black family man," he cannot withstand their various critiques, but neither do they use his homosexuality explicitly against him as part of those critiques.

In her collection of essays titled *Margaret Mead Made Me Gay*, noted lesbian anthropologist Esther Newton relates the story of how she gravitated toward Mead's work of exploring cultural difference. Having felt herself to be different in the "nasty barnyard" of high school, Newton personalizes the anthropological study of otherness as an endeavor that made a special kind of sense *to her*. Mead, as a woman who chose women subjects (and women lovers), became a model for the young Newton, even though, at the time, Newton "knew nothing about Margaret Mead's being bisexual."[55] Female difference attracted Newton to Mead; unarticulated queer similarity lay at the heart of that difference.

Mead and Baldwin met in August of 1970 for a conversation that would be published the following year as *A Rap on Race*. Though the transcript of that meeting has been celebrated and derided, the two-day discussion at least made a certain kind of sense: a superstar anthropologist meets a tour de force of the literary world to discuss the shared subject of much of their thinking and writing. Yet the meeting was also a setup, a performance arranged by an interested party (the publisher) and predicated on a set of potentially productive (yet potentially incendiary) differences between the two participants. An otherwise unremarkable negative review in the *New York Review of Books* in December 1971 stands out for the particular clarity with which it styles Baldwin and Mead not merely as different but, in fact, as opposites.

Baldwin presents himself as male, black, poet, existentialist, slave, exile, ex-Christian. Mead appears as female, white, positivist, Episcopalian, old American, the most famous anthropologist in America. From the beginning they are betrayed by their respective idioms. His is stagy, stale, full of forced rhythms, a parody of the writer's style. Hers is pretentious, inflated; one feels that one is being beaten to death with a pillow. Through most of the dialogue Margaret Mead is full of what can only be called *machismo*, while Baldwin seems as nervous and respectful as a bridegroom.[56]

While being so clear about the speakers' differences, what the reviewer also tries so loudly to whisper is that another difference structures the dialogue's polarity: Mead's lesbianism and Baldwin's homosexuality. Mead had been linked to Ruth Benedict early in her career and, having divorced her third husband in 1950, had been living with Rhoda Metraux (both women were fellow anthropologists and collaborators) since 1955, one year before Baldwin's literary coming-out with the publication of *Giovanni's Room*. Mead and Metraux would live together until Mead's death in 1978. As public or semi-public queer intellectuals, Mead, "full of what can only be called *machismo*," becomes the butch to Baldwin's nelly "nervous and respectful . . . bridegroom." Differences abound.

But I wonder whether an unarticulated queer similarity such as the one that drew Esther Newton to Mead also drew the macho Mead and the effeminized Baldwin together around the issue of racial difference. In other words, did the very "expertise" metaphorized by the snide reviewer above nevertheless provide the logic for their discussion? Their talk is frequently exasperating and perhaps ultimately exhausting as they circle around, as a climactic moment exemplifies, the (a)symmetries of racial oppression. Baldwin insists, characteristically, that he and Mead have both been victimized in their own ways and that "we are both exiles," he because of "the terms on which my life was offered to me in my country"[57] and she "because of what you know." For Baldwin, Mead knows something that makes her an outsider "from the mainstream of the life in this country." The ostensible topic being race, Mead rebukes Baldwin again and again: "I am not an exile. I am absolutely not an exile. I live here and I live in Samoa and I live in New Guinea. I live everywhere on this planet that I have ever been, and I am no exile."[58] Baldwin can only respond with, "I am not at home. I am not at home."[59]

Was Baldwin reaching, in this exchange, toward a queer common ground, one stabilized by the more obvious considerations of race and gender that placed him in the room with Mead? If so, that queer meeting place becomes quicksand. In his discussion with Mead as in his dealings with Hansberry, Giovanni, and Lorde, Baldwin ultimately stands alone (stubbornly? blindly? longingly?) in a place of shared queerness. But how did queer similarity—a meeting of queer imaginative minds—fail to sustain Baldwin, thereby throwing him into relief against lesbian feminism rather than in line with it? The answer I have been considering is the paradox of Baldwin's black gay masculinism and, more generally, the gay male conundrum.

This point, that Baldwin engages Hansberry, Mead, Giovanni, and

Lorde—so different from each other—as a gay man addressing lesbians, cannot be proved. His need for queer collaboration, if it is a need, go unspoken. Neither can it be proved that Baldwin's extended exchanges with Norman Mailer exist because Mailer was straight. Yet, to offer but one illuminating counterexample, Baldwin's "love letter" to the famously, helplessly straight Mailer, written as an essay titled "The Black Boy Looks at the White Boy," clearly suggests that truth. Likewise, the gay-lesbian connection allowed for the Baldwin-lesbian dialogues to be imagined. The queer imagination created not the raison d'être for the dialogues but, rather, one important condition of their very possibility. That these conversations were "about" race and gender does not change the queer conditions that facilitated the engagements. One of the points I am trying to make in this conclusion crystallizes here: the queer imagination both enables and disables; it creates possibilities for thought even as it ruptures in the very specificity of queer need. Queerness brought these thinkers together, and queerness kept them apart in an agon of queer doing and undoing.

In her dialogue with Baldwin, Giovanni pleads for rationality about the power differentials that structure gender. Mead, in a more scientific fashion, does the same for race. I want to repeat Baldwin's explicit response to Giovanni (and his implicit response to Mead): "I said we are not being rational." If we are looking for a rational answer to why Baldwin does not represent lesbians in his fiction, we might theorize that absence as a vacuum created by forces of sexism, racism, and homophobia. Though Baldwin demonstrates, time and again, that he is tethered to these interwoven oppressions, I have wanted, in this conclusion and in this book, to suggest the incongruity of these limitations with the expansiveness of Baldwin's queer imagination. If we are to explain the absence of lesbians in his fiction, we might need to explain how Baldwin could manage not to feel pinned in his own chair by Hansberry's final smile at Bobby Kennedy. To do this, we might need to look beyond the "rational" rewards of gay male misogyny to a more paradoxical interplay of interest and disinterest. Adapting Lear's psychoanalytic model, we might consider another explanation. Perhaps Baldwin's twin motivations—to engage with and to disengage from lesbians—have another meaning, an irrational one. Further, perhaps it is not the *discrepancy* between the two actions that provide the basis for understanding Baldwin's treatment of lesbians as irrational. Instead, perhaps Baldwin's strategy of "doing and undoing" is not so much agonistic as dependent, integral, indivisible. The "twin" acts of speaking with and silencing lesbians may not in fact be two; rather, they may index, without explaining, the more general paradox—a paradox that is not a pattern— of the queer imagination. Leo Bersani, who provides an epigraph to this chapter, writes in *Homos* that

> gay male sexuality is as prone as any other mode of sexual expression to contradictions not entirely reducible to bad social arrangements. By attributing the inevitable suffering and struggle for power between intimately related individuals to the nefarious influence of patriarchal culture, gay and lesbian activists have found a convenient if rather mean-spirited way of denying human distress. To admit that being a gay man or a lesbian involves a certain sexual specificity, and even to go so far as to wonder about the psychic structures and origins of that specificity, might implicate us in that distress by forcing us to see the gay take on what is politically unfixable in the human.[60]

While my argument in this conclusion primarily has exposed the "convenient" (though I hope I have made clear not always "mean-spirited") ways Baldwin was able to deny lesbians and their distress—and I am not at all backing away from that argument—there is yet light between those explanations of Baldwin's gay male conundrum and my sense of the man I have spent every day with for many years. This further aspect of the paradox of Baldwin is the indivisibility of his success and his failure, the paradox of his specific unfixability, which must be set alongside that which is fixable in his queer vision. Insofar as specificity provides the logic of unfixibility, the queer imagination will continue to rupture in specific, unpredictable, irrational ways. Much as we might hope for it, Baldwin's paradox will not emerge in exactly the same form ever again. Our future work as queer theorists—the work of articulating queer paradox, of fixing what is fixable, and of facing what is not—has not yet been cut out for us.

Baldwin's deepest artistic interests were his deepest erotic interests. Why should they not be? His eroticism is, after all, no light or easy thing. Baldwin saw it as absolutely central to American history and national identity, as the crux of the American question, because he worked from the assumption that the sexual and the racial were inseparable, because he understood the black man—made into "a walking phallic symbol"[61]—as *the* symbol of the combustible union of sex and race, and because he was himself queer. In exploring how his sexual identity as a black man shot through his national identity and was shot through by it, he was able to bring to light the homo-erotics of that violent union as perhaps no one else has done. This is to say that Baldwin's artistic vision was formed as and informed by a black queer imaginative capacity. That his erotic interest was specific (or what he called "personal") is beyond criticism; that his artistic interest tracked closely with the erotic is unexceptional as well. That this connection is made within a complex dynamic of power relations, including with black and white lesbians, and that Baldwin's writing replays those unequal power relations *in the very field of queerness* has been, in the more general case, the source of my fascination in this book. I have wanted to do several things: to map the queer imaginative field created and reflected in Baldwin's fiction, to suggest that the topography of that map is rich and varied and simultaneously thin and inconsistent, and to complicate the queerness of the map's borders by examining its expansive as well as its unpredictable, even ufixable, ruptures. Beyond the simplistic hierarchies that Baldwin worked tirelessly to dismantle, differences and differentials persist, altered yet unexpectedly resilient, in queer imaginative paradox.

Notes

Introduction

1. Cathy Cohen, "Punks, Bulldaggers, and Welfare Queens: The Radical Potential of Queer Politics?," 438.

2. Ibid., 441 (my emphasis).

3. José Esteban Muñoz , *Cruising Utopia: The Then and There of Queer Futurity*, 1.

4. Jasbir K. Puar, "Queer Times, Queer Assemblages," 526.

5. See Jack Halberstam's study of queer temporalities and postmodern geographies, *In a Queer Time and Place: Transgender Bodies, Subcultural Lives*, for a related exploration of the contradictory, messy ways queerness and norms are imbricated.

6. Judith Butler, *Bodies That Matter: On the Discursive Limits of "Sex,"* 237.

7. Valerie Traub, "The New Unhistoricism in Queer Studies," 34.

8. See, for example, Jonathan Dollimore's seminal *Sexual Dissidence: Augustine to Wilde, Freud to Foucault*, which posits a process of "transgressive reinscription" that relies on a relationship of proximity between dominant and subordinate to effect both a displacement (i.e., a construction of the marginal "other") and a recuperation of difference (a "tracking back of the 'other' into the 'same'") (33).

9. Michael Warner, "Queer and Then? The End of Queer Theory?," accessed July 21, 2013.

10. Cathy Cohen, 448.

11. Judith Halberstam, *The Queer Art of Failure*, 105.

12. It was only quite late in the process of writing this book that I came to understand its place within queer theoretical discussions of reparative reading practices versus critique. Robyn Wiegman, whose work has been important to me in a number of ways, helpfully refuses to oppose (or temporally distinguish) these interpretive traditions of hope and suspicion. In her talk, "Affective Atmospheres," at the Queer Methods conference, organized by Heather Love and hosted by the University of Pennsylvania (October

31–November 1, 2013), Wiegman suggested the necessity of both queer methods of reading, especially as together they can help us understand and intervene in our own painful histories of traumatic interpretation.

13. If Baldwin's scholarly reception has reflected two oddly divergent paths, his presence within literary anthologies, which act as gatekeepers of the canon, continues to be quite singular. Baldwin's sexuality is rarely discussed in the introductory biographical remarks typical of the genre, so that the anthologized Baldwin has been the raced, not sexed, Baldwin.

14. Magdalena Zaborowska, *James Baldwin's Turkish Decade: Erotics of Exile*, 19 (my emphasis).

15. Marlon B. Ross, "White Fantasies of Desire: Baldwin and the Racial Identities of Sexuality," 15.

16. The introduction to the indispensable *Black Queer Studies: A Critical Anthology*, edited by E. Patrick Johnson and Mae G. Henderson, offers a brief history of the ways African American studies and queer studies have avoided each other. Marlon Ross's "White Fantasies of Desire," in that same volume, presents a more thorough discussion of the reception of *Giovanni's Room* in African American literary and cultural studies.

17. Ross, 16.

18. Ibid., 22.

19. Dwight A. McBride, *James Baldwin Now*, 2.

20. James Baldwin, "Here Be Dragons," 690.

21. James Baldwin, *The Devil Finds Work*, 606.

22. Hilton Als, "The Enemy Within: The Making and Unmaking of James Baldwin," 72.

23. See Baldwin's famous query, "Who is the Nigger?," in his 1963 interview for *Take This Hammer*.

24. Robert Corber, "Everybody Knew His Name: Reassessing James Baldwin," 168–69.

25. James Baldwin, "The Black Boy Looks at the White Boy," 298.

26. James Baldwin, *The Fire Next Time*, 375.

27. Ibid., 362.

28. James Baldwin, *The Evidence of Things Not Seen*, 6.

29. D. H. Lawrence, *Studies in Classic American Literature*, 1. Lawrence's distinction between the "blood-self" and the "nerve-brain self" implicitly hovers over much of Baldwin's work, particularly the novel I take up in my second chapter, *Giovanni's Room*.

30. Ibid., 171.

31. David A. Gerstner, *Queer Pollen: White Seduction, Black Male Homosexuality, and the Cinematic*, 14. Gerstner brings the conceptual tool of "the cinematic" to bear on the works of Richard Bruce Nugent and Marlon Riggs as well as Baldwin.

32. Ibid., 94 (quoting from Jacques Derrida, *Aporias*, 70).

33. Ibid., 95.

34. Audre Lorde, "Uses of the Erotic: The Erotic as Power" in *Sister Outsider: Essays*

and Speeches, 58–59. Amber Musser's unpublished work ("Embodying a Movement: Lesbianism and Queer of Color Critique." Modern Language Association Annual Convention. January 12, 2014) on the pragmatic, disembodied, and de-sexualized uses of Lorde's erotic promises a much-needed reintroduction of black lesbian feminist sexuality into queer theory.

35. Richard Hall's "The Language Animal," collected in his *Fidelities*, is the perhaps perfectly named short story inspired by Baldwin's life and work.

36. Baldwin makes a similar point about what is owed to the absent subject of one's inquiry in a comparison of Billie Holiday's autobiography, *Lady Sings the Blues*, to the film adaptation of that book. He privileges the former because it contains "her testimony, for that is what we are compelled to deal with, and respect, and whatever others may imagine themselves to know of these matters cannot compare with the testimony of the person who was there" (*Devil Finds Work*, 131).

37. Lee Edelman, *No Future: Queer Theory and the Death Drive*, 2.

38. Ibid., 3.

39. However, Baldwin's social vision diverges from Edelman's. In contrast to Baldwin's vision of the hard-won but positive social gains to be made from the nearly impossible work of queer imagination, Edelman proposes a "queer negativity" that "refuses to reinforce some positive social value," specifically "futurism's unquestioned good" (ibid., 6–7).

40. See Robyn Wiegman's "Queering the Academy," "Un-remembering Monique Wittig," "Interchanges: Heteronormativity and the Desire for Gender," and the introduction to *Women's Studies on Its Own*.

41. Wiegman, "Interchanges," 92.

42. Wiegman, "Un-remembering Monique Wittig," 505–6.

43. Wiegman, "Interchanges," 100.

44. Wiegman, "Un-remembering Monique Wittig," 514.

45. Ibid., 515.

46. Kathryn Bond Stockton, *Beautiful Bottom, Beautiful Shame: Where "Black" Meets "Queer,"* 32.

47. Ibid., 33.

48. Ibid., 25.

49. Thomas Piontek's *Queering Gay and Lesbian Studies* offers an accessible jumping-off point for further research into this debate.

50. Judith Butler, "Imitation and Gender Insubordination," 19.

51. E. Patrick Johnson and Mae G. Henderson, *Black Queer Studies*, 1.

52. Ibid., 1.

53. See, in particular, ibid., 3–6, for a discussion of this disciplinary relationship.

54. Dwight A. McBride, "Straight Black Studies: On African American Studies, James Baldwin, and Black Queer Studies," 87.

55. E. Patrick Johnson, "'Quare' Studies, or (Almost) Everything I Know about Queer Studies I Learned from My Grandmother," 126.

56. Michael Warner, *Fear of a Queer Planet: Queer Politics and Social Theory*, vii.

Chapter 1

1. Emmanuel Nelson, "Critical Deviance: Homophobia and the Reception of James Baldwin's Fiction," 91.

2. Ibid.

3. Robert F. Reid Pharr, *Black Gay Man: Essays*, 92.

4. Sharon Patricia Holland, *Raising the Dead: Readings of Death and (Black) Subjectivity*, 115.

5. Ibid., 110.

6. Ibid., 104–5.

7. Ibid., 107.

8. Ibid., 104.

9. Ibid.

10. Ibid., 118 (my emphasis).

11. Ibid., 111.

12. Ibid., 104.

13. Though I will address it more fully in this book's conclusion, I want to foreshadow here that I am thinking in particular about the place of women in the black gay male literary tradition over which Baldwin looms so large.

14. Colin Robinson, Cary Alan Johnson, and Terence Taylor, eds., *Other Countries: Black Gay Voices*, 1.

15. Emmanuel Nelson, "James Baldwin," accessed August 8, 2011.

16. John Keene, "This Week, Pt1: Als on Baldwin + Reading @ Temple," accessed August 10, 2011.

17. Thomas Glave, *Words to Our Now: Imagination and Dissent*, 26. Glave borrows the phrase "giantless time" from an unpublished poem by Gwendolyn Brooks.

18. Essex Hemphill's *Brother to Brother* has recently been given new life, having been republished by Lisa C. Moore at RedBone Press in 2007. Subsequent page references in this chapter are to that more recent edition.

19. Hemphill, xliv.

20. Ibid., xliii.

21. Beam's introduction to *In the Life* is titled "Leaving the Shadows Behind."

22. Myriam J. A. Chancy, "Brother/Outsider: In Search of a Black Gay Legacy in James Baldwin's *Giovanni's Room*," 155–56.

23. Beam, *In the Life*, 14.

24. Hemphill, xlix.

25. Beam, "Making Ourselves from Scratch," 335.

26. Ibid., 336.

27. *Carry the Word: A Bibliography of Black LGBTQ Books* is a seminal reference work edited by Steven G. Fullwood, Reginald Harris, and Lisa C. Moore, featuring titles by

and about black same-gender-loving (SGL) and lesbian, gay, bisexual, transgender, and queer-identified (LGBTQ) writers and culture, as well as interviews and articles about black SGL authors.

28. See Carol Hanisch, "The Personal Is the Political," accessed July 21, 2013.

29. Steven Fullwood, personal conversation, March 5, 2009. Fullwood adds that "[c]ontemporary writers are adapting new language as a way, often, of *not* saying 'gay.'"

30. Marlon B. Ross, "White Fantasies of Desire: Baldwin and the Racial Identities of Sexuality," 15.

31. Ibid., 15–16.

32. Dwight A. McBride, "Can the Queen Speak? Racial Essentialism, Sexuality, and the Problem of Authority," 36.

33. James Baldwin, *The Fire Next Time*, 370.

34. D. Quentin Miller, *Re-viewing James Baldwin: Things Not Seen*, 4.

35. James Baldwin, *Go Tell It on the Mountain*, back cover.

36. Miller, 3.

37. Steven Seidman, *Difference Troubles: Queering Social Theory and Sexual Politics*, 135.

38. James Baldwin, "'Go the Way Your Blood Beats': An Interview with James Baldwin," 174.

39. James Baldwin, "Race, Hate, Sex, and Colour: A Conversation with James Baldwin and Colin MacInnes," 54.

40. Baldwin, "Go the Way Your Blood Beats," 174.

41. Ibid., 175.

42. Ibid., 173.

43. Ibid., 179.

44. Glave, 39.

45. I borrow this phrase from the title of A. B. Christa Schwarz's important study *Gay Voices of the Harlem Renaissance*.

46. Herb Boyd, *Baldwin's Harlem*, especially 23–46 (for an account of Baldwin's relationship with Cullen and Hughes).

47. James Baldwin, "James Baldwin—Reflections of a Maverick," 223.

48. In "Wrestling with 'The Love That Dare Not Speak Its Name': John, Elisha, and the 'Master,'" Bryan Washington attributes Baldwin's reticence to speak "homosexual" in *Go Tell It on the Mountain* as an act of discipleship committed in deference to the famously tight-lipped James.

49. Discussions of the "agon" between Baldwin and Wright are well rehearsed. My key point here is that none of Baldwin's major literary influences occupy the racial and sexual intersection that he does.

50. Samuel Delany, "Samuel R. Delany: The Possibility of Possibilities," 197.

51. Ibid., 185.

52. Bayard Rustin, "An Interview with Bayard Rustin," 14.

53. Thomas H. Wirth, *Gay Rebel of the Harlem Renaissance: Selections from the Work of Richard Bruce Nugent*, 57.

54. Thomas H. Wirth, personal conversation, December 5, 2008.

55. Douglas Field, "James Baldwin in His Time," 27.

56. This description comes from D. Quentin Miller, "James Baldwin's Critical Reception," 95.

57. Darryl Pinckney, "James Baldwin: The Risks of Love," 401.

58. James Baldwin, *The Price of the Ticket*, xi.

59. Ibid., x.

60. James Baldwin, "An Interview with James Baldwin," 5–6.

61. Robert F. Reid-Pharr, *Once You Go Black: Desire, Choice, and Black Masculinity in Post-War America*, 15

62. Carolyn Wedin Sylvander, *James Baldwin*, 36.

63. James Baldwin, *Go Tell It on the Mountain*, 3. Subsequent page references in this chapter appear parenthetically in the text.

64. James Baldwin, "The Art of Fiction LXXVIII: James Baldwin," 240.

65. Quoted in Scott Bravmann, *Queer Fictions of the Past: History, Culture, and Difference*, 3.

66. James Baldwin, "White Man's Guilt," 410.

67. Baldwin, *Fire Next Time*, 336.

68. James Baldwin, "Every Good-Bye Ain't Gone," 642–43.

69. Roderick Ferguson, "The Nightmares of the Heteronormative," 420.

70. Ibid., 423.

71. Ibid., 427.

72. Ibid., 437.

73. Ibid., 432.

74. Ibid., 440.

75. Ibid., 439.

76. Ibid.

77. Ibid.

78. Ibid., 432.

79. Christopher Nealon, "Queer Tradition," 619.

80. Ibid., 621.

81. He also has the potential to signify as *racially different*, insofar as male homosexuality can be interpreted within African American communities as a rejection of a masculine-overdetermined black identity.

Chapter 2

1. Donald Hall's hermeneutic ethics in *Reading Sexualities: Hermeneutic Theory and the Future of Queer Studies* elaborates just such a journey to self-knowledge, one neces-

sarily routed through the very self/other interrelationships that David has spent a life-time avoiding. See Hall's Gadamerian reading of *Giovanni's Room* in *Reading Sexualities* (66–71).

2. I here use the term "queer studies" to refer to a broad academic enterprise that engages diverse perspectives and interests, including gay and transgender studies. My use of the term "queer theory" in this chapter refers to a more discrete approach within queer studies.

3. James Baldwin, "'Go the Way Your Blood Beats': An Interview with James Baldwin," 13.

4. Baldwin, *Giovanni's Room*, 11. Subsequent page references in this chapter appear parenthetically in the text.

5. We should note, however, that these are not equal and opposite forces.

6. James Baldwin, "Everybody's Protest Novel," 33.

7. James Baldwin, "Is *A Raisin in the Sun* a Lemon in the Dark?," 25–26.

8. Marlon B. Ross, "White Fantasies of Desire: Baldwin and the Racial Identities of Sexuality," 36.

9. James Baldwin, "Here Be Dragons," 678.

10. Donald Hall, *Queer Theories*, 156.

11. Ibid., 160.

12. William B. Turner, *A Genealogy of Queer Theory*, 32.

13. Though Baldwin does not explicitly state it, David's dilemma must be set against the backdrop, identified by Max Weber, of the Protestant ethic in which the work of self-denial and the value of cleanliness contribute to the rigorous pursuit of a secular vocation and, consequently, worldly success.

14. David Leverenz, *Manhood and the American Renaissance*, 4.

15. See Kathryn Bond Stockton's *Beautiful Bottom, Beautiful Shame: Where "Black" Meets "Queer"* for a fascinating study of the ways tropes of decomposition and decay operate in queer black narratives.

16. See Lee Edelman, *Homographesis: Essays in Gay and Literary Cultural Theory*.

17. Kaja Silverman, *Male Subjectivity at the Margins*, 9.

18. Michael Warner, "Homo-Narcissism; or, Heterosexuality," 200.

19. Ibid., 197.

20. Mae G. Henderson, "James Baldwin's *Giovanni's Room*: Expatriation, 'Racial Drag,' and Homosexual Panic," 299.

21. James Baldwin, "The Male Prison," 103.

22. Ibid., 104.

23. http://www.publishingtriangle.org/100best.asp and http://latimesblogs.latimes.com/jacketcopy/2010/08/20-classic-works-of-gay-literature.html, accessed July 7, 2011.

24. Thomas Piontek, *Queering Gay and Lesbian Studies*, 28.

25. For a trenchant critique of this trend, see Valerie Traub's "The New Unhistoricism in Queer Studies."

26. Heather Love, *Feeling Backward: Loss and the Politics of Queer History*, 147.

27. James Baldwin, "Preservation of Innocence," 45.

28. Ibid.

29. The counterpoint to Baldwin's perspective in this regard is that of his exact contemporary Jean Genet.

30. Baldwin, "The Preservation of Innocence," 45.

31. See, in particular, Eva Kosofsky Sedgwick, *Epistemology of the Closet*, 67–90.

32. James Baldwin, *The Fire Next Time*, 335.

33. Ibid., 336.

34. Baldwin, "Male Prison," 104.

35. James Baldwin, "Disturber of the Peace: James Baldwin—An Interview," 79.

36. Ibid., 80.

37. Baldwin, "Here Be Dragons," 688–89.

38. Baldwin, "Preservation of Innocence," 45.

39. See Amin Ghaziani, "Post-Gay Collective Identity Construction"; Amin Ghaziani and Matt Brim, "The Problems with 'Post-Gay.'"

40. Sarah Schulman, "The Lady Hamlet," 15.

41. Ibid., 82.

42. I will here be using "transgender" or "trans" as broadly inclusive terms, differentiating between "transgender" and "transsexual" where that distinction holds. However, as I will argue, part of the power of trans critique is its applicability to interpretive situations that might not be considered "properly" transgender or transsexual.

43. Jay Prosser, *Second Skins: The Body Narratives of Transsexuality*, 58. Prosser offers a thorough push back against what he considers the appropriative uses that queer theory has made of transgender as a figure or trope, a move that allows queer academics to pursue a poststructuralist project of producing the body as a discursive construct rather than as material substance, effectively disembodying, deliteralizing, and fictionalizing trans bodies that Prosser takes to be irreducible. In this chapter, I follow Prosser in turning back to the materiality of the body.

44. Susan Stryker and Stephen Whittle, *The Transgender Studies Reader*, 1.

45. Prosser, 138.

46. Ibid., 150.

47. Ibid., 151.

48. Anna Margarita Albelo, *Hooters! The Making Older, Wiser, Lesbian Cinema*, DVD.

49. Genny Beemyn and Susan Rankin's groundbreaking study *The Lives of Transgender People* (2011) describes not only the "myriad ways that those who transgress choose to gender identify" (27) but also the complex dynamics of how transgender identity relates to sexual orientation (22–35). I want to reiterate Halberstam's point that this relationship must increasingly be thought of as multidirectional, as proliferating transgender identities inform and inflect the sexual identities of people who identify as non-trans.

50. In his article "*Folles*, Swells, Effeminates, and Homophiles in Saint-Germain-des-Prés of the 1950s: A New 'Precious' Society?," Georges Sidéris attributes David's read of *les folles* to Baldwin himself: "Baldwin subscribed here to a 'virile' vision of homosexuality and of human love in general, a vision that might today be qualified as 'hetero-centric.' He could not imagine that the *folles* could be attractive to other men, either heterosexual or homosexual" (221).

51. Leslie Feinberg, *Trans Liberation: Beyond Pink or Blue*, 7.

52. Jacob Hale, "Suggested Rules for Non-Transsexuals Writing about Transsexuals, Transsexuality, Transsexualism, or Trans_____," accessed June 8, 2011.

53. Viviane K. Namaste, *Invisible Lives: The Erasure of Transsexual and Transgendered People*, 13.

54. Ibid., 11.

55. Ibid., 13.

56. Sidéris, 219.

57. Ibid., 220. For an invaluable study of a slightly earlier Paris, see William A. Peniston's *Pederasts and Others: Urban Culture and Sexual Identity in Nineteenth-Century Paris*.

58. Quoted in ibid., 220.

59. Ibid., 220.

60. Ibid., 226.

61. Ibid., 222–27.

62. In his 1983 book *Les Amies de Place Blanche*, Swedish photographer Christer Strömholm alludes to the women with whom he lived and worked in Paris from the late 1950s to the late 1960s as "transsexuals." The term would have been current, for some at least, during that decade. Strömholm, of course, simply called these women "friends."

63. Sidéris, 227.

64. James Campbell, *Exiled in Paris: Richard Wright, James Baldwin, Samuel Beckett, and Others on the Left Bank*, 118.

65. Prosser, 17.

66. Henderson, 315.

67. Ibid., 316.

68. Ibid., 300.

69. See Judith Butler, "Imitation and Gender Insubordination."

70. Henderson, 300.

71. Ibid., 319.

72. Prosser makes the important point that people often read surgical refashioning or "resexing" of the body as removal or "desexing" and thus misconceive of sex reassignment surgery as mutilation or loss.

73. Prosser, 73.

74. Stryker and Whittle, 12.

75. Prosser, 167.

76. Judith Halberstam, *Female Masculinity*, 151.

77. Prosser, 4.

78. Ibid., 7.

79. Of course, framing these questions in the singular for clarity, I have drastically oversimplified them.

80. My point here is that the postreassignment transsexual's body may not simply recover the individual's real body but may also allow that body to align with a previously sensed but disembodied sexual identity.

81. Prosser, 84.

82. Ibid., 85.

83. As George Chauncey notes in *Gay New York*, the invention in the 1960s of the isolating metaphor of the closet, which makes coming out an individual responsibility, also turned gay men away from an understanding of coming out as an initiation *into* the gay world (6–8). One wonders if the de-materialized gay body might be linked to the increasingly individualized gay coming out experience.

84. I want to add here the important qualifications that not all gay people identify as such based on desire, that not all gay people desire bodies, that not all desire stems from or can be reduced to bodily desire, and that not all gay bodies are desiring bodies. My theory of gay embodiment is meant to relate, not confine, gay identity to bodies.

Chapter 3

1. See Marjorie Garber's *Bisexuality and the Eroticism of Everyday Life* for a detailed discussion of the various models and myths of bisexuality that are current in culture.

2. David A. Gerstner, *Queer Pollen: White Seduction, Black Male Homosexuality, and the Cinematic*, 3.

3. James Baldwin, "'Go the Way Your Blood Beats': An Interview with James Baldwin," 178.

4. Throughout "White Fantasies of Desire: Baldwin and the Racial Identities of Sexuality," Marlon Ross persuasively cautions against readings of Baldwin in which race and sexuality are made to displace one another rather than exist in more complex relation. In my reading, sexuality and race are integral to each other, yet I argue they must be treated in their specificity as well.

5. Robert F. Reid-Pharr, *Black Gay Man: Essays*, 96.

6. The precursors Reid-Pharr points to include David R. Roediger, Alexander Saxton, Richard Dyer, Toni Morrison, and Eric Lott.

7. Reid-Pharr, *Black Gay Man*, 88.

8. Ibid., 94.

9. James A. Dievler. "Sexual Exiles: James Baldwin and *Another Country*," 179.

10. For excellent introductions to the liberatory potential of queer theory, see Annamarie Jagose's *Queer Theory: An Introduction*, William Turner's *A Genealogy of Queer Theory*, Nikki Sullivan's *A Critical Introduction to Queer Theory*, Donald Hall's *Queer*

Theories, and the essays collected in *Fear of a Queer Planet*, especially editor Michael Warner's introduction to that volume.

11. Eve Kosofsky Sedgwick, *Between Men: English Literature and Male Homosocial Desire*, ix.

12. Sedgwick, "Queer and Now," 11–12.

13. William Cohen, "Liberalism, Libido, Liberation: Baldwin's *Another Country*," 14.

14. Eldridge Cleaver, *Soul on Ice*, 132.

15. Ross reminds us that while Cleaver's early homophobic position is often taken as representative of Black Power movements' attitudes toward gay people, the picture was actually far more complex (47–48). For example, Huey P. Newton's 1970 essay "The Women's Liberation and Gay Liberation Movements," collected in his *To Die for the People: The Writings of Huey P. Newton*, argues for the necessary linkages among those fighting race, gender, and sexual oppression.

16. Reid-Pharr, *Black Gay Man*, 104.

17. Ibid., 98.

18. Ibid., 97.

19. James Baldwin, *Another Country*, 67. Subsequent page references in this chapter appear parenthetically in the text.

20. Rufus's suicide is modeled after that of Baldwin's early love interest, Eugene Worth, who jumped from the George Washington Bridge in 1946.

21. Mikko Tuhkanen, "Binding the Self: Baldwin, Freud, and the Narrative of Subjectivity," 556.

22. See, for instance, Susan Amper, "Love and Death Reconsidered"; William Cohen; Susan Feldman, "Another Look at *Another Country*"; D. Quentin Miller, *Reviewing James Baldwin: Things Not Seen*; Terry Rowden, "A Play of Abstractions: Race, Sexuality, and Community in James Baldwin's *Another Country*," accessed June 22, 2011.

23. Jeffrey Hole ("Select Bibliography of Works by and on James Baldwin," 394–95) attributes this critical focus to the rise of postmodernism and cultural studies in the mid-1980s, as does Dwight A. McBride (*James Baldwin Now*).

24. See Laura Quinn, "'What Is Going on Here?': Baldwin's *Another Country*."

25. William Cohen, 17.

26. David Leeming, *James Baldwin: A Biography*, 203.

27. Dievler, 179.

28. Leeming, 200.

29. Ibid., 204.

30. For commentary on and critique of the notion of transcendent identity in *Another Country*, see Kevin Ohi, "I'm Not the Boy You Want': Sexuality, 'Race,' and Thwarted Revelation in Baldwin's *Another Country*." See also Michael F. Lynch, "Beyond Guilt and Innocence: Redemptive Suffering and Love in Baldwin's *Another Country*"; Emmanuel Nelson, "Critical Deviance: Homophobia and the Reception of James Baldwin's Fiction." It should be noted that Baldwin's race lesson is learned only through *male* same-sex exploration.

31. While most critics have agreed on the absence of a gay black man in *Another Country*, that LeRoy shares both Ida/Rufus's racial perspective and Eric's revelatory sexuality would seem to situate him as the unexpected gay black figure for which *Another Country* longs.

32. Didier Eribon, *Insult and the Making of the Gay Self*, 59.

33. Ibid., 111, 137.

34. Ibid., 50.

35. Ohi, 274.

36. Ibid., 279.

37. Ibid., 280.

38. Quinn, 58.

39. Ibid., 55.

40. Sara Ahmed, *Queer Phenomenology: Orientations, Objects, Others*, 2.

41. Ibid., 67–68.

42. Ibid., 87.

43. Ibid., 56.

44. Ibid., 38.

45. Ibid., 87.

46. Ibid., 172.

47. Ibid., 92.

48. Ibid., 91.

49. Ibid., 88.

50. Eribon, 9.

51. Dievler, 180–81.

52. Rowden, "A Play of Abstractions."

53. Reid-Pharr, *Black Gay Man*, 17.

54. Dievler, 178.

55. In Paris, Eric falls in love with and rescues the young French prostitute Yves, who recounts how, thanks to Eric, he has come to the realization of his own self-worth: "I have not to be a whore just because I come from whores. I am better than that. . . . I learned that from you" (208). Yet Baldwin did not understand the optimism with which critics read Yves's salvation: "What is going to happen to Yves when he gets [to America]? Something terrible is going to happen to him. Yves comes and he is not prepared. . . . I was bitter. I could not understand how [the critics] could see that as a happy ending. But I am not responsible for my critics if they don't pick up on my messages" (quoted in Tuhkanen, 575). Unlike gay love given to straight white people, gay love between gay men thus contains no emancipatory vision.

56. William Cohen, 7.

57. Dievler, 163.

58. Leo Bersani, *Homos*, 11–12.

59. Quoted in Quinn, 51.

60. Rowden, "A Play of Abstractions."

61. Leeming, 201.

62. Eve Kosofsky Sedgwick, *Epistemology of the Closet*, 32.

63. Leeming, 76.

64. Quoted in Leeming, 74–75.

65. Gerstner, 6.

66. Gerstner, 99.

67. David Kurnick, in *Empty Houses: Theatrical Failure and the Novel*, offers a fascinating reading of the representational obstacles Baldwin faced in *Another Country* and his other novels. Kurnick links the novel form, typically associated with interiority, to Baldwin's theatrical ambitions in order to theorize the yearning toward radical collectivity that marks Baldwin's novels: "Baldwin's vision of collective existence, and that of the novel of interiority more generally, may seem sentimental, doomed to failure by virtue of its abstraction from the details of social and political struggle. But the failure, and that provocation, are those of the literary itself" (206).

Chapter 4

1. James Baldwin, *The Price of the Ticket*, xiv.

2. Marlon B. Ross, "White Fantasies of Desire: Baldwin and the Racial Identities of Sexuality," 25.

3. Hortense Spillers, "Mama's Baby, Papa's Maybe: An American Grammar Book," 80.

4. Ibid., 76.

5. Robert F. Reid-Pharr, *Black Gay Man: Essays*, 12.

6. Spillers, 73.

7. I find it fascinating that, at every stage of this project, readers have questioned the correctness of my use of "papas' baby." In fact, the logic of the possessive form of the plural noun, "papas," is quite clear and unambiguous: the baby belongs to the papas. The confusion points back, obviously enough, to a tacit connection between parenthood and biological reproduction, such that it doesn't quite yet make sense to think of a two-papa parentage. The grammar betrays a breach: the clarity of the rules of possession is pierced by a failure of the queer imagination.

8. As a practical measure and unless otherwise noted, I will use the title of the entire collection, *Going to Meet the Man*, to reference the three stories exclusively under consideration here.

9. "The Rockpile" was probably written in the late 1940s but was unpublished prior to the 1965 collection.

10. Baldwin, *Going to Meet the Man*, 16–17. Subsequent page references in this chapter appear parenthetically in the text.

11. Spillers, 67.

12. Sigmund Freud, *Three Contributions to the Theory of Sex*, 29.

13. Yasmin Y. Degout, "Masculinity and (Im)maturity: 'The Man Child' and Other Stories in Baldwin's Gender Studies Enterprise," 149.

14. Ibid., 137.

15. Ibid., 138.

16. Freud, "On the Universal Tendency to Debasement in the Sphere of Love," 179.

17. Ibid., 179.

18. Lee Edelman, *Homographesis: Essays on Gay and Literary Cultural Theory*, 65.

19. Winthrop D. Jordan, *The White Man's Burden: Historical Origins of Racism in the United States*, 82.

20. Ibid., 80.

21. Baldwin, "The Black Boy Looks at the White Boy," 290.

22. Trudier Harris, *Exorcising Blackness: Historical and Literary Lynching and Burning Rituals*, 20.

23. Steven Weisenberger, "The Shudder and the Silence: James Baldwin on White Terror," 12.

24. Eve Kosofsky Sedgwick, *Between Men: English Literature and Male Homosocial Desire*, 25.

25. William F. Pinar, *The Gender of Racial Politics and Violence in America: Lynching, Prison Rape, and the Crisis of Masculinity*, 8.

26. Gary Taylor, *Castration: An Abbreviated History of Western Manhood*, 52.

27. Ibid., 33.

28. Ibid., 38.

29. Joel Williamson, *New People: Miscegenation and Mulattoes in the United States*, 112.

30. Robyn Wiegman, *American Anatomies: Theorizing Race and Gender*, 12.

31. Ibid., 14.

32. Susan Gubar, *Racechanges: White Skin, Black Face in American Culture*, 175.

33. Pinar, 11.

34. Gubar, 180.

35. Charles Johnson, "The Vanishing Mulatto," 291.

36. Frederick L. Gwynn and Joseph Blotner, *Faulkner in the University*, 118.

37. Williamson, 2.

38. John Brenkman, *Straight Male Modern: A Cultural Critique of Psychoanalysis*, 22.

39. Ross, 14.

Conclusion

1. Hebrews 11:1, http://www.kingjamesbibleonline.org/book.php?book=Hebrews&chapter=11&verse=1.

2. James Baldwin, *The Evidence of Things Not Seen*, 22.

3. James Baldwin, "The Discovery of What It Means to Be an American," 175.

4. Ibid., 176.

5. In arguing for the sustained, paradoxical presence of queer successes and failures, I diverge from Judith Halberstam's reconceptualization of failure as a "queer art" that "embrace[s] a truly political negativity" (*The Queer Art of Failure*, 110). While I agree that failure can be its own kind of success, I do wonder whether queer theory, when it cedes success to total, unadulterated failure—effectively making a success of failure—misses the opportunity to theorize the perplexing simultaneities of failure and success.

6. Lear, *Freud*, 4.

7. Ibid., 5.

8. Trudier Harris, *Black Women in the Fiction of James Baldwin*, 5.

9. Ibid., 206.

10. Ibid., 9.

11. Ibid., 10, 11.

12. Ibid., 207. Ultimately, Harris suggests that Baldwin moves toward a resolution between male and female characters to the extent that he privileges "the extended family, the communal family" over the "repressive nuclear family" (211). It is in Baldwin's larger "familial" context that Harris believes "one kind of black woman" in Baldwin's fiction "has escaped from the limitations of . . . [the black man's] desire for mastery over black women" (211).

13. Ibid., 209.

14. David Ikard, *Breaking the Silence: Toward a Black Male Feminist Criticism*, 13.

15. Ibid., 49.

16. Ibid., 53.

17. Ibid., 50.

18. Harris notes this same erasure: "As lovers, Baldwin's women are always engaged in heterosexual affairs; lesbianism as a concept does not surface in his books. In their roles as lovers, therefore, the women are to be evaluated on the basis of how well they complement, satisfy, and work toward the happiness of the men in their lives—or, in the case of the fanatical lovers of the (masculine) Lord, the extent to which they are committed to Him" (8).

19. Ibid., 205–6.

20. Ibid., 189.

21. James Baldwin and Audre Lorde, "Audre Lorde and James Baldwin: Revolutionary Hope." Baldwin and Lorde met for their discussion at the invitation of *Essence* and thanks to the work of Gloria Joseph and Skip Stackhouse.

22. Ibid., 73.

23. Ibid., 133.

24. Ibid., 130.

25. Ibid., 133.

26. Ibid., 74

27. Ibid., 130.

28. Dwight A. McBride. "Can the Queen Speak? Racial Essentialism, Sexuality, and the Problem of Authority," 29.

29. Ibid., 27.

30. Ibid., 37.

31. The Baldwin-Lorde dialogue of 1984 replays, to a great extent, Lorde's exchange with Robert Staples in *The Black Scholar* in 1979. The Staples essay to which Lorde responded was titled "The Myth of Black Macho: A Response to Angry Black Feminists." Lorde's original response was republished in 1984 under its more recognizable title, "Sexism: An American Disease in Blackface," in Lorde's *Sister Outsider: Essays and Speeches*. It seems unlikely that Baldwin had read the exchange or remembered its details, as his arguments mirror those that were made by Staples and that were so effectively undercut by Lorde in the earlier interaction.

32. James Baldwin and Nikki Giovanni, *James Baldwin/Nikki Giovanni: A Dialogue*, 39–40.

33. Ibid., 43.

34. Ibid., 55.

35. Ibid., 45.

36. Ibid., 55.

37. Later in the dialogue, in a discussion about her father, Giovanni once more positions herself outside the ideals of heteronormativity. "Jones Giovanni," she says, "is a groovy cat, and he's lived with my mother for thirty-five years in holy wedlock. I think that's good for them. . . . I think he's a gas. I just don't want to marry him" (68–69).

38. Ibid., 55.

39. Ibid., 43–44.

40. Ibid., 44.

41. Ibid., 56–57.

42. Ibid., 57.

43. I thank Sarah Schulman for introducing me to this phrase.

44. Lorraine Hansberry, "Letter to the Editor" (May 1957), 26.

45. Ibid., 27.

46. Lorraine Hansberry, "Letter to the Editor" (August 1957), 30.

47. Lisbeth Lipari also makes this connection, in "The Rhetoric of Intersectionality: Lorraine Hansberry's 1957 Letters to the *Ladder*."

48. James Baldwin, "Lorraine Hansberry at the Summit," 112–13.

49. Ibid., 111.

50. I borrow this phrase from Lipari.

51. Lipari suggests that Hansberry's critique, because it stops short of this further analysis, "raise[s] questions both about Hansberry's experiences with gay and lesbian communities of color as well as her imagined audiences of the *Ladder* and *One*" (240).

52. In choosing to "escape" to St. Paul en Vence, an ancient medieval commune on the

French Riviera, Baldwin also undoubtedly bolstered his social and professional status, as the town was well known as a haven for world-famous artists and celebrities.

53. See D. Quentin Miller's "James Baldwin's Critical Reception."

54. Baldwin, *The Fire Next Time*, 341.

55. Esther Newton, *Margaret Mead Made Me Gay*, 2.

56. Stanley Diamond, "Tape's Last Krapp," accessed July 23, 2013.

57. James Baldwin and Margaret Mead, *A Rap on Race*, 220.

58. Ibid., 237.

59. Ibid., 238.

60. Bersani, 71.

61. Baldwin, "The Black Boy Looks at the White Boy," 290.

Bibliography

Ahmed, Sara. *Queer Phenomenology: Orientations, Objects, Others.* Durham, NC: Duke University Press, 2006.

Albelo, Anna Margarita, dir. *Hooters! The Making of Older, Wiser, Lesbian Cinema.* Parliament Film Collective, 2010. DVD.

Als, Hilton. "The Enemy Within: The Making and Unmaking of James Baldwin." *New Yorker,* February 16, 1998, 72–80.

Amper, Susan. "Love and Death Reconsidered: The Union of Lovers in *Another Country.*" *JAISA* 1 (1995): 103–11.

Baldwin, James. *Another Country.* 1962. New York: Vintage, 1993.

Baldwin, James. "The Art of Fiction LXXVIII: James Baldwin." Interview by Jordan Elgrably and George Plimpton. In *Conversations with James Baldwin,* 232–54.

Baldwin, James. "The Black Boy Looks at the White Boy." 1961. In *The Price of the Ticket,* 289–303.

Baldwin, James. *Conversations with James Baldwin.* Edited by Fred L. Standley and Louis H. Pratt. Jackson: University Press of Mississippi, 1989.

Baldwin, James. *The Devil Finds Work.* 1976. In *The Price of the Ticket,* 557–636.

Baldwin, James. "The Discovery of What It Means to Be an American." 1959. In *The Price of the Ticket,* 171–76.

Baldwin, James. "Disturber of the Peace: James Baldwin—An Interview." Interview by Eve Auchincloss and Nancy Lynch. In *Conversations with James Baldwin,* 64–82.

Baldwin, James. "Everybody's Protest Novel." 1949. In *The Price of the Ticket,* 27–33.

Baldwin, James. "Every Good-Bye Ain't Gone." 1977. In *The Price of the Ticket*, 641–46.

Baldwin, James. *The Evidence of Things Not Seen*. Cutchogue, NY: Buccaneer Books, 1985.

Baldwin, James. *The Fire Next Time*. 1963. In *The Price of the Ticket*, 333–79.

Baldwin, James. *Giovanni's Room*. 1956. New York: Delta, 2000.

Baldwin, James. *Going to Meet the Man*. 1965. New York: Dell, 1966.

Baldwin, James. *Go Tell It on the Mountain*. New York: Knopf, 1953.

Baldwin, James. "'Go the Way Your Blood Beats': An Interview with James Baldwin." Interview by Richard Goldstein. 1984. In *James Baldwin: The Legacy*, edited by Quincy Troupe, 173–85. New York: Simon and Schuster, 1989.

Baldwin, James. "Here Be Dragons." 1985. In *The Price of the Ticket*, 677–90.

Baldwin, James. "An Interview with James Baldwin." Interview by Studs Terkel. In *Conversations with James Baldwin*, 2–23.

Baldwin, James. "Is *A Raisin in the Sun* a Lemon in the Dark?" In *The Cross of Redemption: Uncollected Writings*, edited by Randall Kenan, 24–27. New York: Pantheon Books, 2010.

Baldwin, James. "James Baldwin Comes Home." Interview by Jewell Handy Gresham. In *Conversations with James Baldwin*, 159–67.

Baldwin, James. "James Baldwin—Reflections of a Maverick." Interview by Julius Lester. In *Conversations with James Baldwin*, 222–31.

Baldwin, James. "Lorraine Hansberry at the Summit." In *The Cross of Redemption: Uncollected Writings*, edited by Randall Kenan, 109–13. New York: Pantheon Books, 2010.

Baldwin, James. "The Male Prison." 1954. In *The Price of the Ticket*, 101–5.

Baldwin, James. "Preservation of Innocence." 1949. Reprinted with a foreword by Melvin Dixon. *Outlook* 2, no. 3 (1989): 38–45.

Baldwin, James. *The Price of the Ticket: Collected Nonfiction, 1948–1985*. New York: St. Martin's, 1985.

Baldwin, James. "Race, Hate, Sex, and Colour: A Conversation with James Baldwin and Colin MacInnes." Interview by James Mossman. In *Conversations with James Baldwin*, 46–58.

Baldwin, James. "White Man's Guilt." 1965. In *The Price of the Ticket*, 409–14.

Baldwin, James, and Nikki Giovanni. *James Baldwin/Nikki Giovanni: A Dialogue*. Philadelphia: J. B. Lippincott, 1973.

Baldwin, James, and Audre Lorde. "Audre Lorde and James Baldwin: Revolutionary Hope." *Essence* 15 (December 1984): 72–74, 129–33.

Baldwin, James, and Margaret Mead. *A Rap on Race*. Philadelphia: J. B. Lippincott, 1971.

Beam, Joseph, ed. *In the Life: A Black Gay Anthology*. Boston: Alyson Publications, 1986.

Beam, Joseph. "James Baldwin: Not a Bad Legacy, Brother." In *Brother to Brother: New Writings by Black Gay Men*, edited by Essex Hemphill, 229–31. Washington, DC: RedBone, 2007.

Beam, Joseph. "Making Ourselves from Scratch." In *Brother to Brother: New Writings by Black Gay Men*, edited by Essex Hemphill, 335–36. Washington, DC: RedBone, 2007.

Beemyn, Genny, and Susan Rankin. *The Lives of Transgender People*. New York: Columbia University Press, 2011.

Bersani, Leo. *Homos*. Cambridge, MA: Harvard University Press, 1995.

Boyd, Herb. *Baldwin's Harlem*. New York: Atria Books, 2008.

Bravmann, Scott. *Queer Fictions of the Past: History, Culture, and Difference*. Cambridge: Cambridge University Press, 1997.

Brenkman, John. *Straight Male Modern: A Cultural Critique of Psychoanalysis*. New York: Routledge, 1993.

Butler, Judith. *Bodies That Matter: On the Discursive Limits of "Sex."* New York: Routledge, 1993.

Butler, Judith. "Imitation and Gender Insubordination." In *Inside/Out: Lesbian Theories, Gay Theories*, edited by Diana Fuss, 13–31. New York: Routledge, 1991.

Campbell, James. *Exiled in Paris: Richard Wright, James Baldwin, Samuel Beckett, and Others on the Left Bank*. Berkeley: University of California Press, 2003.

Chancy, Myriam J. A. "Brother/Outsider: In Search of a Black Gay Legacy in James Baldwin's *Giovanni's Room*." In *The Gay '90s: Disciplinary and Interdisciplinary Formations in Queer Studies*, edited by Thomas Foster, Carol Siegel, and Ellen E. Berry, 155–90. New York: NYU Press, 1997.

Chauncey, George. *Gay New York: Gender, Urban Culture, and the Making of the Gay Male World*. New York: Basic Books, 1994.

Christian, Barbara. "The Race for Theory." *Feminist Studies* 14, no. 1 (Spring 1988): 67–79.

Cleaver, Eldridge. *Soul on Ice*. 1968. New York: Delta, 1999.

Cohen, Cathy. "Punks, Bulldaggers, and Welfare Queens: The Radical Potential of Queer Politics?" In *GLQ: A Journal of Lesbian and Gay Studies* 3 (1997): 437–65.

Cohen, William A. "Liberalism, Libido, Liberation: Baldwin's *Another Country.*" *Genders* 12 (1991): 1–21.

Corber, Robert. "Everybody Knew His Name: Reassessing James Baldwin." *Contemporary Literature* 42, no. 1 (Spring 2001): 166–75.

Degout, Yasmin Y. "Masculinity and (Im)maturity: 'The Man Child' and Other Stories in Baldwin's Gender Studies Enterprise." In *Reviewing James Baldwin: Things Not Seen*, edited by D. Quentin Miller, 128–53. Philadelphia: Temple University Press, 2000.

Delany, Samuel R. "The Possibility of Possibilities." Interview by Joseph Beam. In *In the Life: A Black Gay Anthology*, edited by Joseph Beam, 185–208. Boston: Alyson Publications, 1986.

Derrida, Jacques. *Aporias*. Stanford: Stanford University Press, 1993.

Diamond, Stanley. "Tape's Last Krapp." *New York Review of Books*, December 2, 1971. Accessed July 23, 2013. http://www.nybooks.com.ezproxy.gc.cuny.edu/articles/archives/1971/dec/02/tapes-last-krapp/.

Dievler, James A. "Sexual Exiles: James Baldwin and *Another Country.*" In *James Baldwin Now*, edited by Dwight A. McBride, 161–83. New York: New York University Press, 1999.

Dollimore, Jonathan. *Sexual Dissidence: Augustine to Wilde, Freud to Foucault*. Oxford: Oxford University Press, 1991.

Dyer, Richard. "White." *Screen* 29, no. 4 (1988): 44–64.

Edelman, Lee. *Homographesis: Essays in Gay and Literary Cultural Theory*. New York: Routledge, 1994.

Edelman, Lee. *No Future: Queer Theory and the Death Drive*. Durham, NC: Duke University Press, 2004.

Eribon, Didier. *Insult and the Making of the Gay Self*. Durham, NC: Duke University Press, 2004.

Feinberg, Leslie. *Trans Liberation: Beyond Pink or Blue*. Boston: Beacon, 1999.

Feldman, Susan. "Another Look at *Another Country*: Reconciling Baldwin's Racial and Sexual Politics." In *Re-viewing James Baldwin: Things Not Seen*, edited by D. Quentin Miller, 88–104. Philadelphia: Temple University Press, 2000.

Ferguson, Roderick. "The Nightmares of the Heteronormative." *Cultural Values* 4 (2000): 419–44.

Fiedler, Leslie. *Love and Death in the American Novel*. 1960. Reprint, Norman, IL: Dalkey Archive Press, 1997.

Field, Douglas. "James Baldwin in His Time." In *Critical Insights: James Baldwin*, edited by Morris Dickstein, 23–38. Pasadena, CA: Salem, 2011.

Freud, Sigmund. "On the Universal Tendency to Debasement in the Sphere of Love." 1912. In *The Standard Edition of the Complete Psychological Works*, edited and translated by James Strachey, 11:179–90. London: Hogarth, 1961.

Freud, Sigmund. *Three Contributions to the Theory of Sex*. Translated by A. A. Brill. 4th ed. 1930. Reprint, New York: Johnson Reprint Corporation, 1970.

Fullwood, Steven G., Reginald Harris, and Lisa C. Moore, eds., *Carry the Word: A Bibliography of Black LGBTQ Books*. Washington, DC: Red-Bone, 2007.

Garber, Marjorie. *Bisexuality and the Eroticism of Everyday Life*. New York: Routledge, 2000.

Gerstner, David A. *Queer Pollen: White Seduction, Black Male Homosexuality, and the Cinematic*. Urbana: University of Illinois Press, 2011.

Ghaziani, Amin. "Post-Gay Collective Identity Construction." *Social Problems* 58, no. 1 (2011): 99–125.

Ghaziani, Amin, and Matt Brim. "'The Problems with 'Post-Gay.'" *Sexual Behavior, Politics, and Communities Division Newsletter of the Society for the Study of Social Problems*, Fall 2011, 2–3, 8–9.

Glave, Thomas. *Words to Our Now: Imagination and Dissent*. Minneapolis: University of Minnesota Press, 2005.

Gubar, Susan. *Racechanges: White Skin, Black Face in American Culture*. New York: Oxford University Press, 1997.

Gwynn, Frederick L., and Joseph Blotner, eds. *Faulkner in the University*. New York: Random House, 1959.

Halberstam, Judith. *Female Masculinity*. Durham, NC: Duke University Press, 1998.

Halberstam, Judith. *In a Queer Time and Place: Transgender Bodies, Subcultural Lives*. New York: New York University Press, 2005.

Halberstam, Judith. *The Queer Art of Failure*. Durham, NC: Duke University Press, 2011.

Hale, Jacob. "Suggested Rules for Non-Transsexuals Writing about Transsexuals, Transsexuality, Transsexualism, or Trans____." Accessed June 8, 2011. http://sandystone.com/hale.rules.html.

Hall, Donald. *Queer Theories*. New York: Palgrave Macmillan, 2003.

Hall, Donald. *Reading Sexualities: Hermeneutic Theory and the Future of Queer Studies.* London: Routledge, 2009.

Hall, Donald E., and Annamarie Jagose. *The Routledge Queer Studies Reader.* London: Routledge, 2013.

Hall, Richard. *Fidelities.* New York: Viking, 1992.

Hanisch, Carol. "The Personal Is the Political." 1970. Accessed July 21, 2013. http://carolhanisch.org/CHwritings/PIP.html.

Hansberry, Lorraine. "Letter to the Editor." *Ladder* 1, no. 8 (May 1957): 26–28.

Hansberry, Lorraine. "Letter to the Editor." *Ladder* 1, no. 11 (August 1957): 26–30.

Harris, Trudier. *Black Women in the Fiction of James Baldwin.* Knoxville: University of Tennessee Press, 1985.

Harris, Trudier. *Exorcising Blackness: Historical and Literary Lynching and Burning Rituals.* Bloomington: Indiana University Press, 1984.

Hemphill, Essex, ed. *Brother to Brother: New Writings by Black Gay Men.* 1991. Washington, DC: RedBone, 2007.

Henderson, Mae G. "James Baldwin's *Giovanni's Room*: Expatriation, 'Racial Drag,' and Homosexual Panic." In *Black Queer Studies: A Critical Anthology,* edited by E. Patrick Johnson and Mae G. Henderson, 298–322. Durham, NC: Duke University Press, 2005.

Hole, Jeffrey. "Select Bibliography of Works by and on James Baldwin." In *James Baldwin Now,* edited by Dwight A. McBride, 393–409. New York: New York University Press, 1999.

Holland, Sharon Patricia. *Raising the Dead: Readings of Death and (Black) Subjectivity.* Durham, NC: Duke University Press, 2000.

Ikard, David. *Breaking the Silence: Toward a Black Male Feminist Criticism.* Baton Rouge: Louisiana State University Press, 2007.

Jagose, Annamarie. *Queer Theory: An Introduction.* New York: New York University Press, 1997.

Johnson, Charles. "The Vanishing Mulatto." *Opportunity* 3 (1925): 291.

Johnson, E. Patrick. "'Quare' Studies, or (Almost) Everything I Know about Queer Studies I Learned from My Grandmother." In *Black Queer Studies: A Critical Anthology,* edited by E. Patrick Johnson and Mae G. Henderson, 124–57. Durham, NC: Duke University Press, 2005.

Johnson, E. Patrick, and Mae G. Henderson, eds. *Black Queer Studies: A Critical Anthology.* Durham, NC: Duke University Press, 2005.

Jordan, June. "*If Beale Street Could Talk.*" *Village Voice*, June 20, 1974, 33–35.

Jordan, Winthrop D. *The White Man's Burden: Historical Origins of Racism in the United States*. New York: Oxford University Press, 1974.

Keene, John. "This Week, Pt1: Als on Baldwin + Reading @ Temple." October 29, 2007. Accessed August 10, 2011. http://jstheater.blogspot.com/2007/10/this-week-pt1-als-on-baldwin-reading.html.

Kenan, Randall, ed. *A Visitation of Spirits*. New York: Grove, 1989.

Kurnick, David. *Empty Houses: Theatrical Failure and the Novel*. Princeton: Princeton University Press, 2012.

Lawrence, D. H. *Studies in Classic American Literature*. 1923. New York: Viking, 1964.

Lear, Jonathan. *Freud*. New York: Routledge, 2005.

Leeming, David. *James Baldwin: A Biography*. New York: Knopf, 1994.

Leverenz, David. *Manhood and the American Renaissance*. Ithaca, NY: Cornell University Press, 1989.

Lipari, Lisbeth. "The Rhetoric of Intersectionality: Lorraine Hansberry's 1957 Letters to the *Ladder.*" In *Queering Public Address: Sexualities in American Historical Discourse*, edited by Charles E. Morris III, 220–48. Columbia: University of South Carolina Press, 2007.

Lorde, Audre. *Sister Outsider: Essays and Speeches*. Berkeley: Crossing Press, 2007.

Lott, Eric. *Love and Theft: Blackface Minstrelsy and the American Working Class*. New York: Oxford University Press, 1993.

Love, Heather. *Feeling Backward: Loss and the Politics of Queer History*. Cambridge, MA: Harvard University Press, 2007.

Lynch, Michael F. "Beyond Guilt and Innocence: Redemptive Suffering and Love in Baldwin's *Another Country.*" *Obsidian II: Black Literature in Review* 7, nos. 1–2 (1992): 1–18.

Mailer, Norman. *The White Negro*. San Francisco: City Lights Books, 1957.

McBride, Dwight A. "Can the Queen Speak? Racial Essentialism, Sexuality, and the Problem of Authority." In *The Greatest Taboo: Homosexuality in Black Communities*, edited by Delroy Constantine-Simms, 24–43. Los Angeles: Alyson Books, 2000.

McBride, Dwight A., ed. *James Baldwin Now*. New York: New York University Press, 1999.

McBride, Dwight A. "Straight Black Studies: On African American Studies, James Baldwin, and Black Queer Studies." In *Black Queer Studies: A Critical Anthology*, edited by E. Patrick Johnson and Mae G. Henderson, 68–89. Durham, NC: Duke University Press, 2005.

Miller, D. Quentin, ed. "James Baldwin's Critical Reception." In *Critical Insights: James Baldwin*, edited by Morris Dickstein, 95–109. Pasadena, CA: Salem, 2011.

Miller, D. Quentin, ed. *Re-viewing James Baldwin: Things Not Seen*. Philadelphia: Temple University Press, 2000.

Morrison, Toni. *Playing in the Dark: Whiteness and the Literary Imagination*. Cambridge, MA: Harvard University Press, 1992.

Muñoz, José Esteban. *Cruising Utopia: The Then and There of Queer Futurity*. New York: New York University Press, 2009.

Namaste, Viviane K. *Invisible Lives: The Erasure of Transsexual and Transgendered People*. Chicago: University of Chicago Press, 2000.

Nealon, Christopher. "Queer Tradition." *GLQ: A Journal of Lesbian and Gay Studies* 14, no. 4 (2008): 617–22.

Nelson, Emmanuel. "Critical Deviance: Homophobia and the Reception of James Baldwin's Fiction." *Journal of American Culture* 14, no. 3 (1991): 91–96.

Nelson, Emmanuel. "James Baldwin." In *GLBTQ: An Encyclopedia of Gay, Lesbian, Bisexual, Transgender, and Queer Culture*, edited by Claude J. Summers. Accessed August 8, 2011. http://www.glbtq.com/literature/african_am_lit_gay,2.html.

Newton, Esther. *Margaret Mead Made Me Gay: Personal Essays, Public Ideas*. Durham, NC: Duke University Press, 2000.

Newton, Huey P. *To Die for the People: The Writings of Huey P. Newton*. Edited by Toni Morrison. New York: Writers and Readers Publishing, 1995.

Nugent, Richard Bruce. "Smoke, Lilies, and Jade." *FIRE!!* 1, no. 1 (1926): 33–39.

Ohi, Kevin. "'I'm Not the Boy You Want': Sexuality, 'Race,' and Thwarted Revelation in Baldwin's *Another Country*." *African American Review* 33 (1999): 261–81.

Peniston, William A. *Pederasts and Others: Urban Culture and Sexual Identity in Nineteenth-Century Paris*. New York: Harrington Park, 2004.

Pinar, William F. *The Gender of Racial Politics and Violence in America: Lynching, Prison Rape, and the Crisis of Masculinity*. New York: Peter Lang, 2001.

Pinckney, Darryl. "James Baldwin: The Risks of Love." In *Critical Insights: James Baldwin*, edited by Morris Dickstein, 400–429. Pasadena, CA: Salem, 2011.

Piontek, Thomas. *Queering Gay and Lesbian Studies*. Urbana: University of Illinois Press, 2006.

Prosser, Jay. *Second Skins: The Body Narratives of Transsexuality*. New York: Columbia University Press, 1998.

Puar, Jasbir K. "Queer Times, Queer Assemblages." In *The Routledge Queer Studies Reader*, edited by Donald E. Hall and Annamarie Jagose, 515–28. London: Routledge, 2013.

Quinn, Laura. "'What Is Going on Here?': Baldwin's *Another Country*." *Journal of Homosexuality* 34 (1998): 51–65.

Reid-Pharr, Robert F. *Black Gay Man: Essays*. New York: New York University Press, 2001.

Reid-Pharr, Robert F. *Once You Go Black: Desire, Choice, and Black Masculinity in Post-War America*. New York: New York University Press, 2007.

Robinson, Colin, Cary Alan Johnson, and Terence Taylor, eds. *Other Countries: Black Gay Voices*. New York: Other Countries, 1988.

Roediger, David R. *The Wages of Whiteness: Race and the Making of the American Working Class*. New York: Verso, 1991.

Ross, Marlon B. "White Fantasies of Desire: Baldwin and the Racial Identities of Sexuality." In *James Baldwin Now*, edited by Dwight A. McBride, 13–55. New York: New York University Press, 1999.

Rowden, Terry. "A Play of Abstractions: Race, Sexuality, and Community in James Baldwin's *Another Country*." *Southern Review* 29 (1993): 41–50. Academic Search Complete, EBSCOhost (accessed June 22, 2011). http://ebscohost.com/.

Rustin, Bayard. "An Interview with Bayard Rustin." Interview by Redvers Jeanmarie. In *Other Countries: Black Gay Voices*, edited by Colin Robinson, Cary Alan Johnson, and Terence Taylor, 3–16. New York: Other Countries, 1988.

Saxton, Alexander. *The Rise and Fall of the White Republic: Class Politics and Mass Culture in Nineteenth-Century America*. New York: Verso, 1990.

Schulman, Sarah. "The Lady Hamlet." Unpublished manuscript, April 9, 2008. Microsoft Word file.

Schwarz, A. B. Christa. *Gay Voices of the Harlem Renaissance*. Bloomington: Indiana University Press, 2003.

Sedgwick, Eve Kosofsky. *Between Men: English Literature and Male Homosocial Desire*. New York: Columbia University Press, 1985.

Sedgwick, Eve Kosofsky. *Epistemology of the Closet*. Berkeley: University of California Press, 1990.

Sedgwick, Eve Kosofsky. "Queer and Now." In *The Routledge Queer Studies Reader*, edited by Donald E. Hall and Annamarie Jagose, 3–17. London: Routledge, 2013.

Seidman, Steven. *Difference Troubles: Queering Social Theory and Sexual Politics*. Cambridge: Cambridge University Press, 1997.

Sidéris, Georges. "*Folles*, Swells, Effeminates, and Homophiles in Saint-Germain-des-Prés of the 1950s: A New 'Precious' Society?" In *Homosexuality in French History and Culture*, edited by Jeffrey Merrick and Michael Sibalis, 219–31. New York: Harrington Park Press, 2001.

Silverman, Kaja. *Male Subjectivity at the Margins*. New York: Routledge, 1992.

Spillers, Hortense. "Mama's Baby, Papa's Maybe: An American Grammar Book." *diacritics* 17 (1987): 65–81.

Stockton, Kathryn Bond. *Beautiful Bottom, Beautiful Shame: Where "Black" Meets "Queer."* Durham, NC: Duke University Press, 2006.

Strömholm, Christer. *Les Amies de Place Blanche*. 1983. Stockport: Dewi Lewis Publishing, 2012.

Stryker, Susan, and Stephen Whittle, eds. *The Transgender Studies Reader*. New York: Routledge, 2006.

Sullivan, Nikki. *A Critical Introduction to Queer Theory*. New York: New York University Press, 2003.

Sylvander, Carolyn Wedin. *James Baldwin*. New York: Frederick Ungar, 1980.

Take This Hammer. Dir. Richard O. Moore. Feat. James Baldwin. National Education Television. KQED, San Francisco, 4 Feb. 1964.

Taylor, Gary. *Castration: An Abbreviated History of Western Manhood*. New York: Routledge, 2000.

Traub, Valerie. "The New Unhistoricism in Queer Studies." *PMLA* 128, no. 1 (2013): 21–39.

Troupe, Quincy, ed. *James Baldwin: The Legacy*. New York: Simon and Schuster, 1989.

Tuhkanen, Mikko. "Binding the Self: Baldwin, Freud, and the Narrative of Subjectivity." *GLQ: A Journal of Lesbian and Gay Studies* 7:4 (2001): 553–91.

Turner, William B. *A Genealogy of Queer Theory*. Philadelphia: Temple University Press, 2000.

Warner, Michael. *Fear of a Queer Planet: Queer Politics and Social Theory*. Minneapolis: University of Minnesota Press, 1993.

Warner, Michael. "Homo-Narcissism; or, Heterosexuality." In *Engendering Men: The Question of Male Feminist Criticism*, edited by Joseph A. Boone and Michael Cadden, 190–206. New York: Routledge, 1990.

Warner, Michael. "Queer and Then? The End of Queer Theory?" *Chronicle of Higher Education*, January 1, 2012. Accessed July 21, 2013. http://chronicle.com/article/QueerThen-/130161.

Washington, Bryan. "Wrestling with 'The Love That Dare Not Speak Its Name': John, Elisha, and the 'Master.'" In *New Essays on "Go Tell It on the Mountain,"* edited by Trudier Harris, 77–95. Cambridge: Cambridge University Press, 1996.

Weisenberger, Steven. "The Shudder and the Silence: James Baldwin on White Terror." *ANQ* 16 (2003): 3–12.

Wiegman, Robyn. *American Anatomies: Theorizing Race and Gender*. Durham, NC: Duke University Press, 1995.

Wiegman, Robyn. "Interchanges: Heteronormativity and the Desire for Gender." *Feminist Theory* 7, no. 1 (2006): 89–103.

Wiegman, Robyn, ed. "Introduction: On Location." In *Women's Studies on Its Own*, 1–45. Durham, NC: Duke University Press, 2002.

Wiegman, Robyn. *Object Lessons*. Durham, NC: Duke University Press, 2012.

Wiegman, Robyn. "Queering the Academy." In *The Gay '90s: Disciplinary and Interdisciplinary Formations in Queer Studies*, edited by Thomas Foster, Carol Siegel, and Ellen E. Berry, 3–22. New York: New York University Press, 1997.

Wiegman, Robyn. "Un-remembering Monique Wittig." *GLQ: A Journal of Lesbian and Gay Studies* 13, no. 4 (2007): 505–18.

Williamson, Joel. *New People: Miscegenation and Mulattoes in the United States*. Baton Rouge: Louisiana State University Press, 1995.

Wirth, Thomas H., ed. *Gay Rebel of the Harlem Renaissance: Selection from the Work of Richard Bruce Nugent*. Durham, NC: Duke University Press, 2002.

Wittig, Monique. *"The Straight Mind" and Other Essays*. Boston: Beacon, 1992.

Zaborowska, Magdalena. *James Baldwin's Turkish Decade: Erotics of Exile*. Durham, NC: Duke University Press, 2009.

Index

African American literature: black gay
male literature and, 24–28; tradition of,
24–27
Ahmed, Sara, 111–15. See also *Queer Phenomenology*
AIDS, 29–30, 32, 38, 73, 95–96
Als, Hilton, 11–12
Anderson, Marian, 41
Another Country (Baldwin): 8, 71–72; assimilationist project of, 118; erasure of black gay
man in, 94, 96, 106, 119–21; gay sex and gay
love in, 93, 96, 100–101, 103–5, 106–11, 115–
18; heteronormativity in, 96, 110–11; homophobia in, 104–5, 117; interracial desire
in, 93, 105–8; intersectionality in, 93–95,
99–105; love in, 98–100; privilege in, 101,
103–5, 114–17, 122; prostitution in, 102–3,
104–5; white liberalism in, 98–105, 115
Armstrong, Louis, 41

Baldwin, James: African American literature
and, 24–27; on androgyny, 11; anthologized, 178n13; black gay male literature and,
1, 9–10, 25–33, 36, 39–42; critical reception
of, 23–24; critics' relation to, 1–2, 15–16, 26;
disciplinarity and, 1, 10–12, 21–22; erotic
vision of, 174–75; as exile, 172; language
and, 12–15, 37–38, 42–43, 45; lesbians
and, 8, 71, 155–75; as protector of women,
160–63, 170–72; queer theory and, 1–2, 18,
97–98; as queer touchstone, 1; queer utility
of, 7, 26–27, 36–39; seeing the invisible, 7,

8, 152–53; on sexual identity, 37–39, 72–73;
universalizing poetic of, 97; as witness, 8,
36, 38
Baldwin's Harlem (Boyd), 39
Baraka, Amiri, 157
Beam, Joseph, 29–32, 36, 38, 40, 42, 156
*Beautiful Bottom, Beautiful Shame: Where
"Black" Meets "Queer"* (Stockton), 18,
183n15
Beemyn, Genny, 184n49
Benedict, Ruth, 172
Bersani, Leo, 118, 174
*Between Men: English Literature and Male
Homosocial Desire* (Sedgwick), 95, 139
binaries: gay/lesbian, 172; hetero/homo, 60,
71, 92–93; interracial masculinities, 145–
46; irreducibility of, 6; man/woman, 79;
queer theory's reliance on, 4–5; self/other
in *Giovanni's Room*, 65–67
bisexuality, 92–93, 159
Bisexuality and the Eroticism of Everyday Life
(Garber), 186n1
"Black Boy Looks at the White Boy, The"
(Baldwin), 12
"Black Feminist Statement" (Combahee River
Collective), 168
Black Gay and Lesbian Archive, 32
black gay male conundrum, the, 167, 169,
170–75
black gay male literature, 24–36; Baldwin's
place in, 1, 9–10, 26–33, 36, 39–
42

Printed and bound by CPI Group (UK) Ltd, Croydon, CR0 4YY

13/04/2025